Kore
Yamazaki

FRAU
FAUST

2

STORY

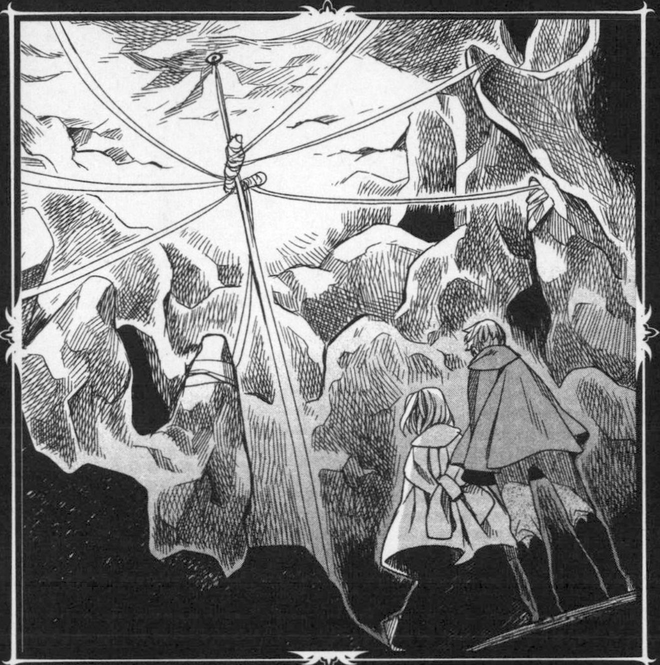

This is the story of a reunion a hundred years in the making…

Johanna Faust is on a journey to find the body of the demon Mephistopheles, whose scattered parts have been sealed away in several locations. Following the trail of one such piece led her to a certain town, where she met a boy named Marion and plotted to use him to retrieve the demon's right arm. After a scuffle with the inquisitor Lorenzo, who attempted to stop her scheme, Johanna escaped with the arm. However, she was unable to ditch Marion, who insisted on sticking around and has joined her on her travels.

To recover from the ordeal, Johanna headed to her safehouse, a place where her homunculus daughter named Nico lived with orphaned children. Their reunion was interrupted, however, when one of the children fell sick. Marion was stunned to learn that the cause of the sickness was a type of plant that Johanna herself brought to the area years ago, causing him to mistrust her way of thinking. Thanks to Nico, Johanna evaded another of Lorenzo's attacks, but the stress of so many battles rendered her unconscious…

CHARACTERS

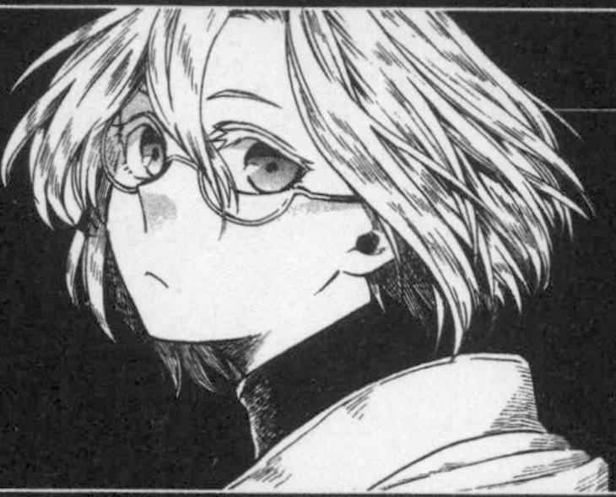

"Don't assume that I'll crumble that easily, demon."

Johanna Faust

Dr. Faust, who supposedly died a century ago. She travels in search of the scattered parts of her demon, Mephistopheles. She is under a curse of immortality, the nature of which is still shrouded in mystery.

Mephistopheles

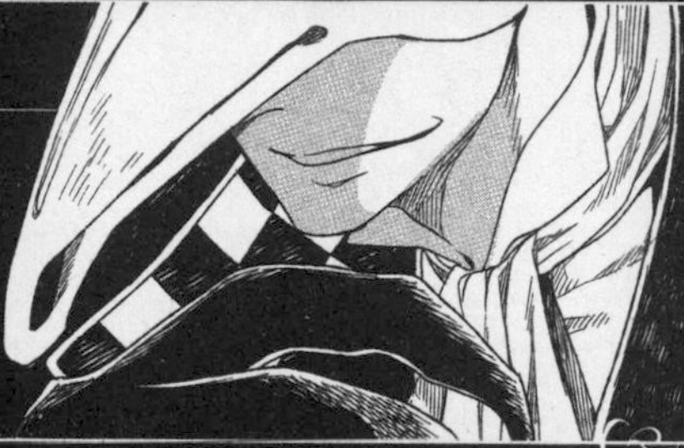

A legendary demon. Over a century ago, he was sentenced for his crimes and quartered in order to remove his powers. His head, left arm, and right leg are still missing. What is the nature of the game that he plays with his master, Johanna?

"As you command, Master."

Inquisitors

Vito

Lorenzo's partner. Undertaking his own research into Mephistopheles.

Lorenzo

Pursues Johanna to prevent her from reviving the demon. Silent and deadly serious. Catastrophically bad art skills.

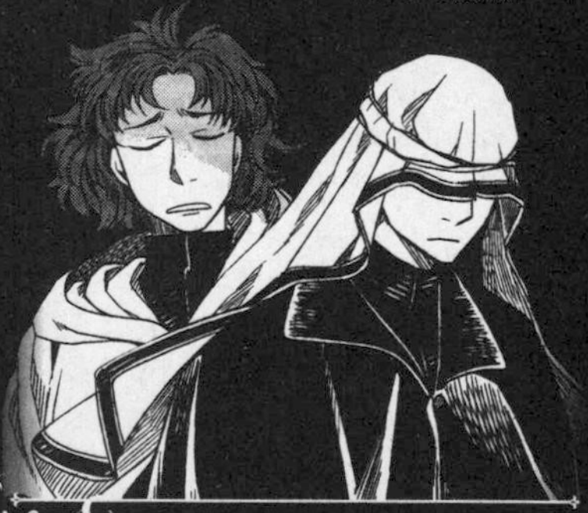

Marion

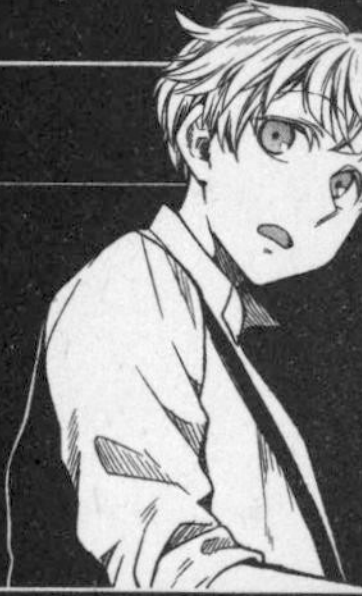

A pure-hearted, kind, and curious youth. Johanna uses and abuses him, but his thirst for knowledge drives him to accompany her on her journey.

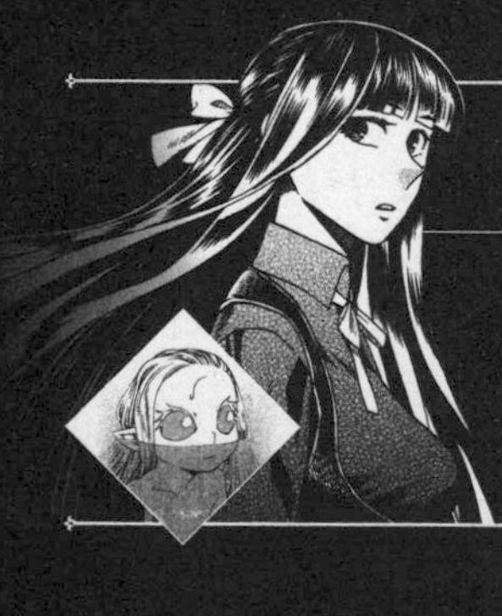

Nico Bernstein

Johanna's daughter. Or rather, Johanna's creation—a homunculus. She normally relies on the body of an automaton (moving doll) to get around.

contents

FRAU FAUST

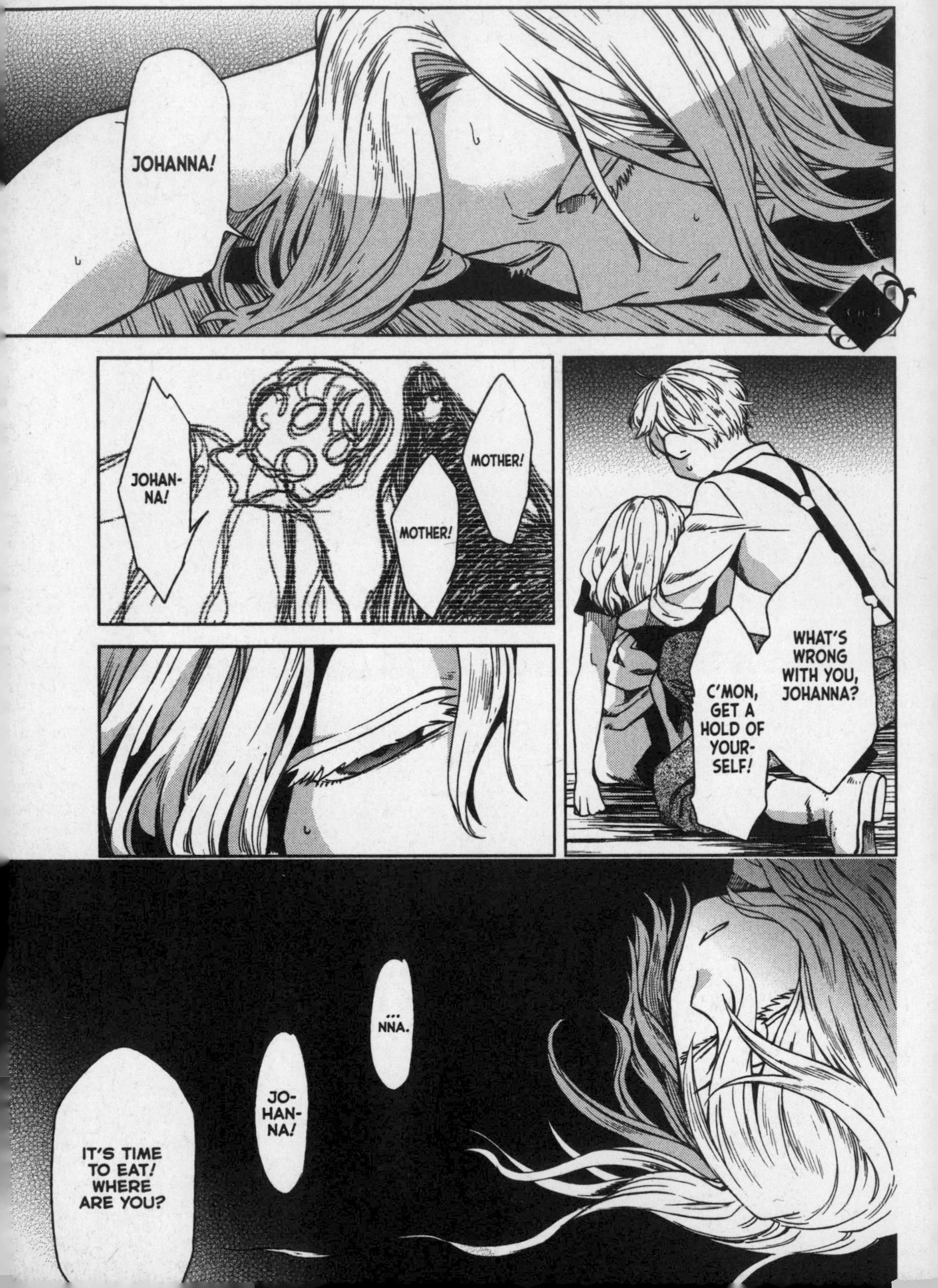
JOHANNA!
WHAT'S WRONG WITH YOU, JOHANNA?
C'MON, GET A HOLD OF YOUR-SELF!
MOTHER!
MOTHER!
JOHAN-NA!
...NNA.
JO-HAN-NA!
IT'S TIME TO EAT! WHERE ARE YOU?

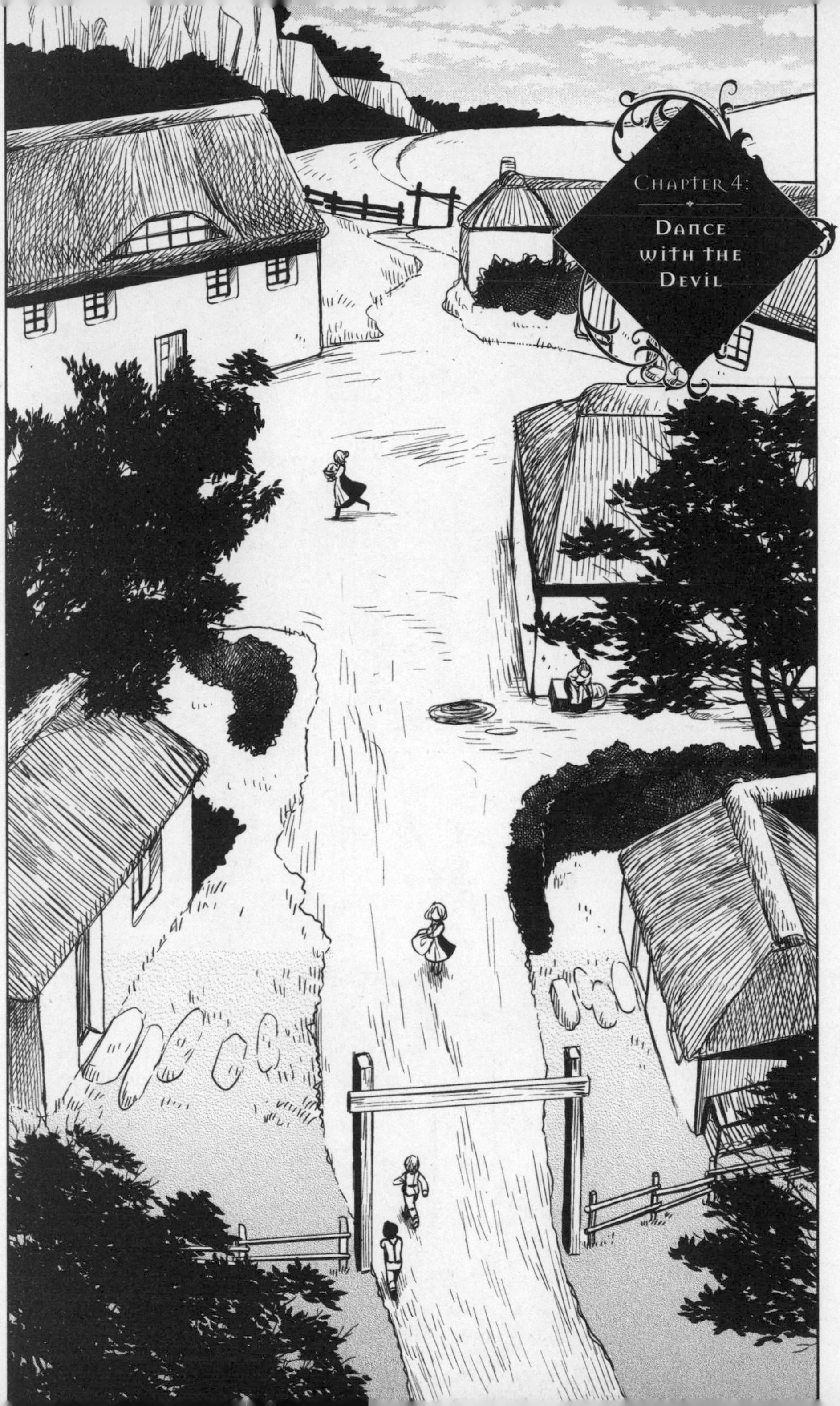
Chapter 4:
Dance with the Devil

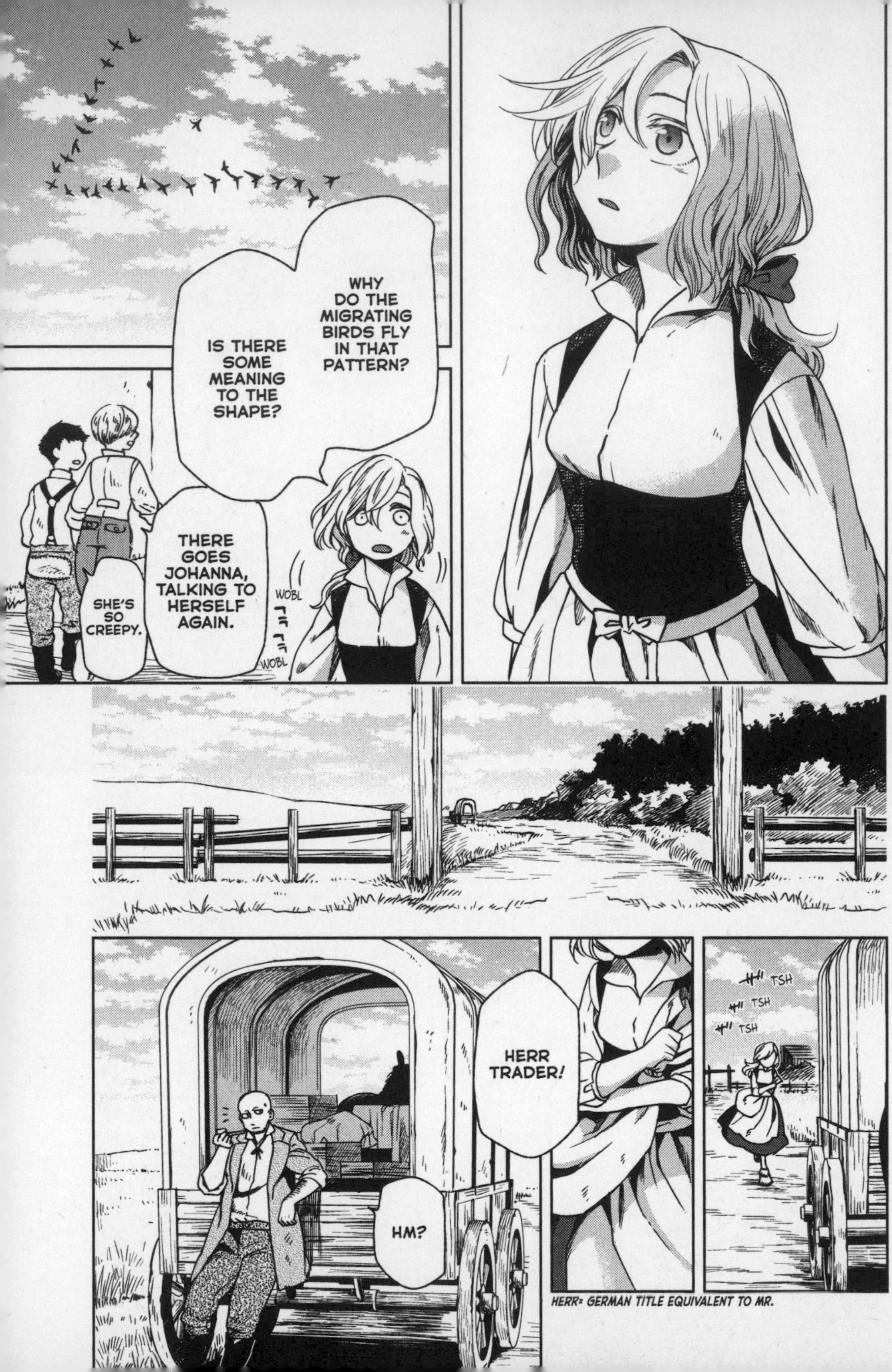
WHY DO THE MIGRATING BIRDS FLY IN THAT PATTERN?
IS THERE SOME MEANING TO THE SHAPE?
WOBL
WOBL
THERE GOES JOHANNA, TALKING TO HERSELF AGAIN.
SHE'S SO CREEPY.
TSH
TSH
TSH
HERR TRADER!
HM?

HERR= GERMAN TITLE EQUIVALENT TO MR.

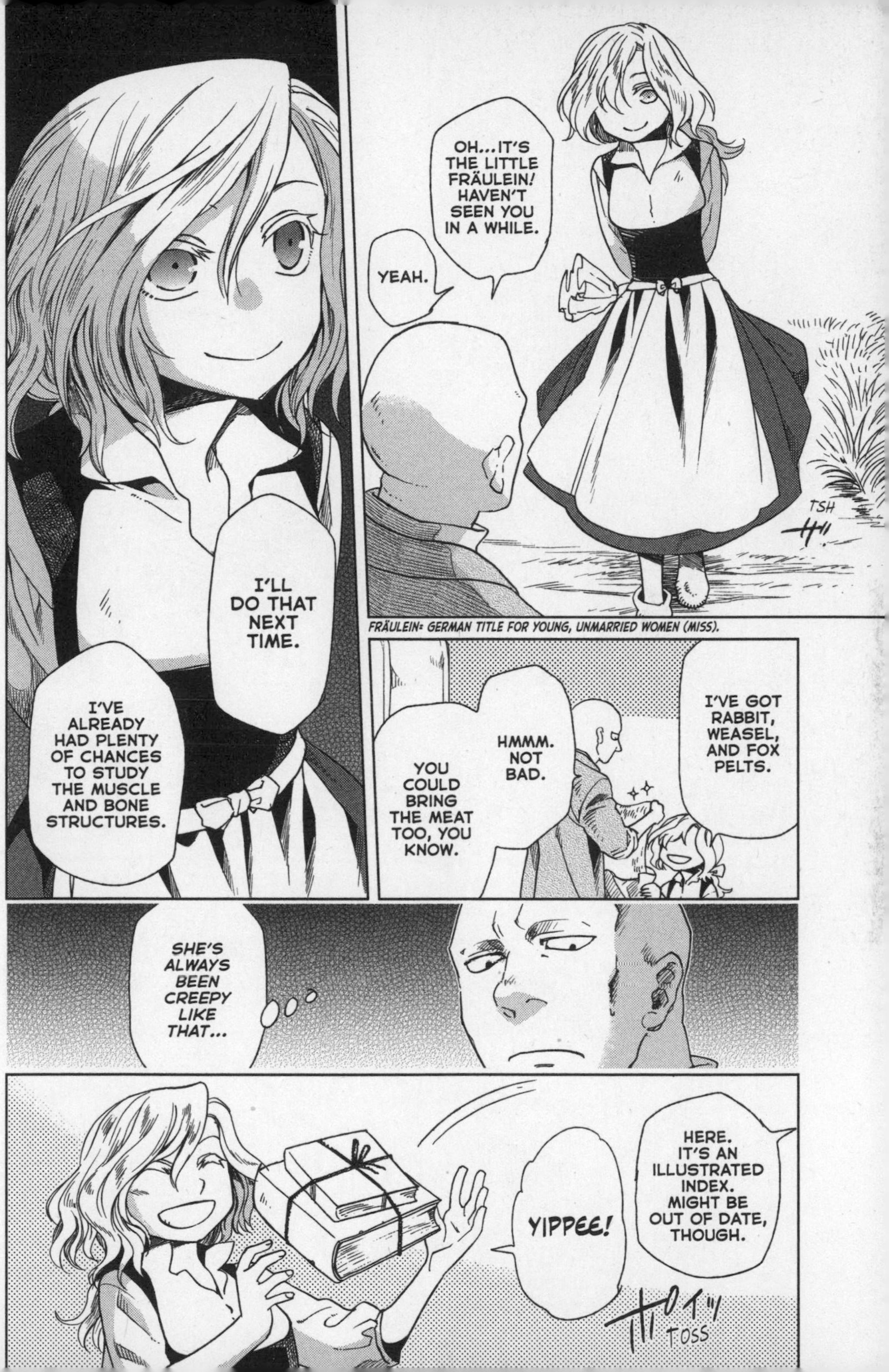
OH...IT'S THE LITTLE FRÄULEIN! HAVEN'T SEEN YOU IN A WHILE.
YEAH.
TSH
I'VE GOT RABBIT, WEASEL, AND FOX PELTS.
HMMM. NOT BAD.
YOU COULD BRING THE MEAT TOO, YOU KNOW.
I'LL DO THAT NEXT TIME.
I'VE ALREADY HAD PLENTY OF CHANCES TO STUDY THE MUSCLE AND BONE STRUCTURES.
SHE'S ALWAYS BEEN CREEPY LIKE THAT...
HERE. IT'S AN ILLUSTRATED INDEX. MIGHT BE OUT OF DATE, THOUGH.
YIPPEE!
TOSS
FRÄULEIN: GERMAN TITLE FOR YOUNG, UNMARRIED WOMEN (MISS).

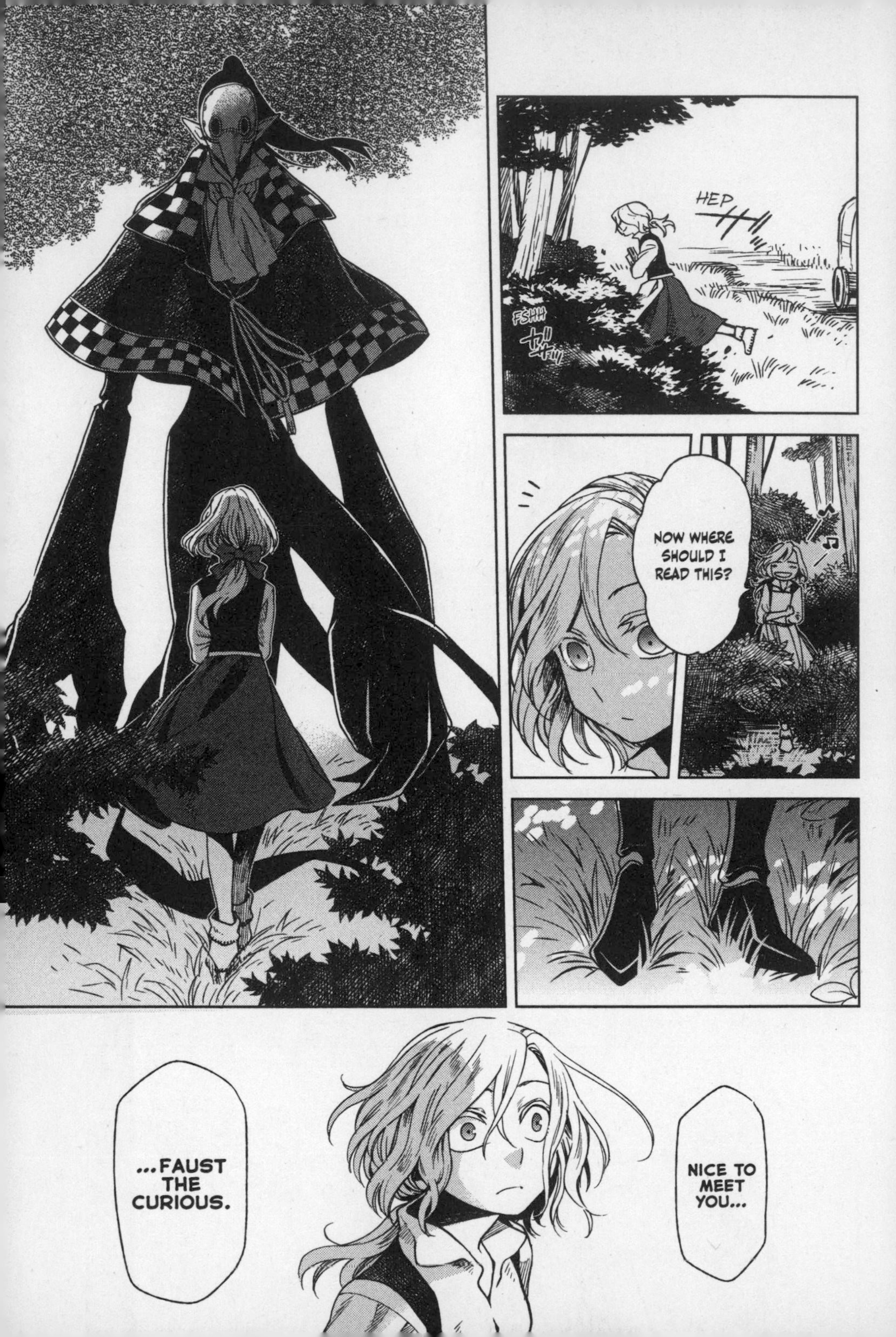

HEP
FSHH
NOW WHERE SHOULD I READ THIS?
NICE TO MEET YOU...
...FAUST THE CURIOUS.

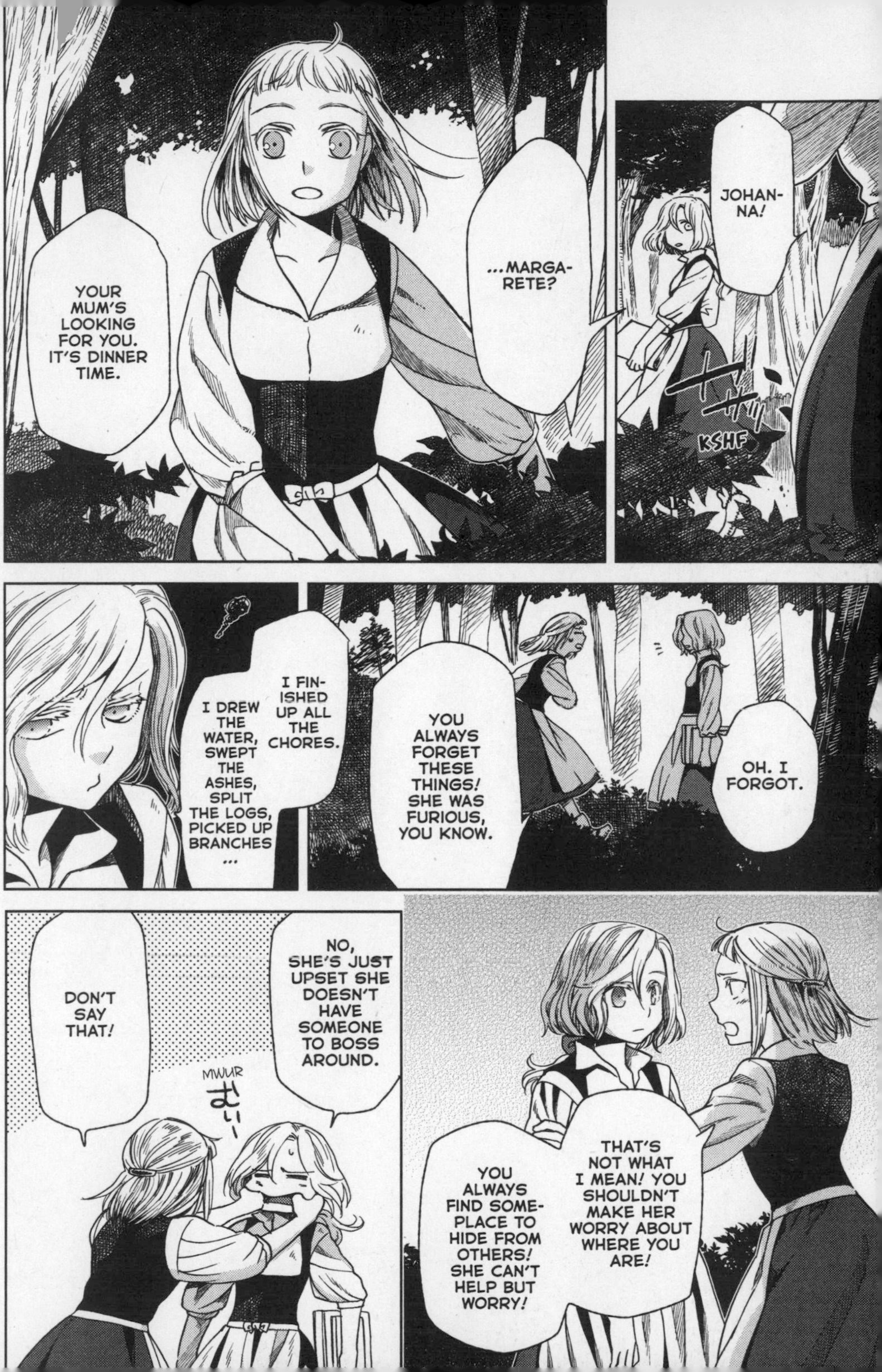
JOHANNA!
KSHF
...MARGARETE?
YOUR MUM'S LOOKING FOR YOU. IT'S DINNER TIME.
OH. I FORGOT.
YOU ALWAYS FORGET THESE THINGS! SHE WAS FURIOUS, YOU KNOW.
I FINISHED UP ALL THE CHORES.
I DREW THE WATER, SWEPT THE ASHES, SPLIT THE LOGS, PICKED UP BRANCHES...
THAT'S NOT WHAT I MEAN! YOU SHOULDN'T MAKE HER WORRY ABOUT WHERE YOU ARE!
YOU ALWAYS FIND SOMEPLACE TO HIDE FROM OTHERS! SHE CAN'T HELP BUT WORRY!
NO, SHE'S JUST UPSET SHE DOESN'T HAVE SOMEONE TO BOSS AROUND.
DON'T SAY THAT!
MWUR
むいー

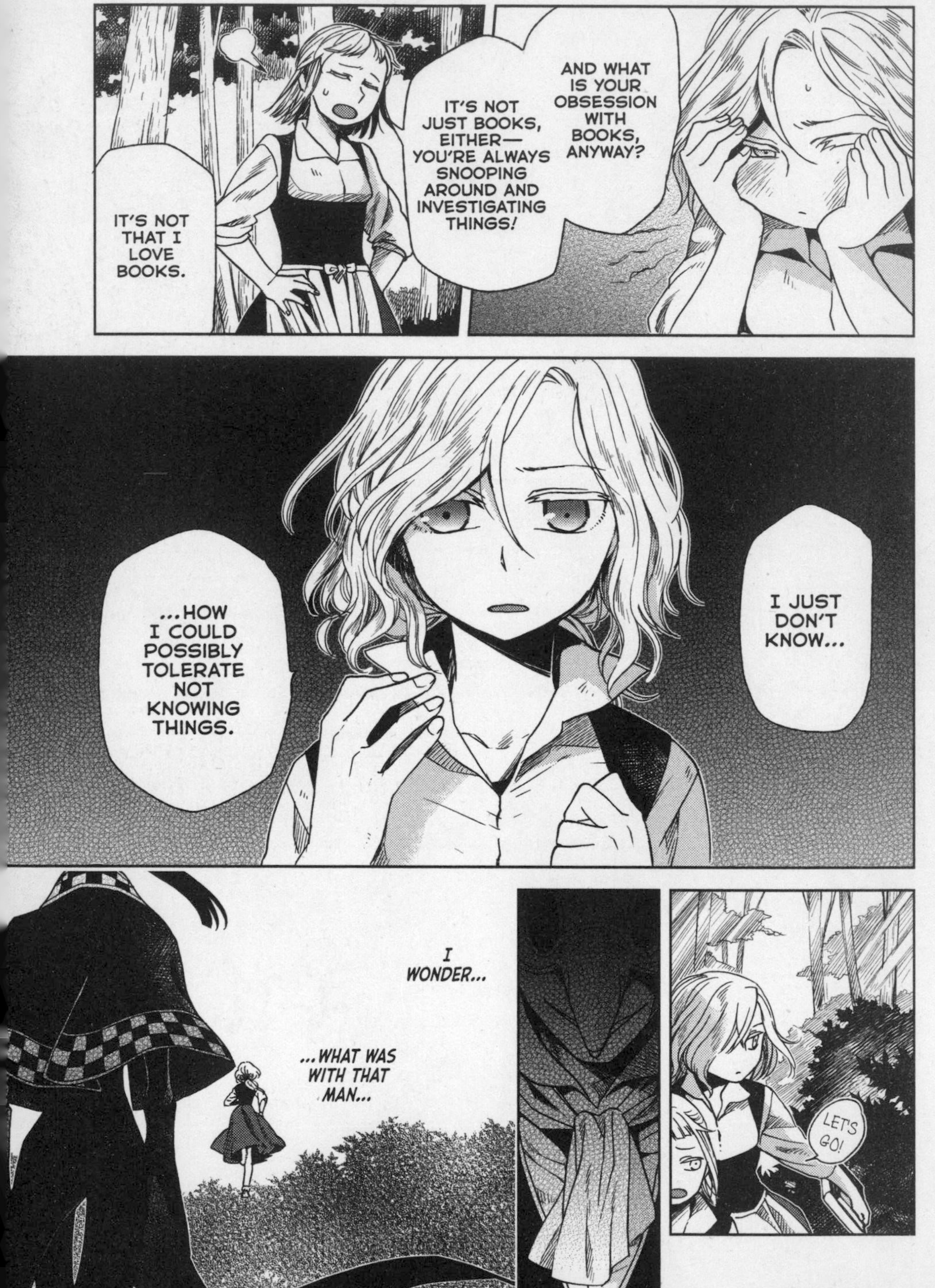
AND WHAT IS YOUR OBSESSION WITH BOOKS, ANYWAY?
IT'S NOT JUST BOOKS, EITHER—YOU'RE ALWAYS SNOOPING AROUND AND INVESTIGATING THINGS!
IT'S NOT THAT I LOVE BOOKS.
I JUST DON'T KNOW...
...HOW I COULD POSSIBLY TOLERATE NOT KNOWING THINGS.
LET'S GO!
I WONDER...
...WHAT WAS WITH THAT MAN...

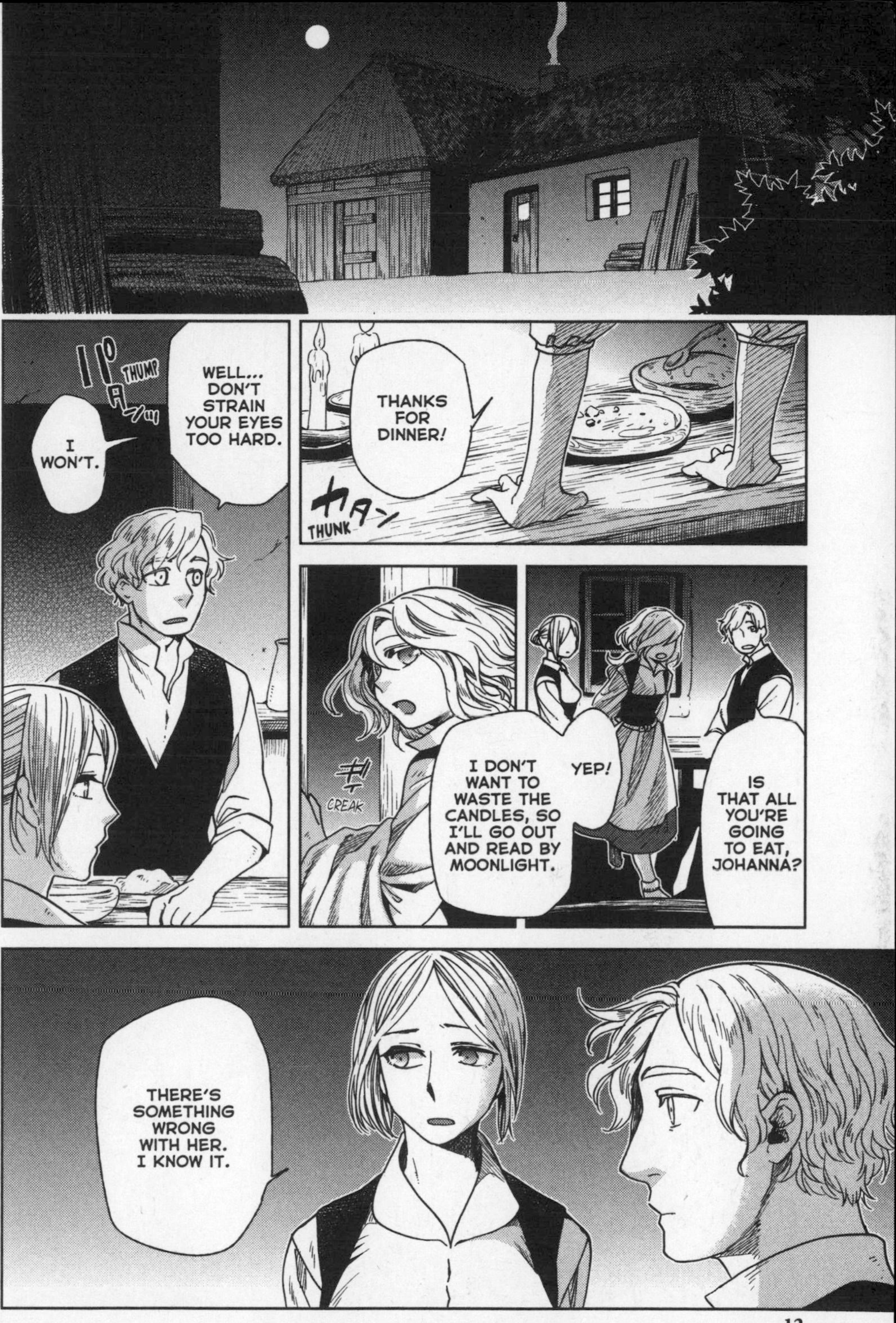
THANKS FOR DINNER!
THUNK
IS THAT ALL YOU'RE GOING TO EAT, JOHANNA?
YEP!
I DON'T WANT TO WASTE THE CANDLES, SO I'LL GO OUT AND READ BY MOONLIGHT.
CREAK
WELL... DON'T STRAIN YOUR EYES TOO HARD.
THUMP
I WON'T.
THERE'S SOMETHING WRONG WITH HER. I KNOW IT.

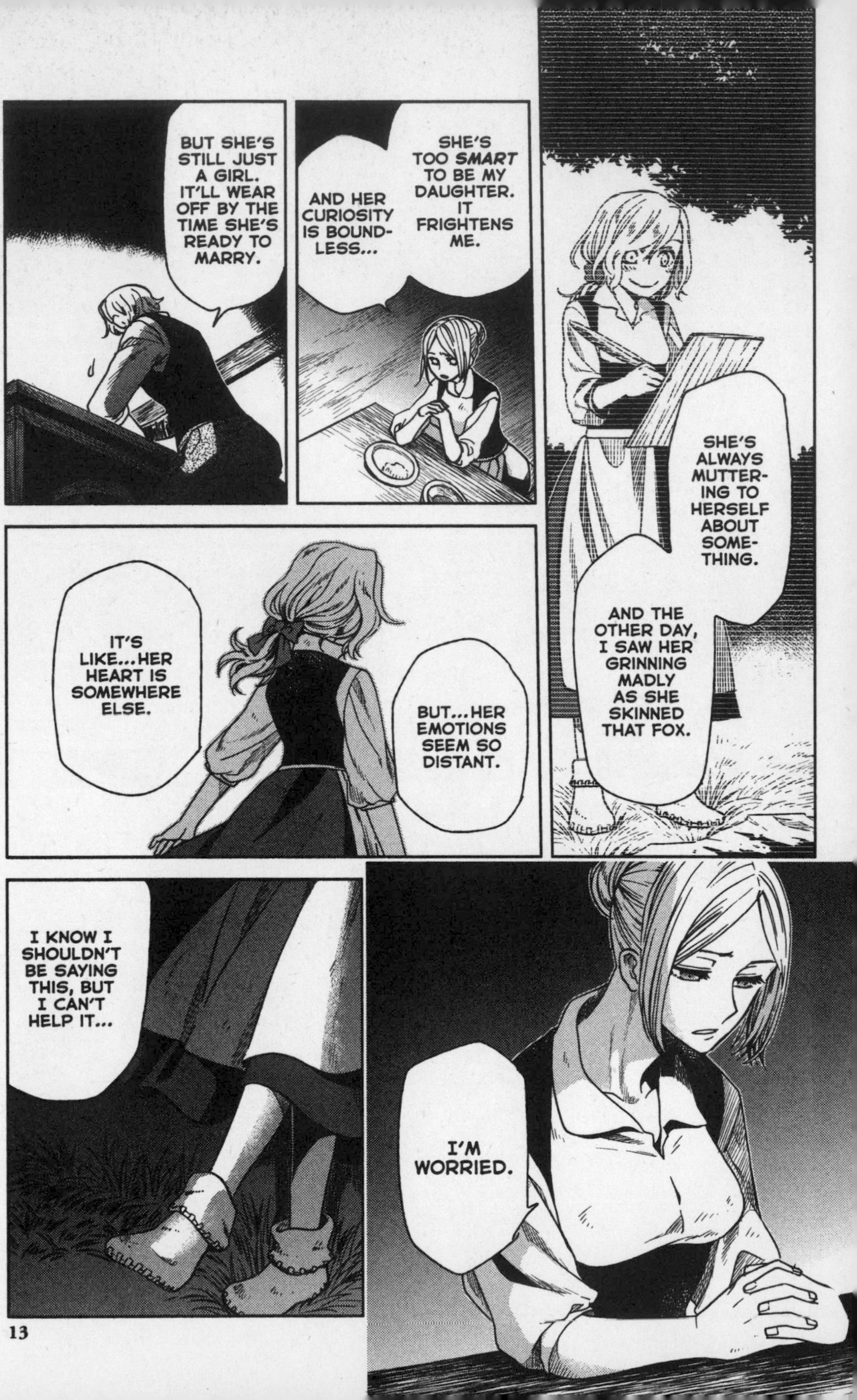
SHE'S ALWAYS MUTTERING TO HERSELF ABOUT SOMETHING.
AND THE OTHER DAY, I SAW HER GRINNING MADLY AS SHE SKINNED THAT FOX.
SHE'S TOO *SMART* TO BE MY DAUGHTER. IT FRIGHTENS ME.
AND HER CURIOSITY IS BOUNDLESS...
BUT SHE'S STILL JUST A GIRL. IT'LL WEAR OFF BY THE TIME SHE'S READY TO MARRY.
BUT...HER EMOTIONS SEEM SO DISTANT.
IT'S LIKE...HER HEART IS SOMEWHERE ELSE.
I'M WORRIED.
I KNOW I SHOULDN'T BE SAYING THIS, BUT I CAN'T HELP IT...

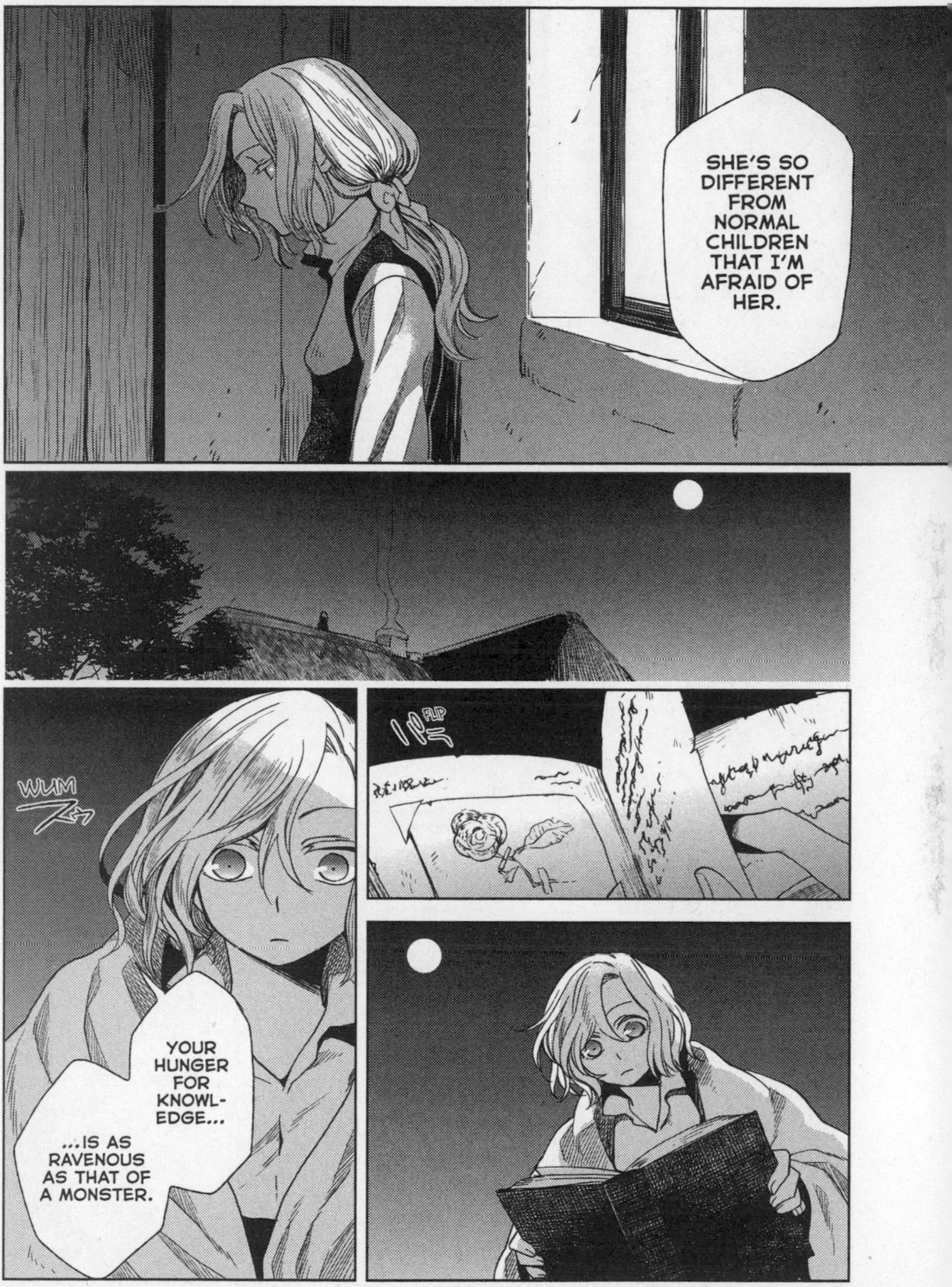
SHE'S SO DIFFERENT FROM NORMAL CHILDREN THAT I'M AFRAID OF HER.
FLIP
WUM
YOUR HUNGER FOR KNOWL-EDGE...
...IS AS RAVENOUS AS THAT OF A MONSTER.

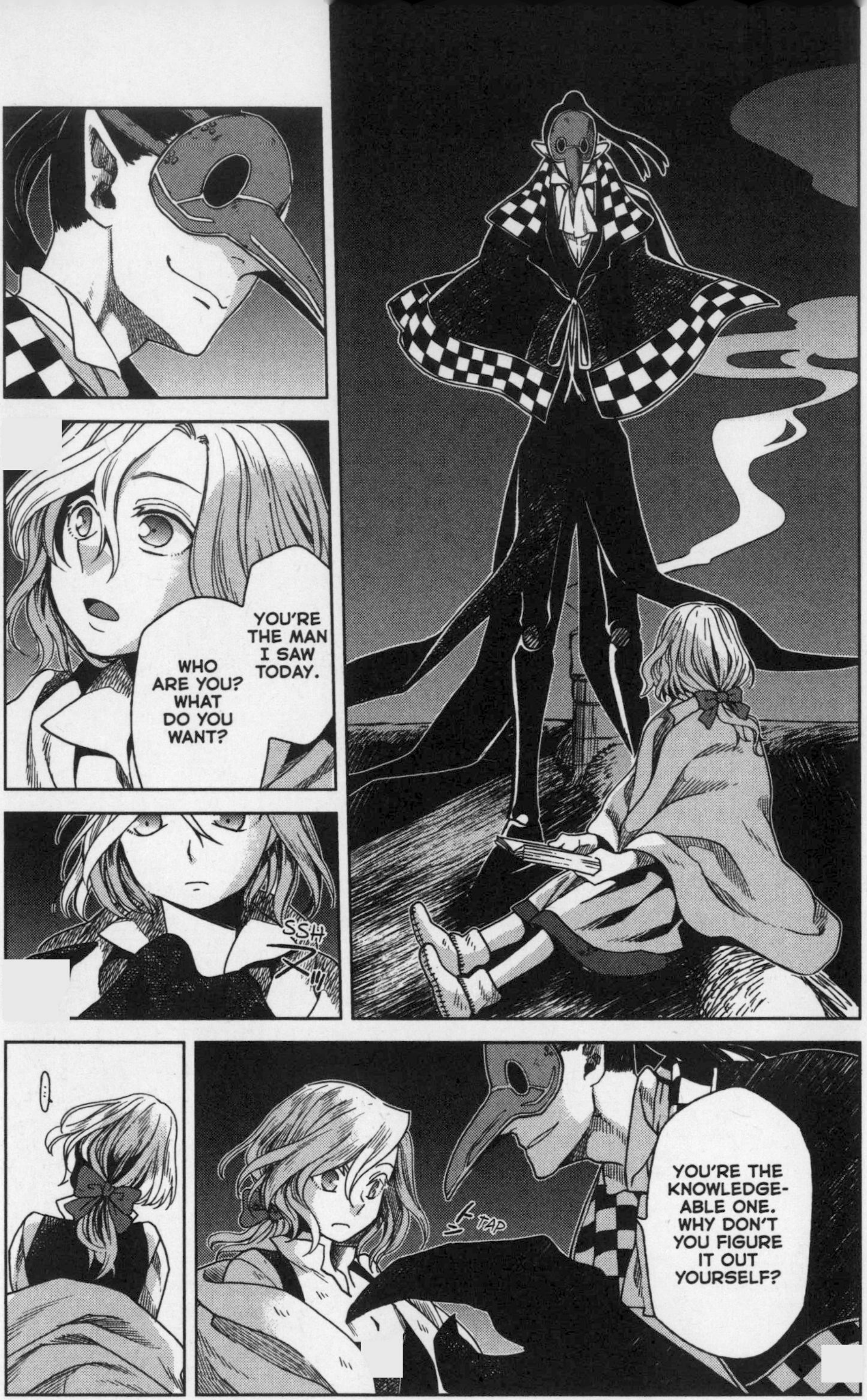
YOU'RE THE MAN I SAW TODAY.
WHO ARE YOU? WHAT DO YOU WANT?
SSH
YOU'RE THE KNOWLEDGE-ABLE ONE. WHY DON'T YOU FIGURE IT OUT YOURSELF?
TAP
...

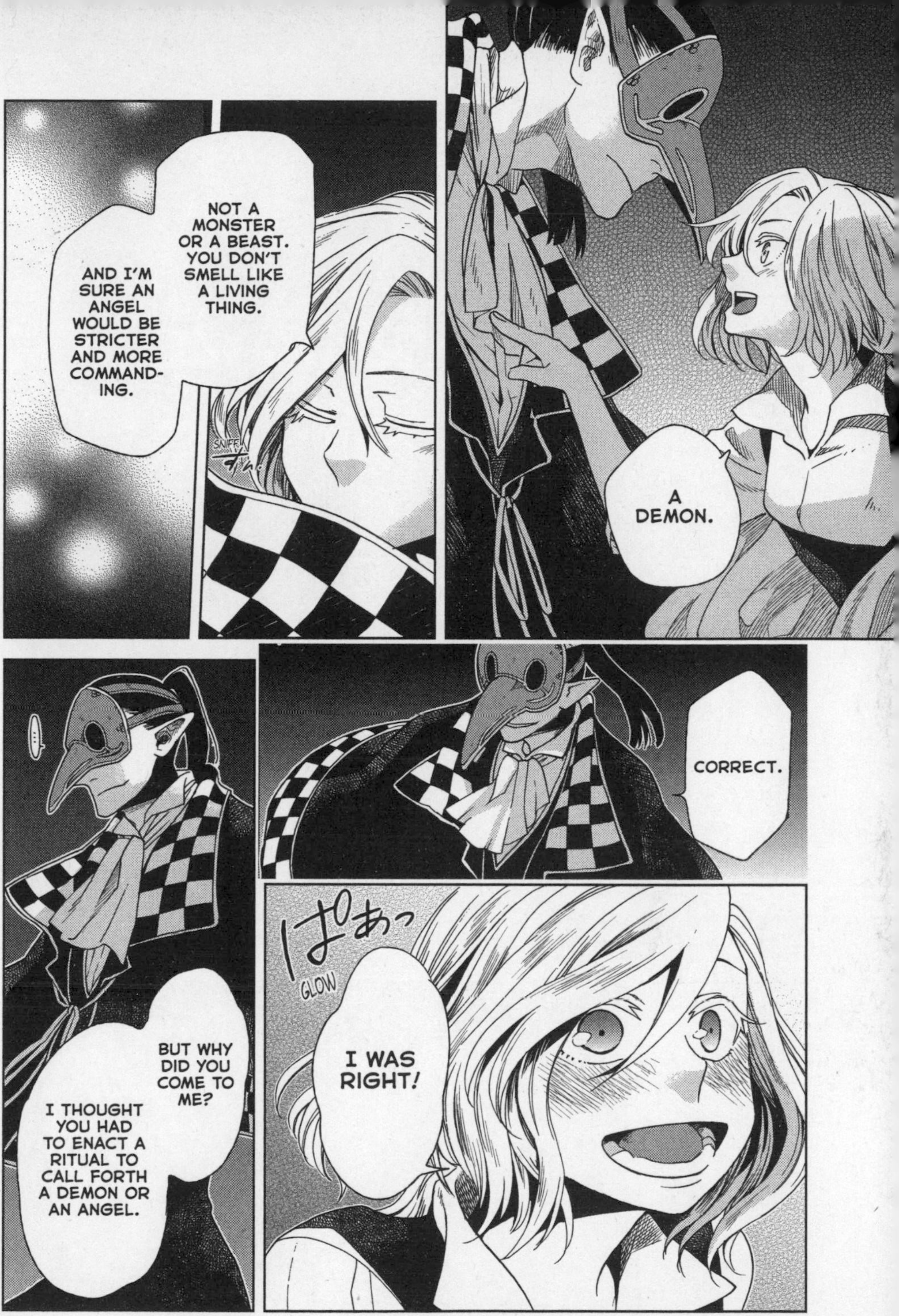
A DEMON.
NOT A MONSTER OR A BEAST. YOU DON'T SMELL LIKE A LIVING THING.
AND I'M SURE AN ANGEL WOULD BE STRICTER AND MORE COMMAND-ING.
SNIFF
CORRECT.
GLOW
I WAS RIGHT!
...
BUT WHY DID YOU COME TO ME?
I THOUGHT YOU HAD TO ENACT A RITUAL TO CALL FORTH A DEMON OR AN ANGEL.

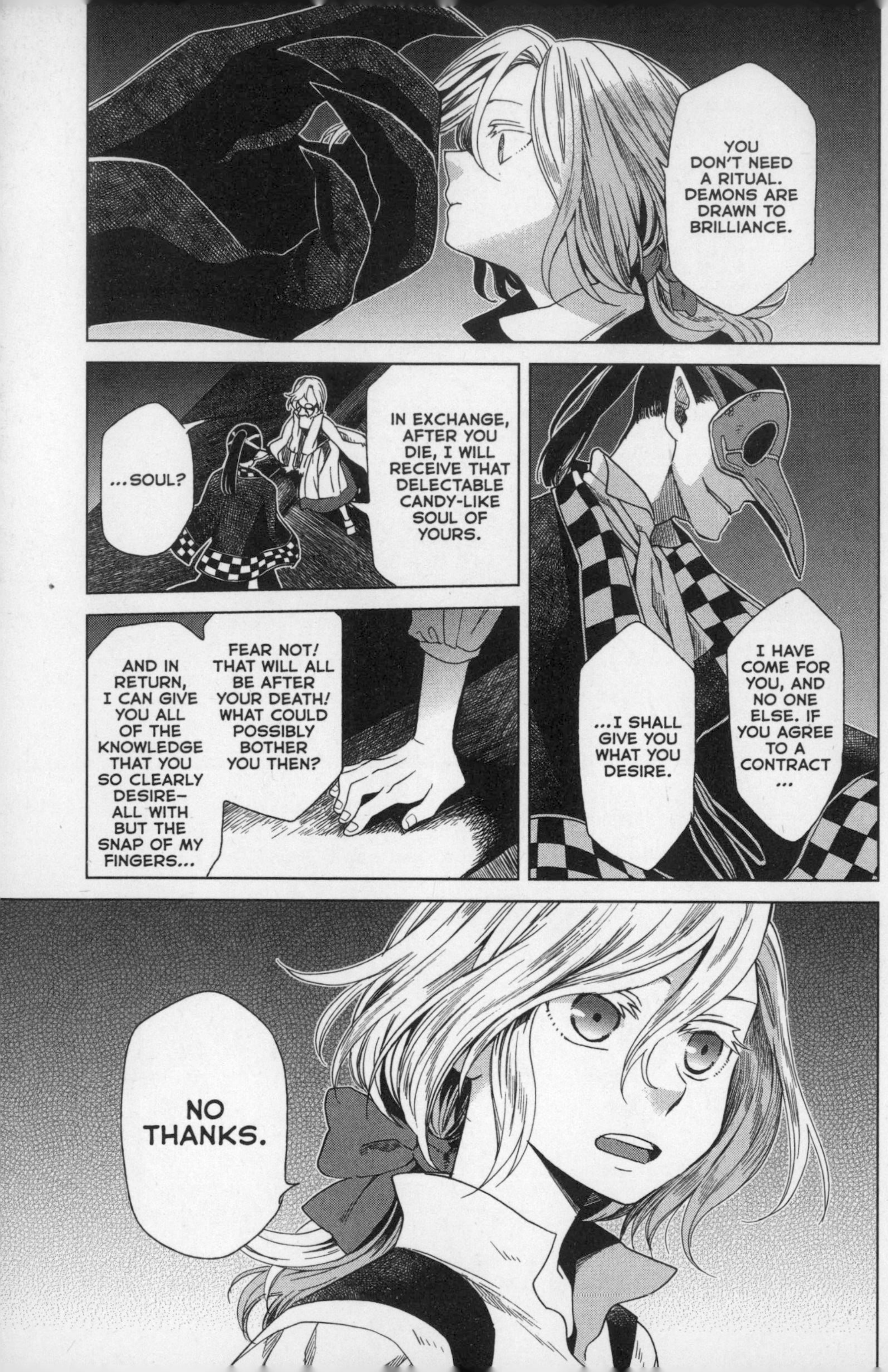
YOU DON'T NEED A RITUAL. DEMONS ARE DRAWN TO BRILLIANCE.
I HAVE COME FOR YOU, AND NO ONE ELSE. IF YOU AGREE TO A CONTRACT ...
...I SHALL GIVE YOU WHAT YOU DESIRE.
IN EXCHANGE, AFTER YOU DIE, I WILL RECEIVE THAT DELECTABLE CANDY-LIKE SOUL OF YOURS.
...SOUL?
FEAR NOT! THAT WILL ALL BE AFTER YOUR DEATH! WHAT COULD POSSIBLY BOTHER YOU THEN?
AND IN RETURN, I CAN GIVE YOU ALL OF THE KNOWLEDGE THAT YOU SO CLEARLY DESIRE–ALL WITH BUT THE SNAP OF MY FINGERS...
NO THANKS.

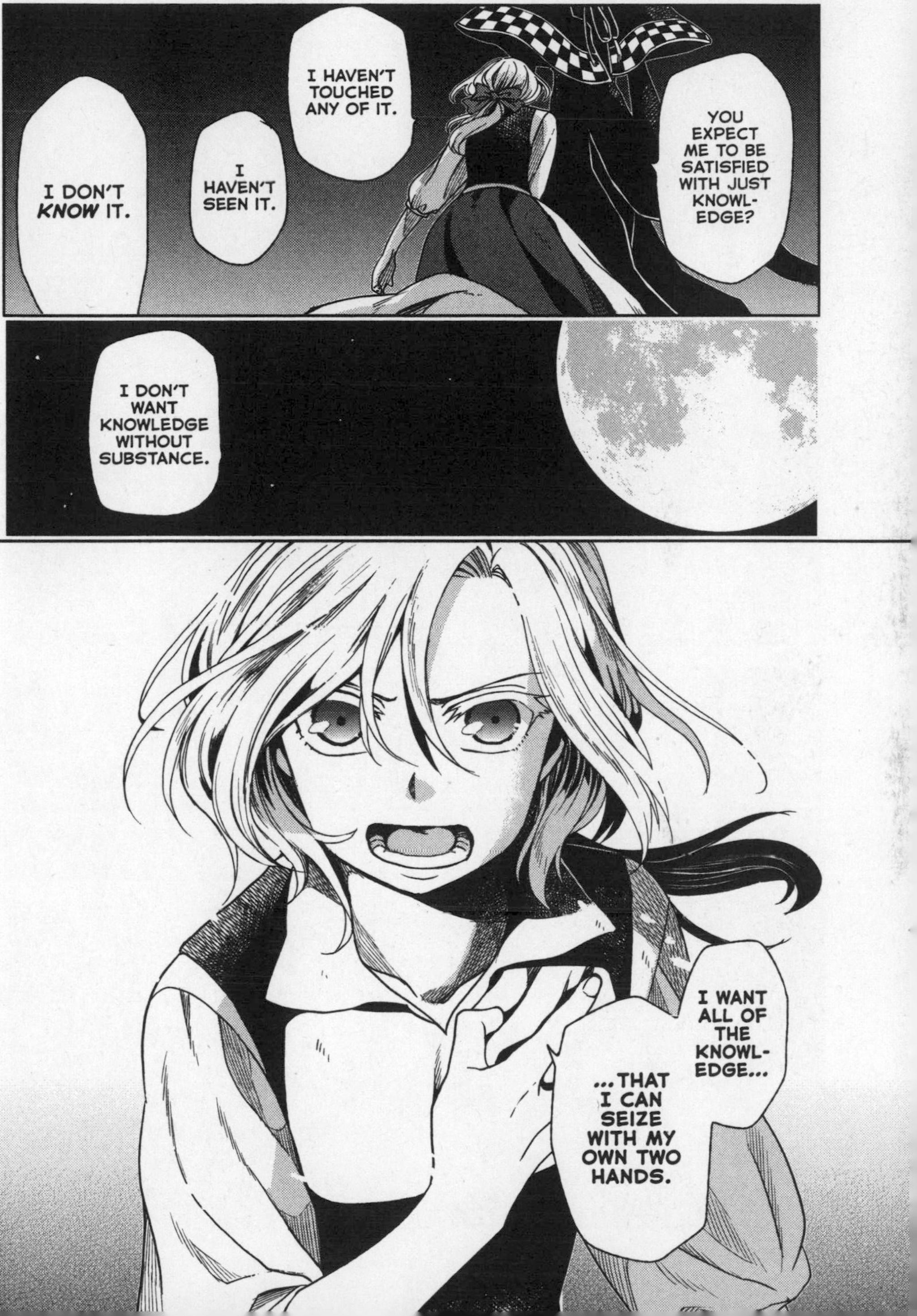
YOU EXPECT ME TO BE SATISFIED WITH JUST KNOWL-EDGE?
I HAVEN'T TOUCHED ANY OF IT.
I HAVEN'T SEEN IT.
I DON'T *KNOW* IT.
I DON'T WANT KNOWLEDGE WITHOUT SUBSTANCE.
I WANT ALL OF THE KNOWL-EDGE...
...THAT I CAN SEIZE WITH MY OWN TWO HANDS.

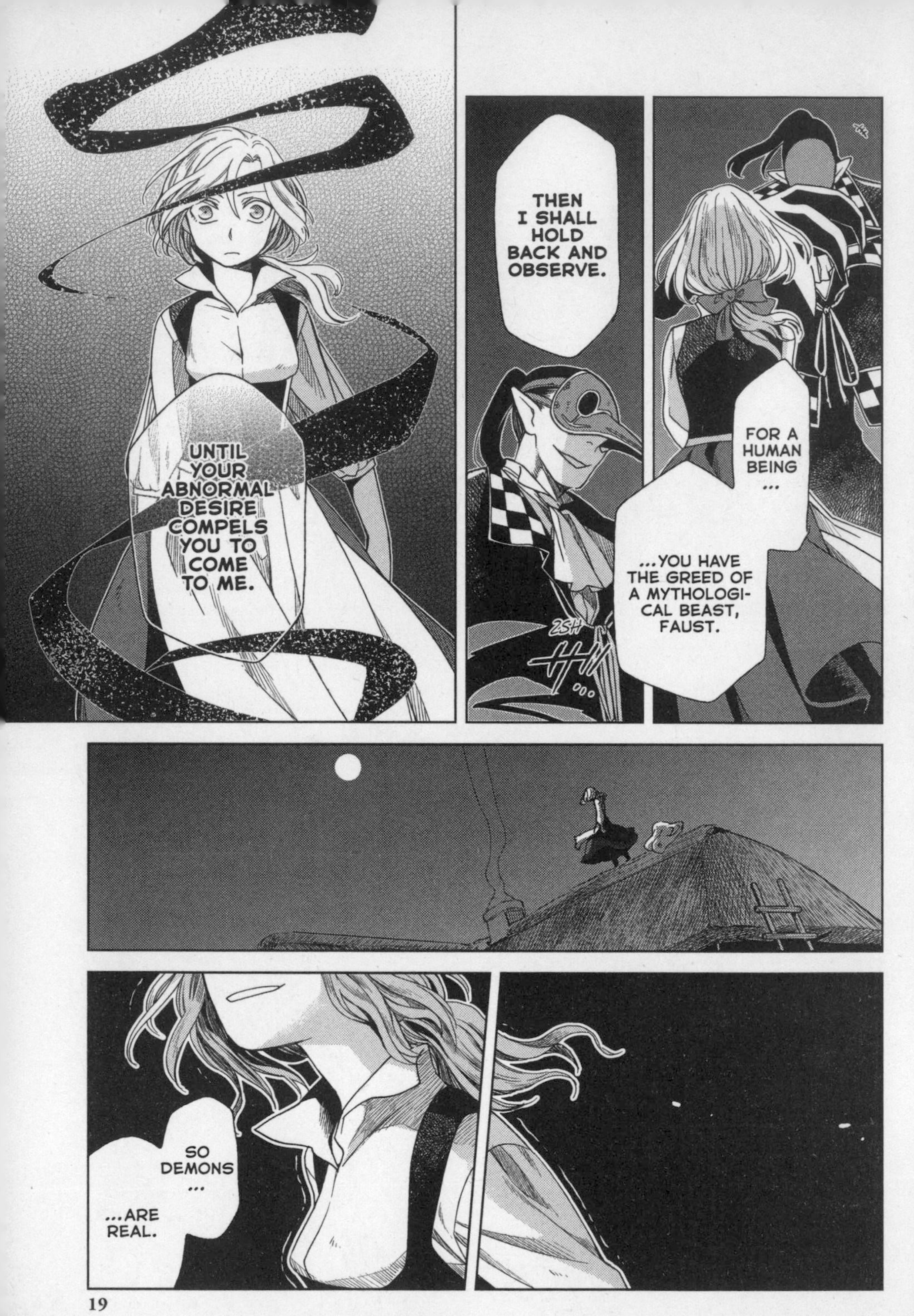
FOR A HUMAN BEING ...
...YOU HAVE THE GREED OF A MYTHOLOGICAL BEAST, FAUST.
THEN I SHALL HOLD BACK AND OBSERVE.
ZSH
UNTIL YOUR ABNORMAL DESIRE COMPELS YOU TO COME TO ME.
SO DEMONS ...
...ARE REAL.

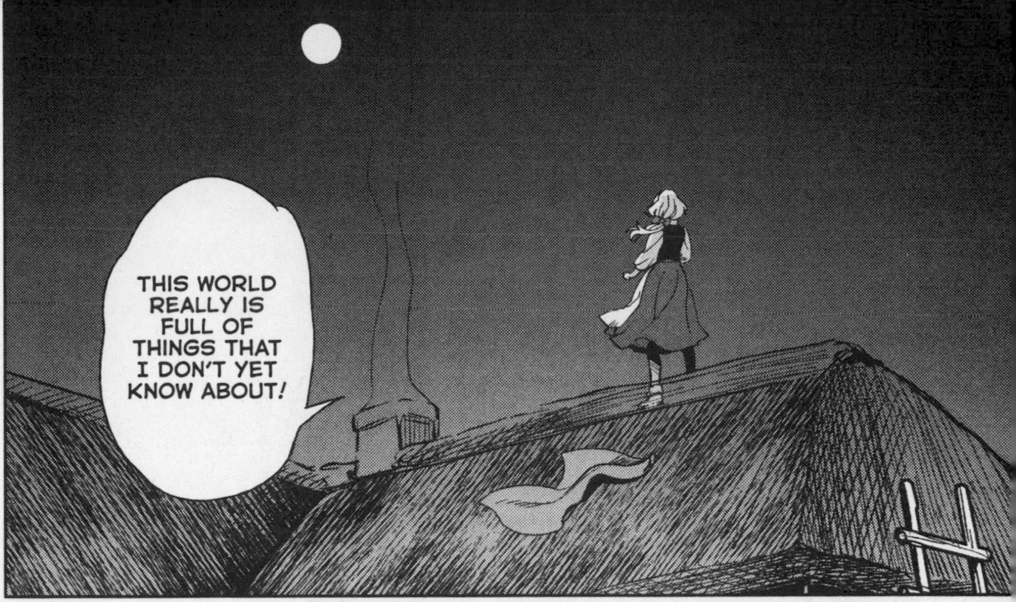
THIS WORLD REALLY IS FULL OF THINGS THAT I DON'T YET KNOW ABOUT!

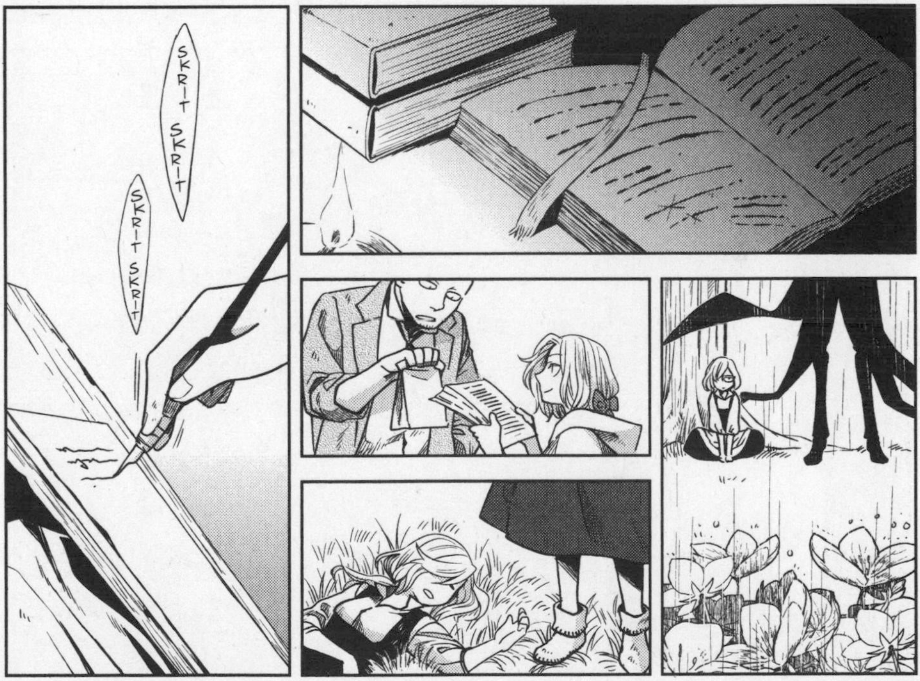
SKRIT SKRIT
SKRIT SKRIT

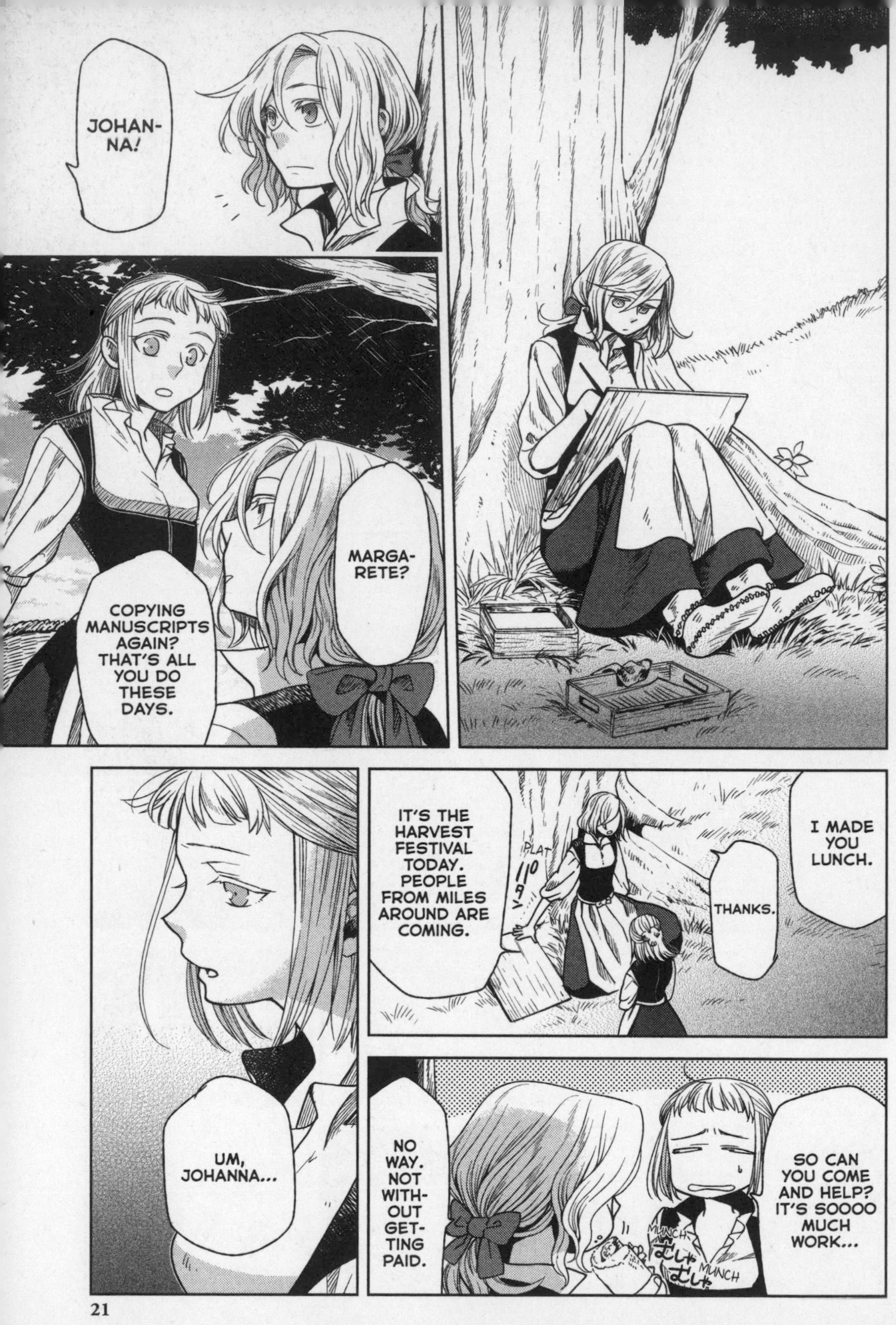
JOHAN-NA!
MARGA-RETE?
COPYING MANUSCRIPTS AGAIN? THAT'S ALL YOU DO THESE DAYS.
I MADE YOU LUNCH.
THANKS.
IT'S THE HARVEST FESTIVAL TODAY. PEOPLE FROM MILES AROUND ARE COMING.
PLAT
SO CAN YOU COME AND HELP? IT'S SOOOO MUCH WORK...
MUNCH
MUNCH
NO WAY. NOT WITH-OUT GET-TING PAID.
UM, JOHANNA...

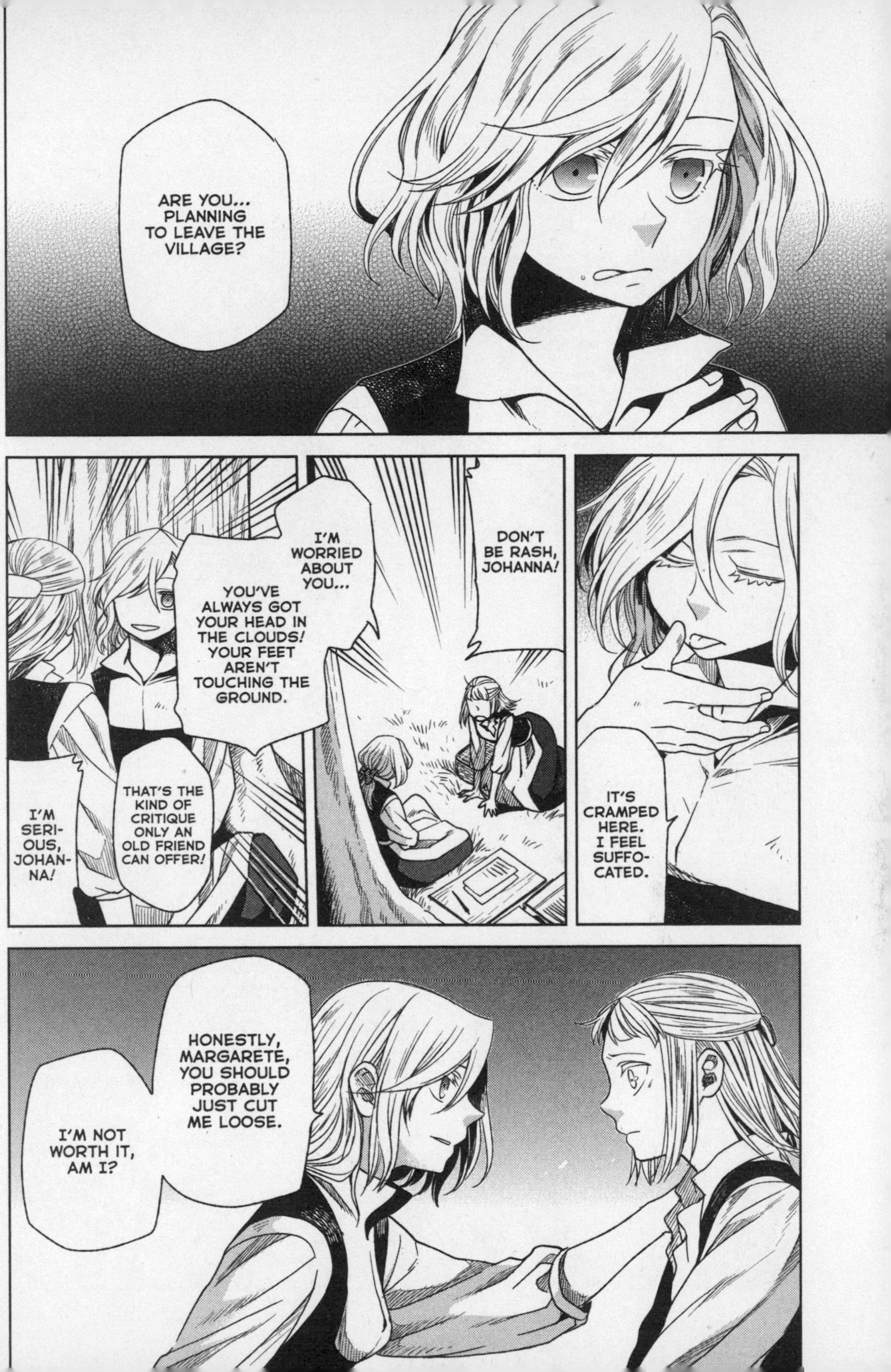
ARE YOU... PLANNING TO LEAVE THE VILLAGE?
IT'S CRAMPED HERE. I FEEL SUFFOCATED.
DON'T BE RASH, JOHANNA!
I'M WORRIED ABOUT YOU... YOU'VE ALWAYS GOT YOUR HEAD IN THE CLOUDS! YOUR FEET AREN'T TOUCHING THE GROUND.
THAT'S THE KIND OF CRITIQUE ONLY AN OLD FRIEND CAN OFFER!
I'M SERI-OUS, JOHAN-NA!
HONESTLY, MARGARETE, YOU SHOULD PROBABLY JUST CUT ME LOOSE.
I'M NOT WORTH IT, AM I?

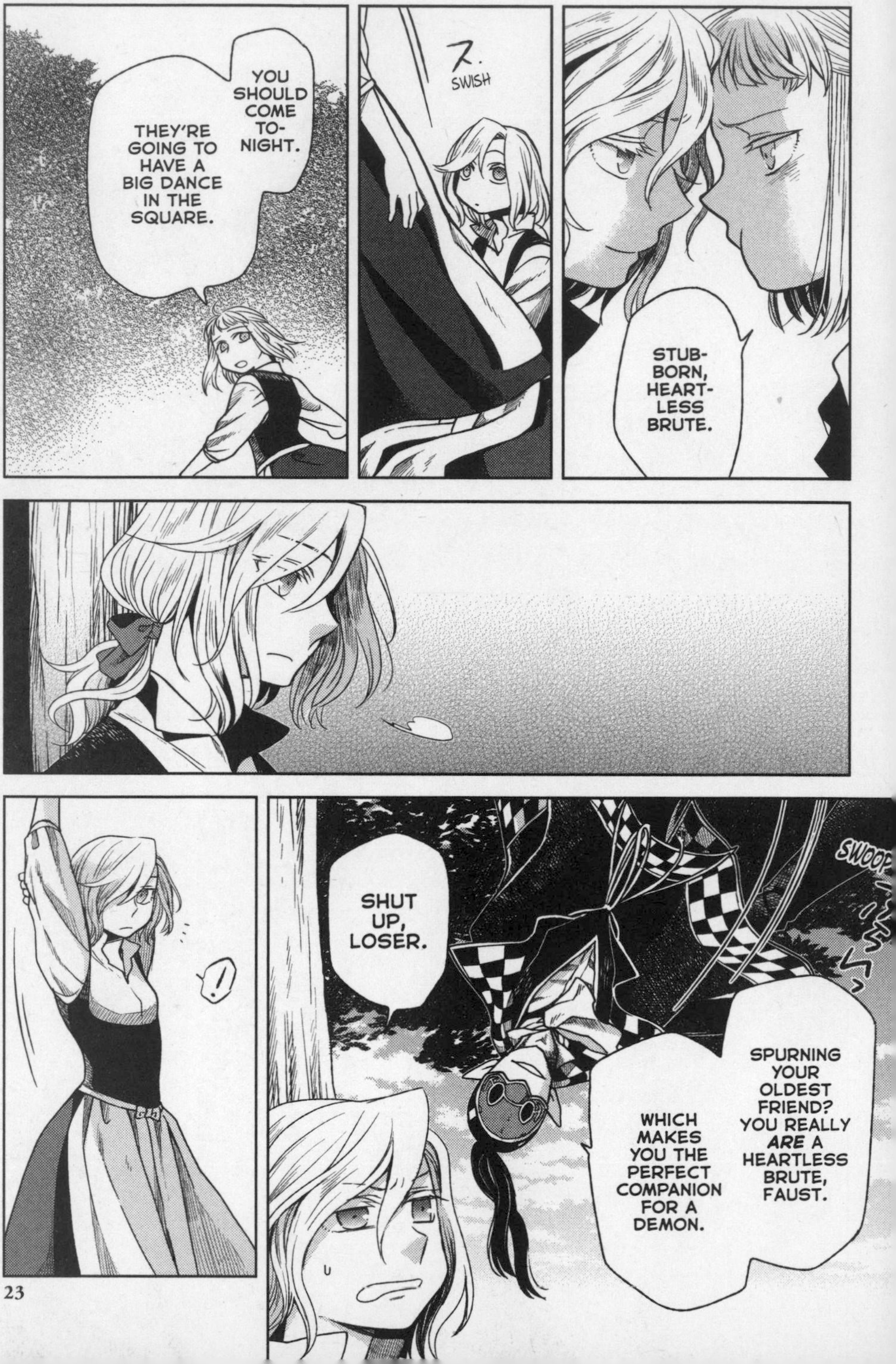
STUB-BORN, HEART-LESS BRUTE.
ス.
SWISH
YOU SHOULD COME TO-NIGHT.
THEY'RE GOING TO HAVE A BIG DANCE IN THE SQUARE.
SWOOP
SHUT UP, LOSER.
SPURNING YOUR OLDEST FRIEND? YOU REALLY *ARE* A HEARTLESS BRUTE, FAUST.
WHICH MAKES YOU THE PERFECT COMPANION FOR A DEMON.
!

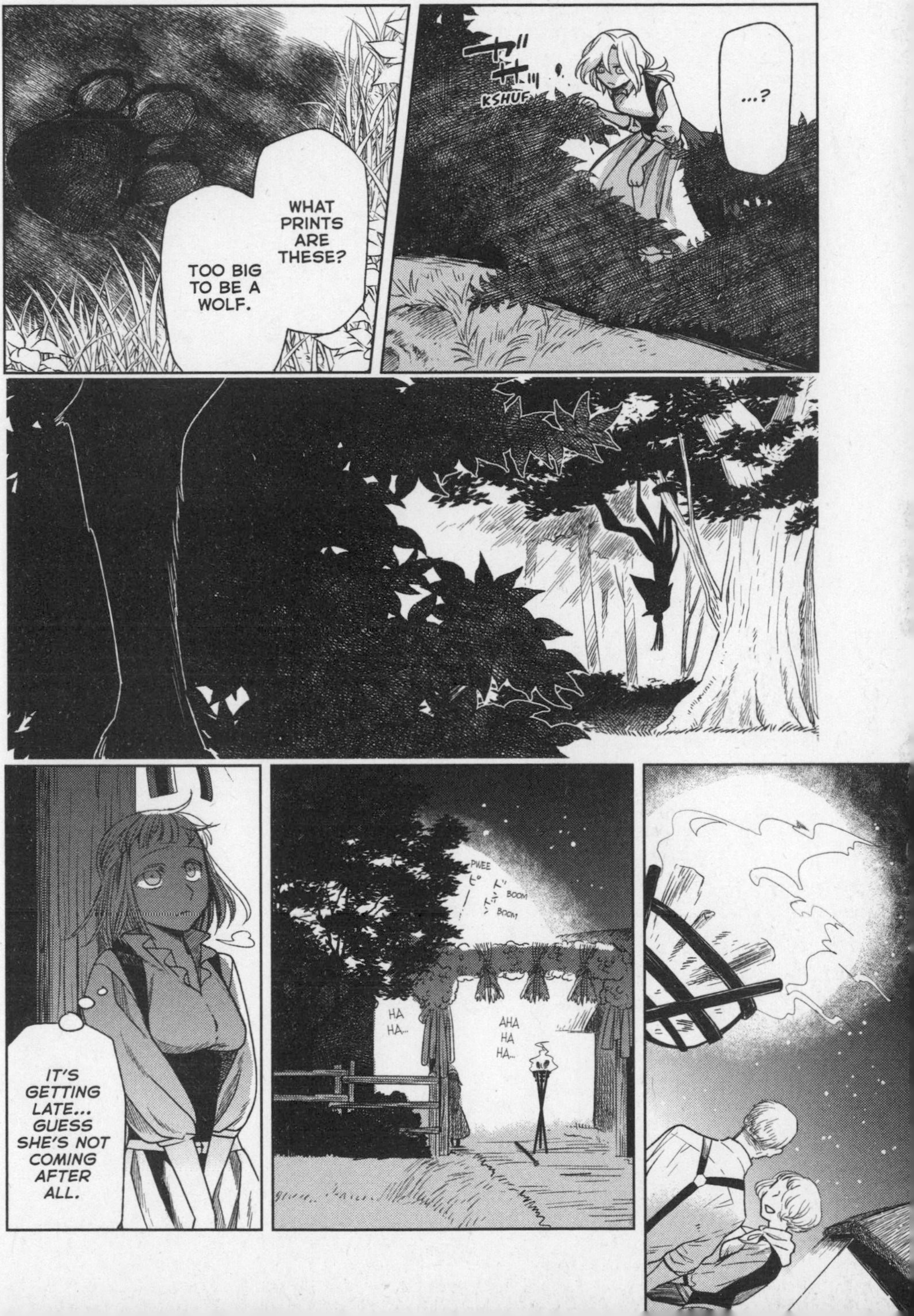
KSHUF
...?
WHAT PRINTS ARE THESE?
TOO BIG TO BE A WOLF.
PWEE
BOOM
BOOM
HA HA...
AHA HA HA...
IT'S GETTING LATE... GUESS SHE'S NOT COMING AFTER ALL.

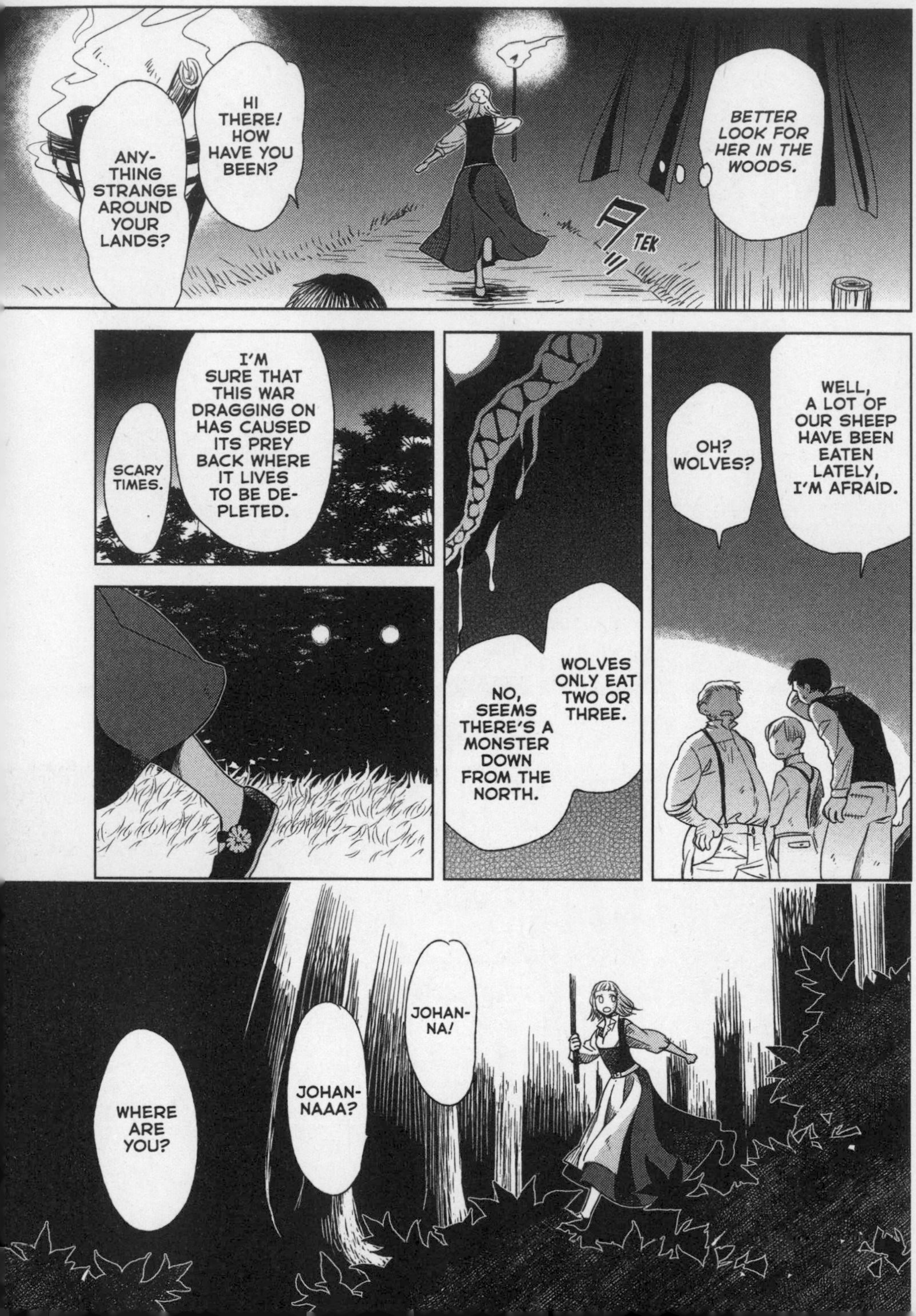
BETTER LOOK FOR HER IN THE WOODS.
TEK
HI THERE! HOW HAVE YOU BEEN?
ANYTHING STRANGE AROUND YOUR LANDS?
WELL, A LOT OF OUR SHEEP HAVE BEEN EATEN LATELY, I'M AFRAID.
OH? WOLVES?
WOLVES ONLY EAT TWO OR THREE.
NO, SEEMS THERE'S A MONSTER DOWN FROM THE NORTH.
I'M SURE THAT THIS WAR DRAGGING ON HAS CAUSED ITS PREY BACK WHERE IT LIVES TO BE DEPLETED.
SCARY TIMES.
JOHANNA!
JOHANNAAA?
WHERE ARE YOU?

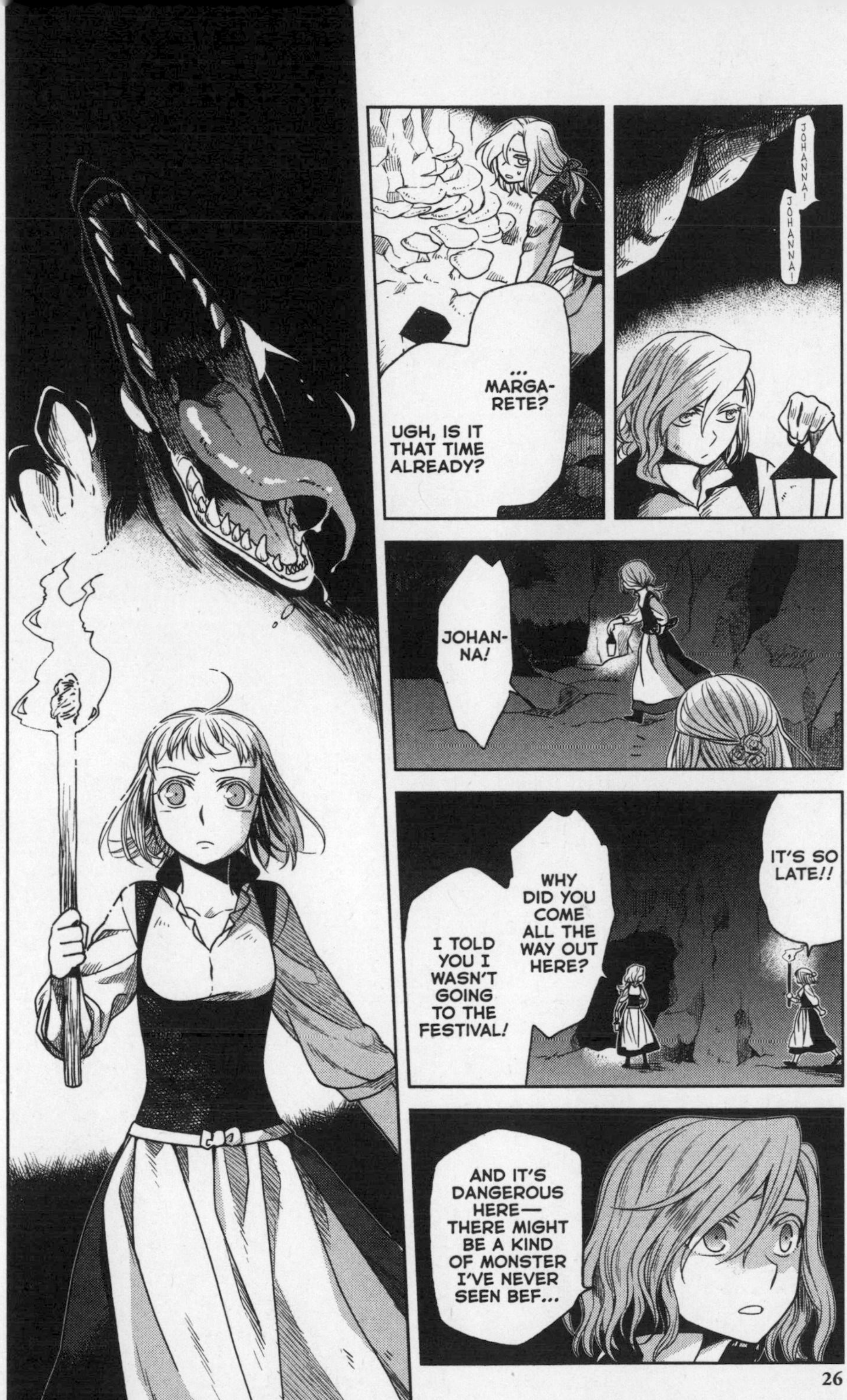
JOHANNA! JOHANNA!
... MARGARETE?
UGH, IS IT THAT TIME ALREADY?
JOHANNA!
IT'S SO LATE!!
WHY DID YOU COME ALL THE WAY OUT HERE?
I TOLD YOU I WASN'T GOING TO THE FESTIVAL!
AND IT'S DANGEROUS HERE—THERE MIGHT BE A KIND OF MONSTER I'VE NEVER SEEN BEF...

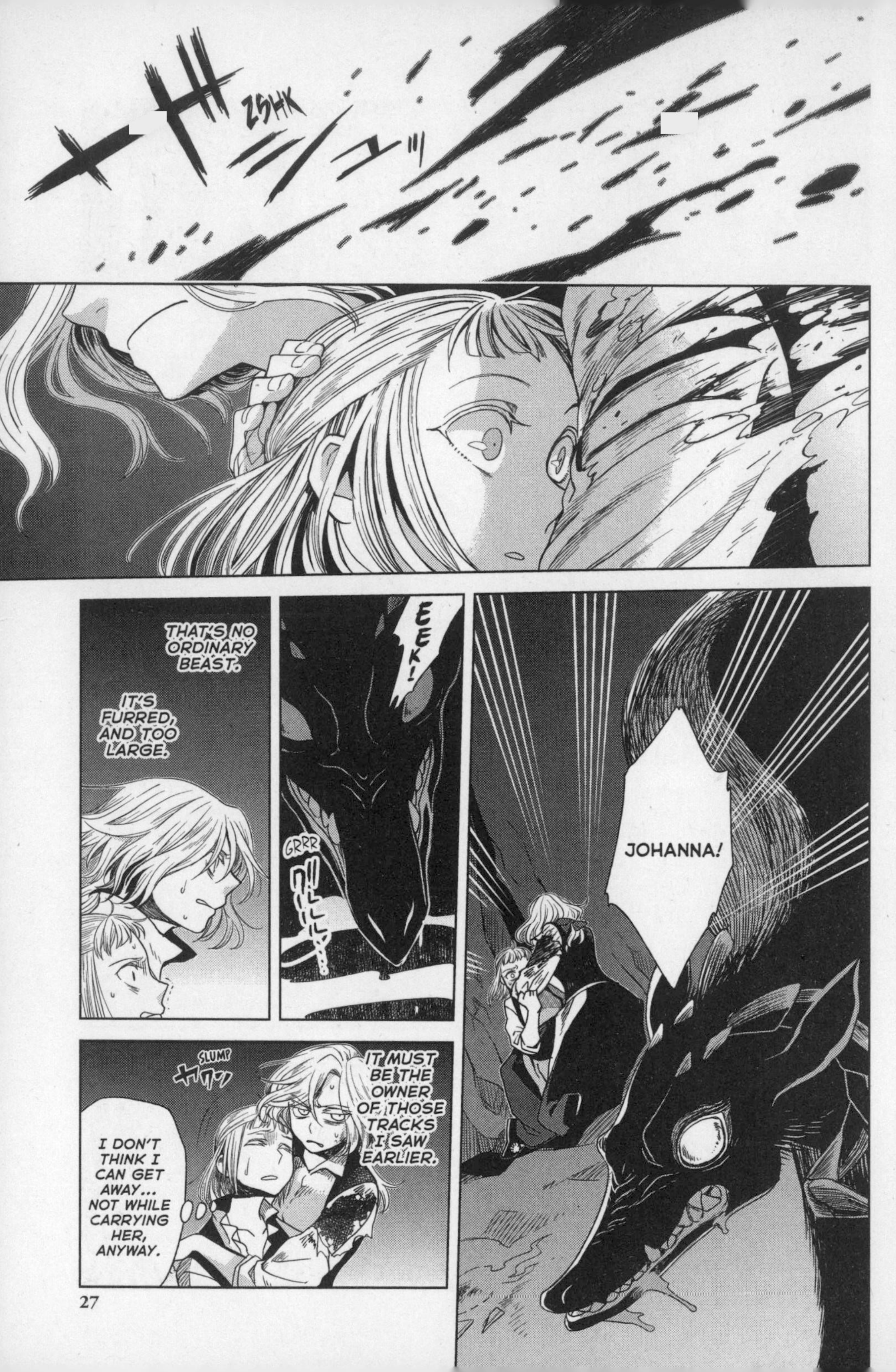
ZSHK
JOHANNA!
EEK!
GRRR
THAT'S NO ORDINARY BEAST.
IT'S FURRED, AND TOO LARGE.
IT MUST BE THE OWNER OF THOSE TRACKS I SAW EARLIER.
SLUMP
I DON'T THINK I CAN GET AWAY... NOT WHILE CARRYING HER, ANYWAY.

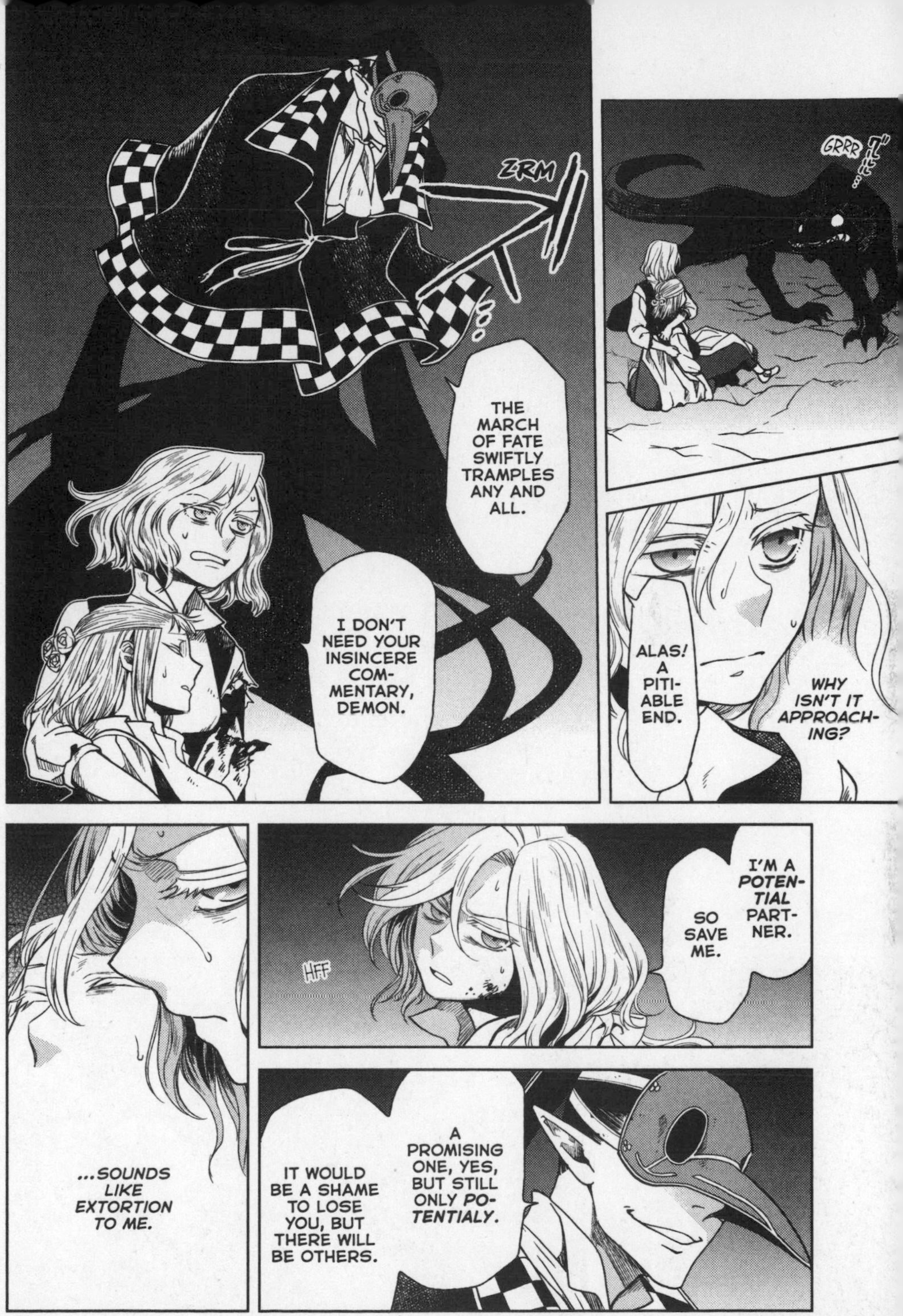
GRRR
ALAS! A PITIABLE END.
WHY ISN'T IT APPROACHING?
ZRM
THE MARCH OF FATE SWIFTLY TRAMPLES ANY AND ALL.
I DON'T NEED YOUR INSINCERE COMMENTARY, DEMON.
I'M A *POTENTIAL* PARTNER.
SO SAVE ME.
HFF
A PROMISING ONE, YES, BUT STILL ONLY *POTENTIALY*.
IT WOULD BE A SHAME TO LOSE YOU, BUT THERE WILL BE OTHERS.
...SOUNDS LIKE EXTORTION TO ME.

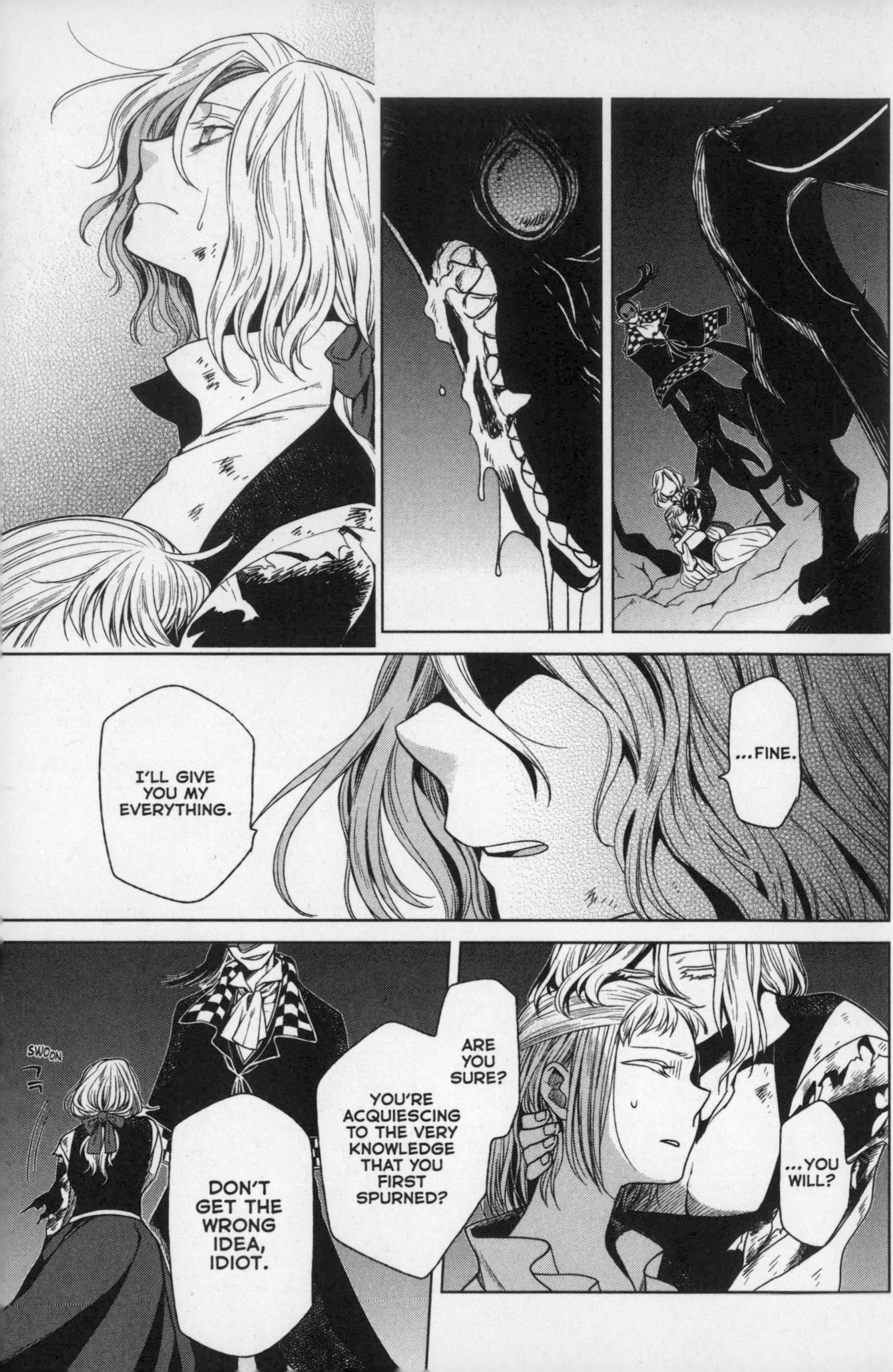
...FINE.
I'LL GIVE YOU MY EVERYTHING.
...YOU WILL?
ARE YOU SURE?
YOU'RE ACQUIESCING TO THE VERY KNOWLEDGE THAT YOU FIRST SPURNED?
DON'T GET THE WRONG IDEA, IDIOT.
SWOON

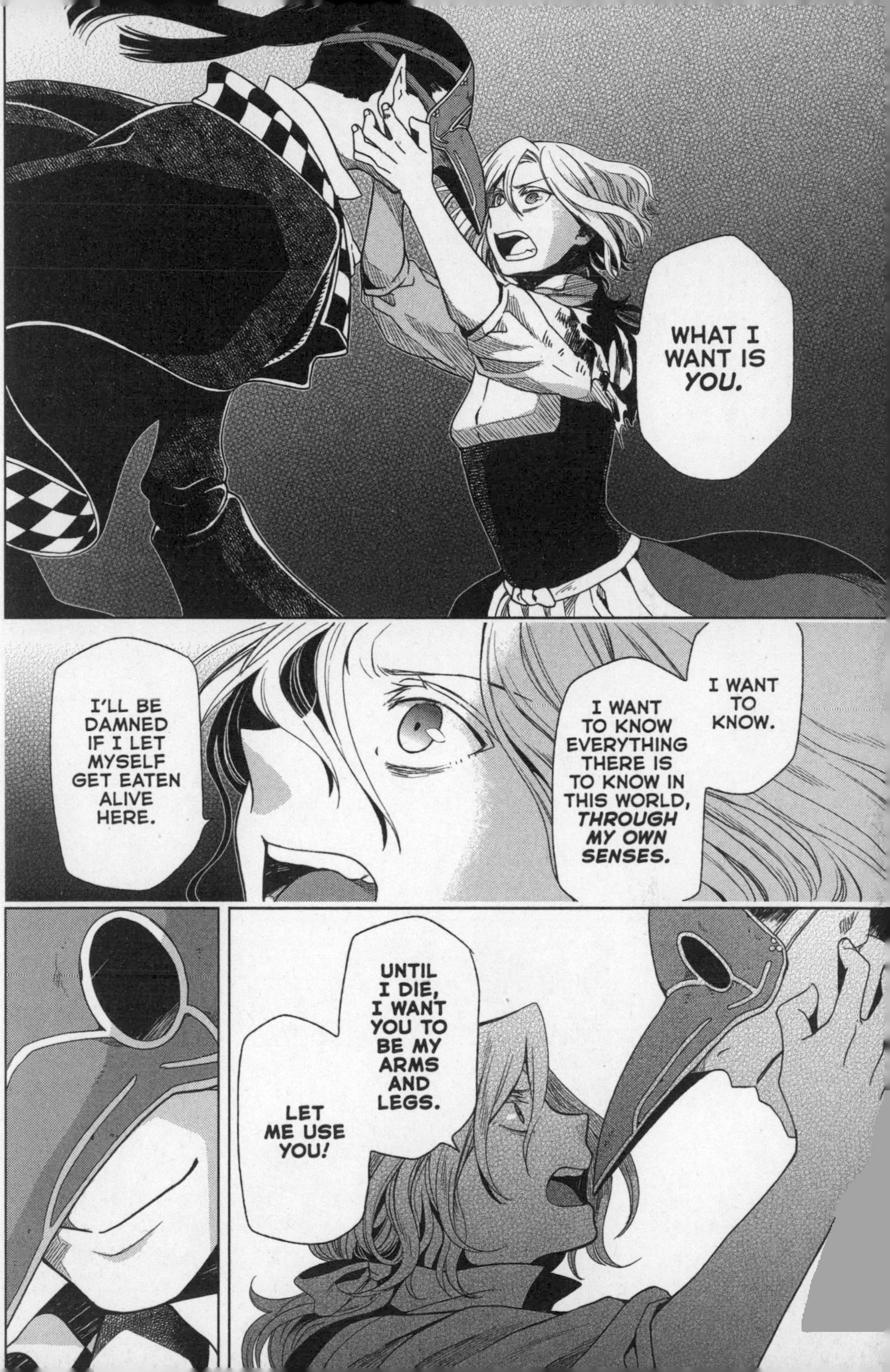
WHAT I WANT IS *YOU.*
I WANT TO KNOW.
I WANT TO KNOW EVERYTHING THERE IS TO KNOW IN THIS WORLD, *THROUGH MY OWN SENSES.*
I'LL BE DAMNED IF I LET MYSELF GET EATEN ALIVE HERE.
UNTIL I DIE, I WANT YOU TO BE MY ARMS AND LEGS.
LET ME USE YOU!

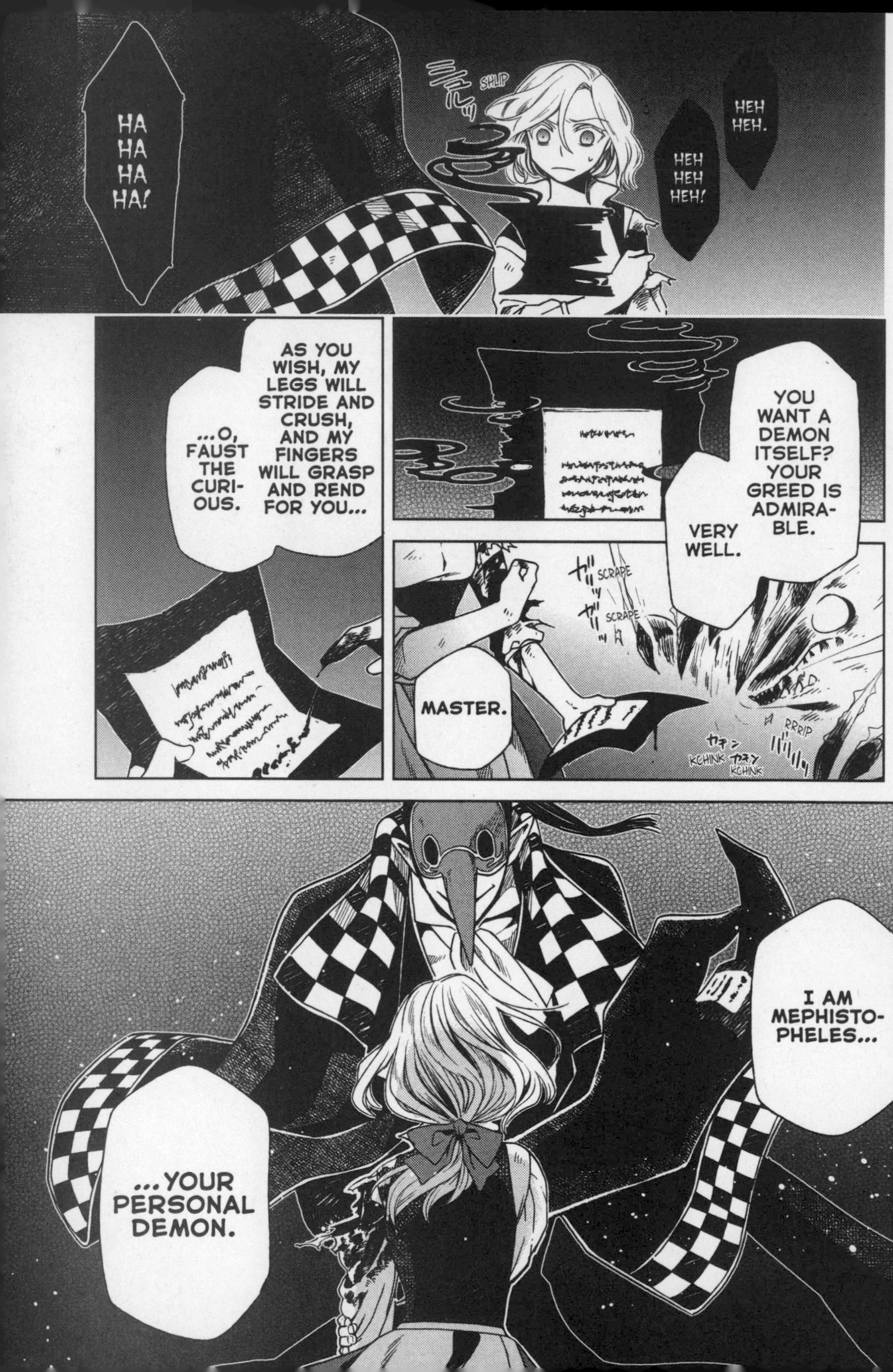
HEH HEH.
HEH HEH HEH!
SHLP
HA HA HA HA!
YOU WANT A DEMON ITSELF? YOUR GREED IS ADMIRABLE.
VERY WELL.
SCRAPE
SCRAPE
RRRIP
KCHINK
KCHINK
MASTER.
AS YOU WISH, MY LEGS WILL STRIDE AND CRUSH, AND MY FINGERS WILL GRASP AND REND FOR YOU...
...O, FAUST THE CURIOUS.
I AM MEPHISTOPHELES...
...YOUR PERSONAL DEMON.

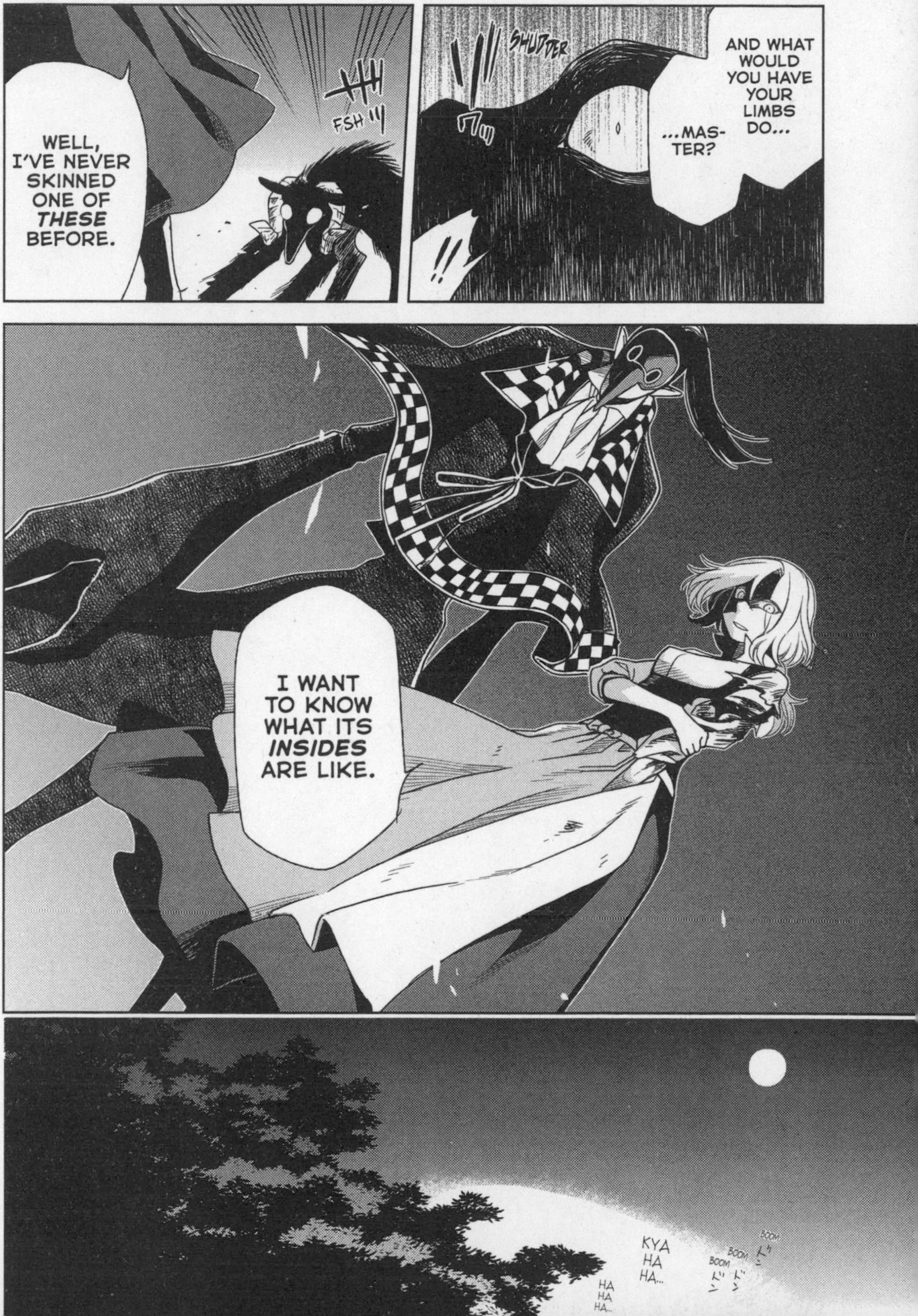
SHUDDER
AND WHAT WOULD YOU HAVE YOUR LIMBS DO...
...MAS-TER?
FSH
WELL, I'VE NEVER SKINNED ONE OF *THESE* BEFORE.
I WANT TO KNOW WHAT ITS *INSIDES* ARE LIKE.
BOOM
BOOM
BOOM
KYA HA HA...
HA HA HA...

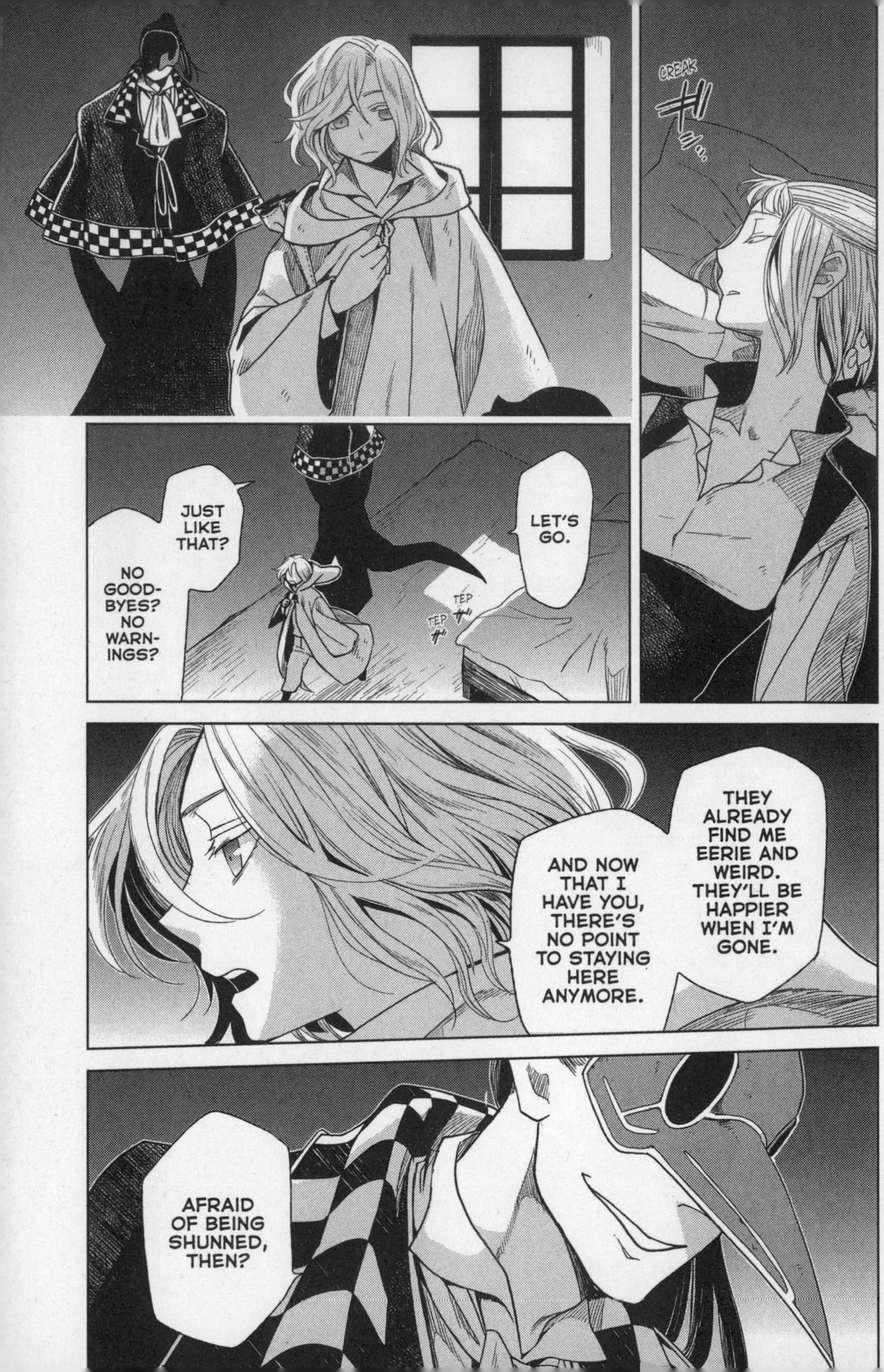
CREAK
LET'S GO.
TEP
TEP
JUST LIKE THAT?
NO GOOD-BYES? NO WARN-INGS?
THEY ALREADY FIND ME EERIE AND WEIRD. THEY'LL BE HAPPIER WHEN I'M GONE.
AND NOW THAT I HAVE YOU, THERE'S NO POINT TO STAYING HERE ANYMORE.
AFRAID OF BEING SHUNNED, THEN?

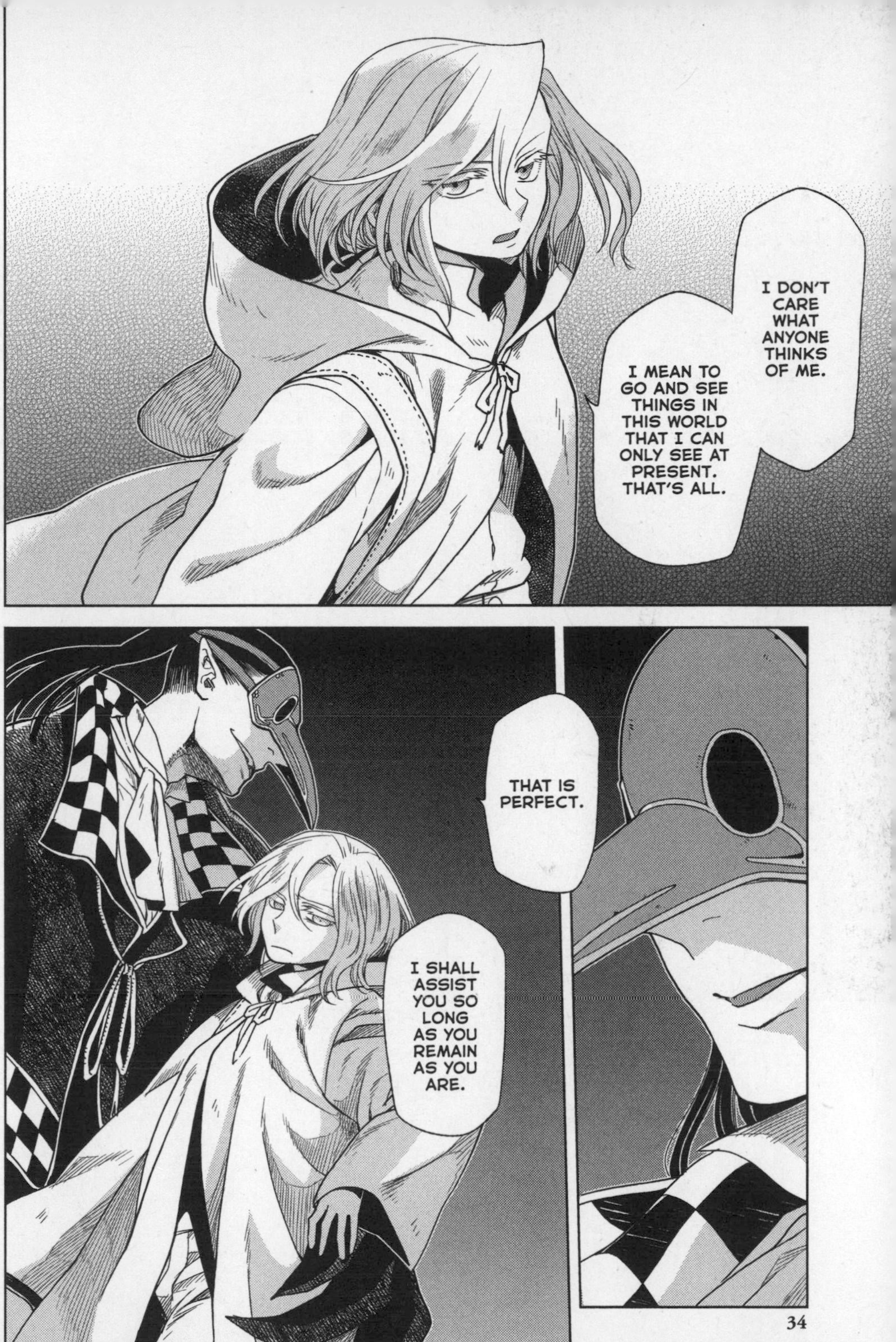
I DON'T CARE WHAT ANYONE THINKS OF ME.
I MEAN TO GO AND SEE THINGS IN THIS WORLD THAT I CAN ONLY SEE AT PRESENT. THAT'S ALL.
THAT IS PERFECT.
I SHALL ASSIST YOU SO LONG AS YOU REMAIN AS YOU ARE.

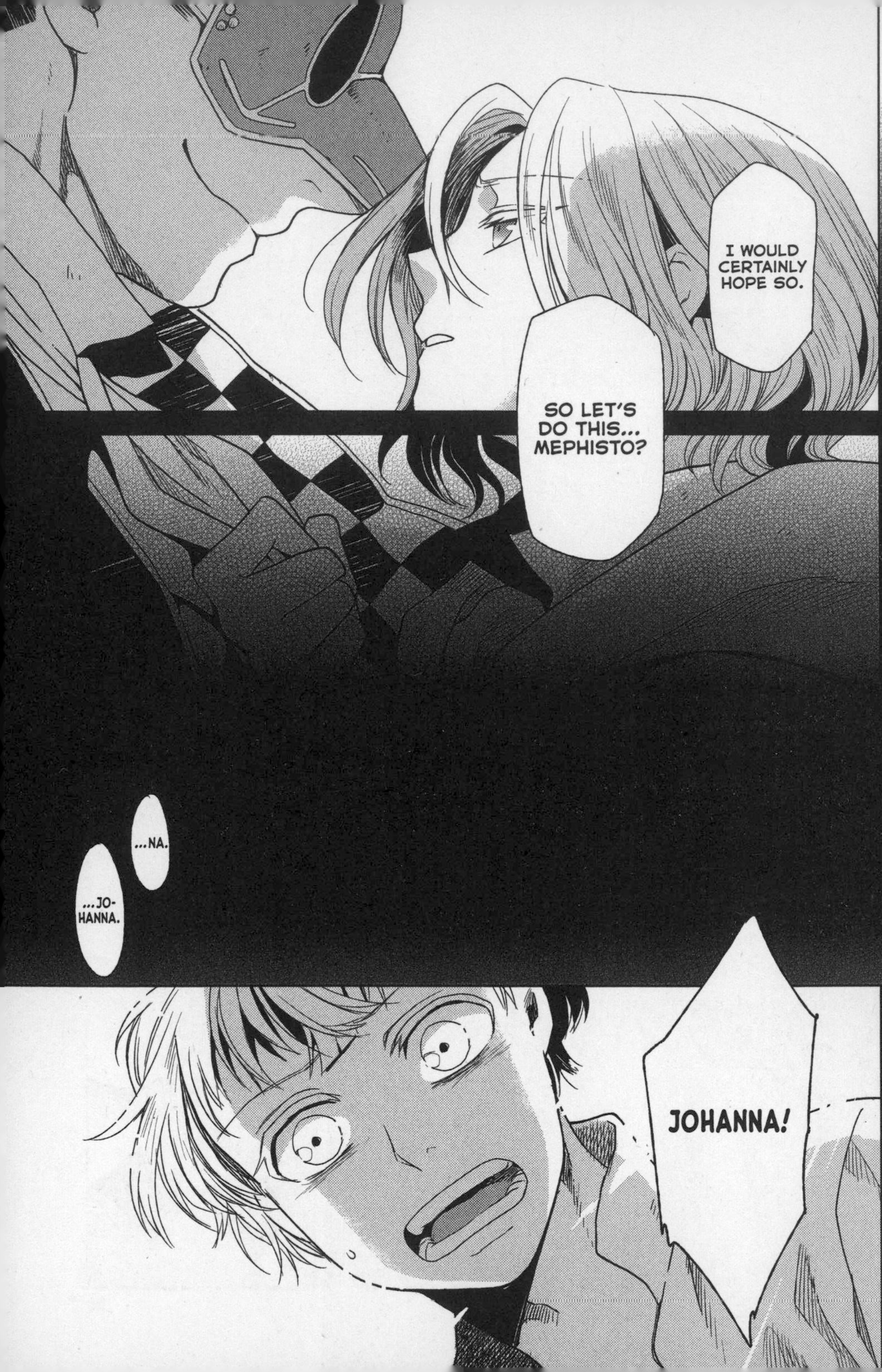
I WOULD CERTAINLY HOPE SO.
SO LET'S DO THIS... MEPHISTO?
...NA.
...JO-HANNA.
JOHANNA!

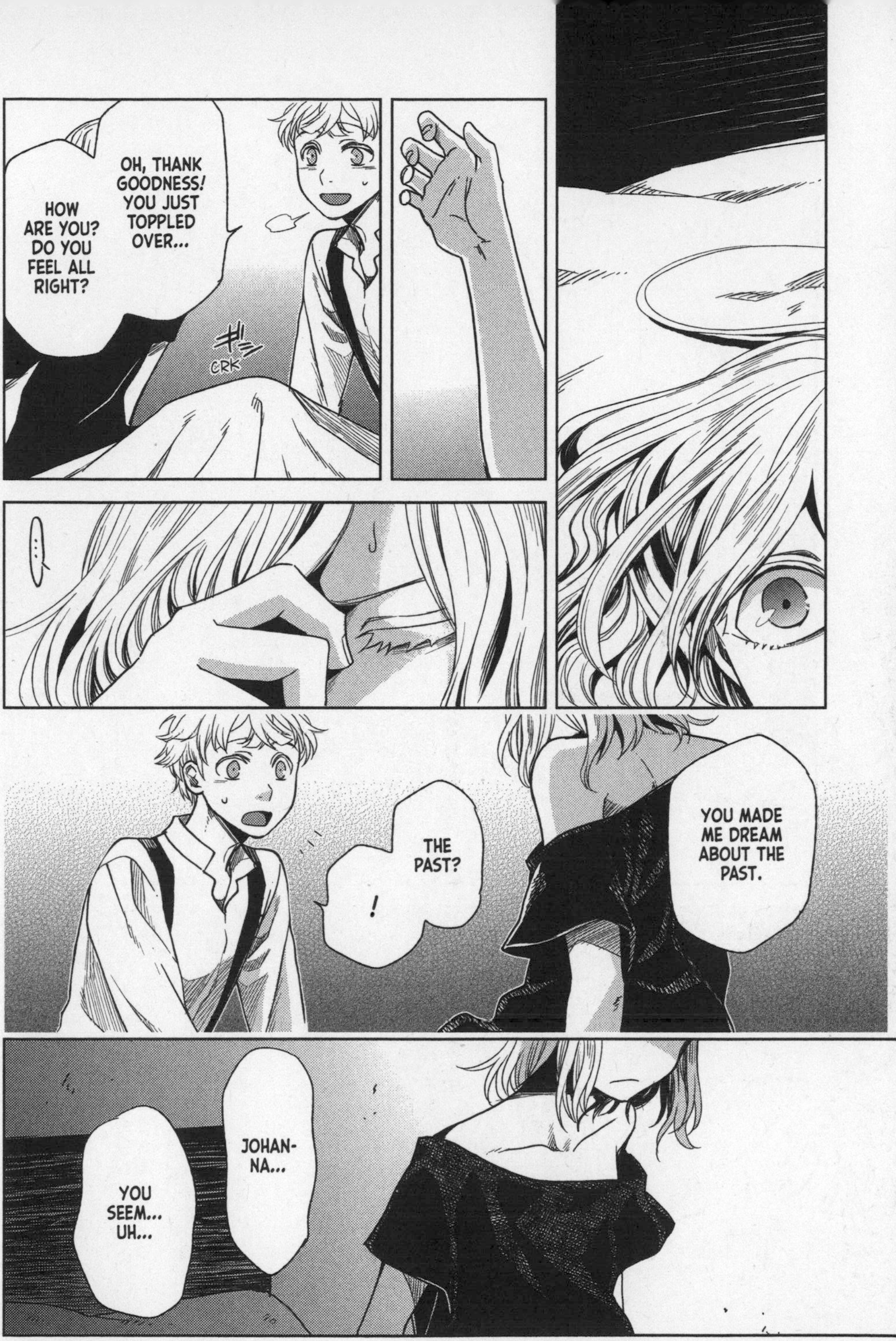
OH, THANK GOODNESS! YOU JUST TOPPLED OVER...
HOW ARE YOU? DO YOU FEEL ALL RIGHT?
CRK
...
YOU MADE ME DREAM ABOUT THE PAST.
THE PAST?
!
JOHAN-NA...
YOU SEEM... UH...

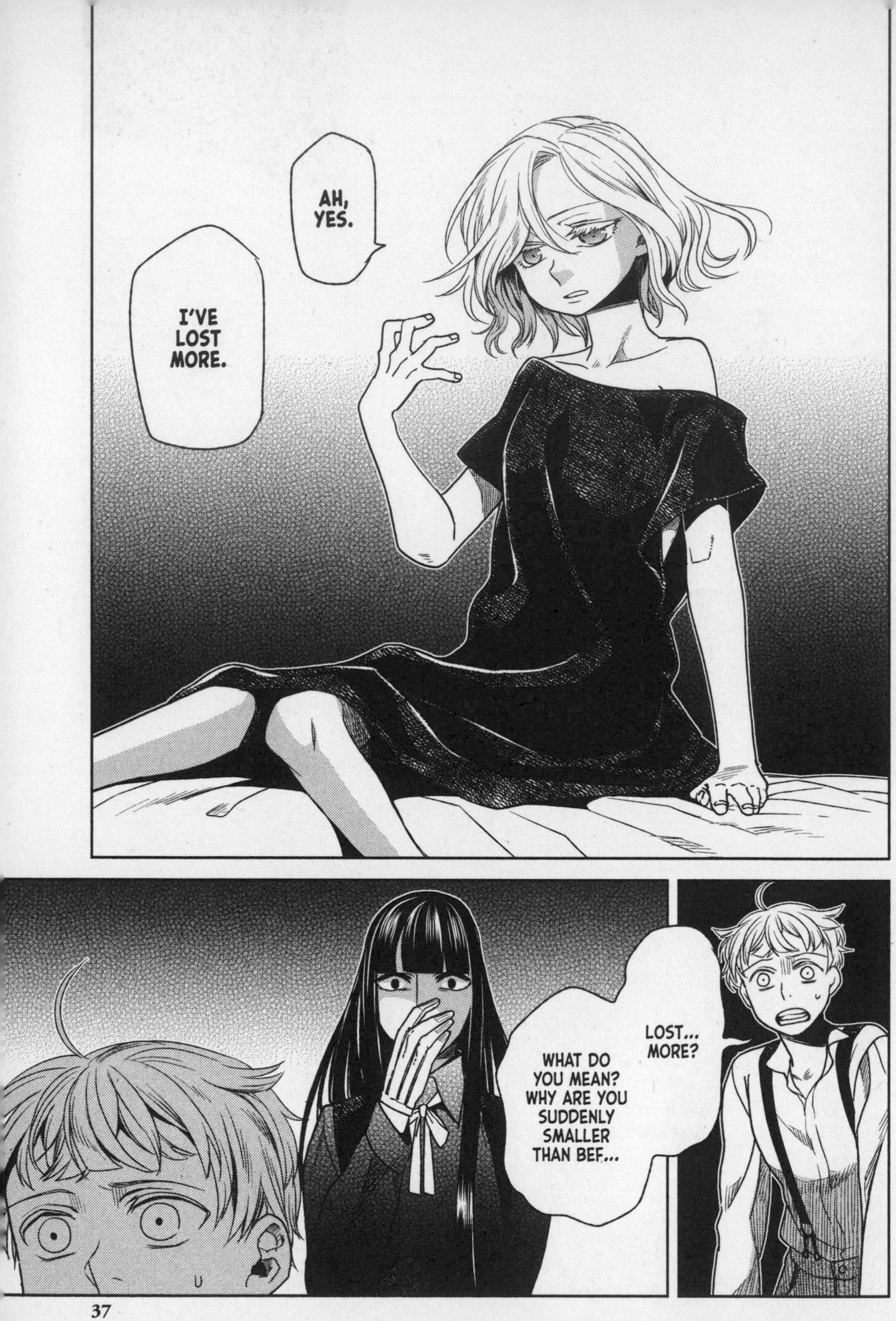
AH, YES.
I'VE LOST MORE.
LOST... MORE?
WHAT DO YOU MEAN? WHY ARE YOU SUDDENLY SMALLER THAN BEF...

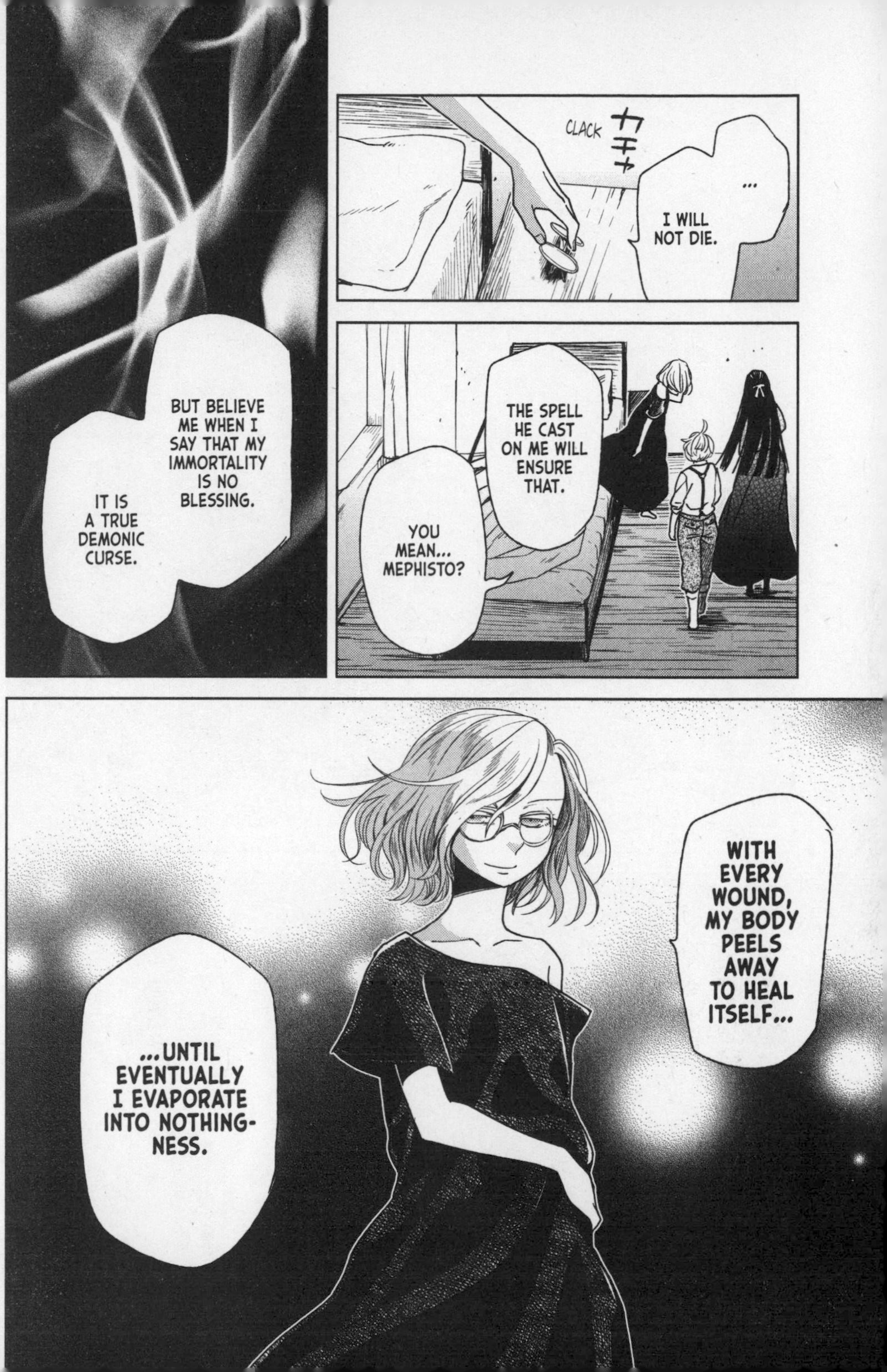

カチャ
CLACK
...
I WILL NOT DIE.
THE SPELL HE CAST ON ME WILL ENSURE THAT.
YOU MEAN... MEPHISTO?
BUT BELIEVE ME WHEN I SAY THAT MY IMMORTALITY IS NO BLESSING.
IT IS A TRUE DEMONIC CURSE.
WITH EVERY WOUND, MY BODY PEELS AWAY TO HEAL ITSELF...
...UNTIL EVENTUALLY I EVAPORATE INTO NOTHING-NESS.

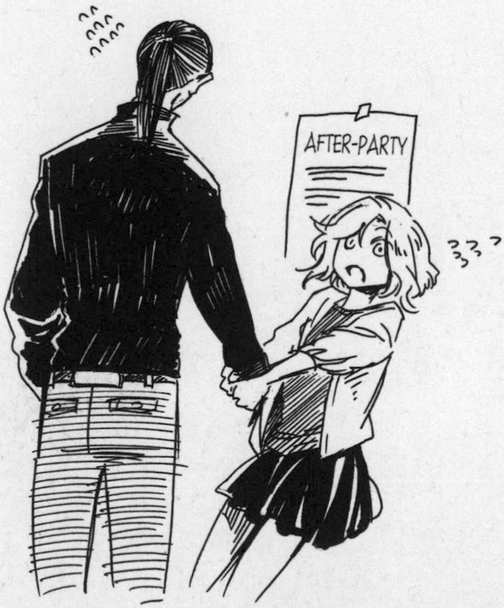
AFTER-PARTY

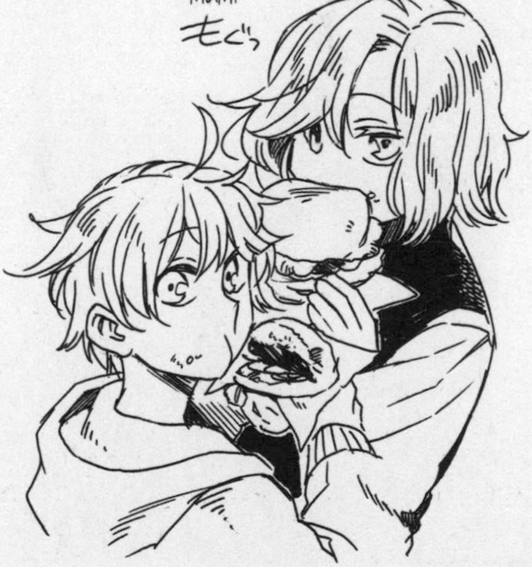
MUMF
もぐっ

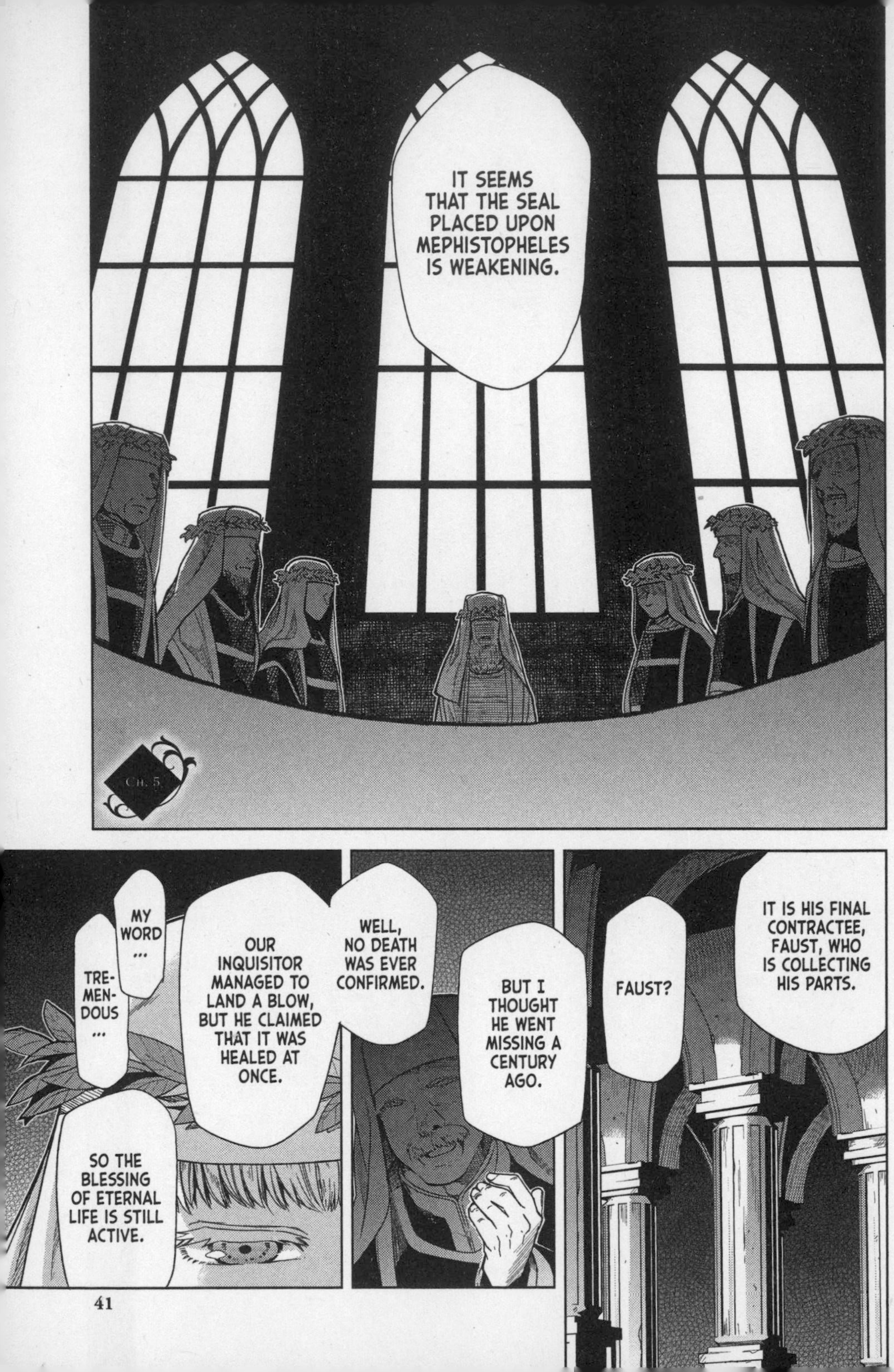
IT SEEMS THAT THE SEAL PLACED UPON MEPHISTOPHELES IS WEAKENING.
Ch. 5
IT IS HIS FINAL CONTRACTEE, FAUST, WHO IS COLLECTING HIS PARTS.
FAUST?
BUT I THOUGHT HE WENT MISSING A CENTURY AGO.
WELL, NO DEATH WAS EVER CONFIRMED.
OUR INQUISITOR MANAGED TO LAND A BLOW, BUT HE CLAIMED THAT IT WAS HEALED AT ONCE.
MY WORD ...
TRE-MEN-DOUS ...
SO THE BLESSING OF ETERNAL LIFE IS STILL ACTIVE.

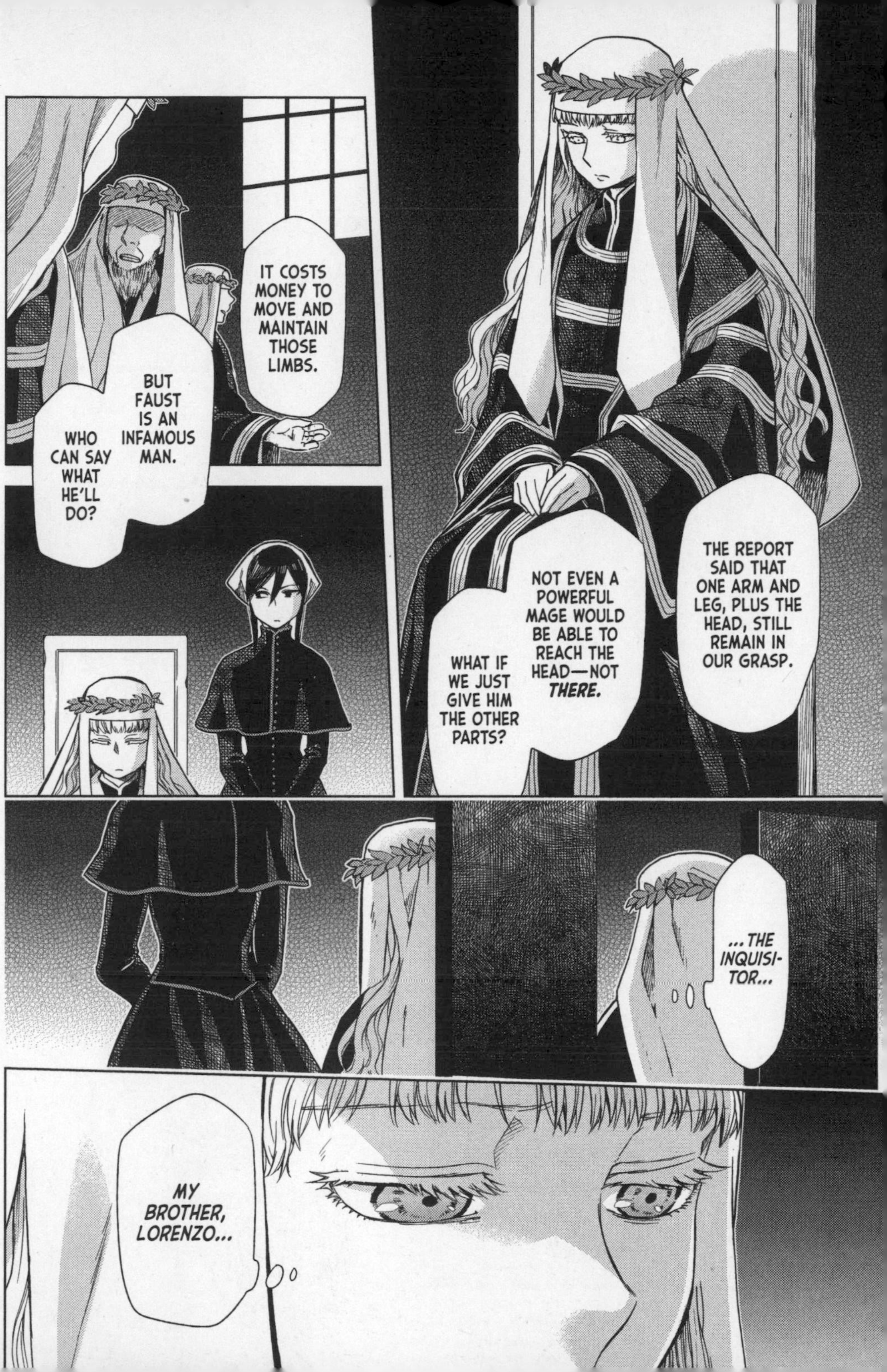
THE REPORT SAID THAT ONE ARM AND LEG, PLUS THE HEAD, STILL REMAIN IN OUR GRASP.
NOT EVEN A POWERFUL MAGE WOULD BE ABLE TO REACH THE HEAD—NOT *THERE.*
WHAT IF WE JUST GIVE HIM THE OTHER PARTS?
IT COSTS MONEY TO MOVE AND MAINTAIN THOSE LIMBS.
BUT FAUST IS AN INFAMOUS MAN.
WHO CAN SAY WHAT HE'LL DO?
...THE INQUISITOR...
MY BROTHER, LORENZO...

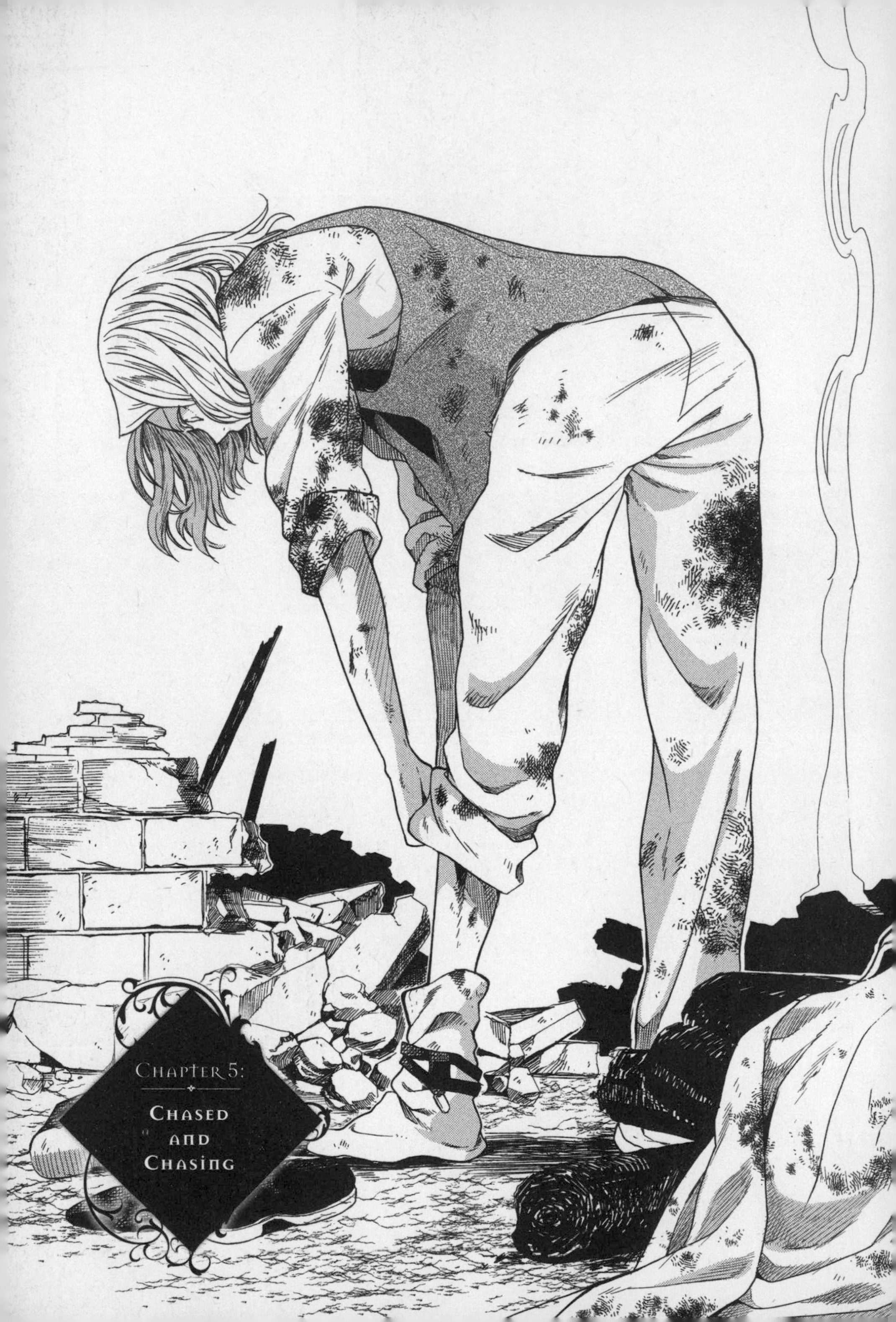
Chapter 5:
Chased and Chasing

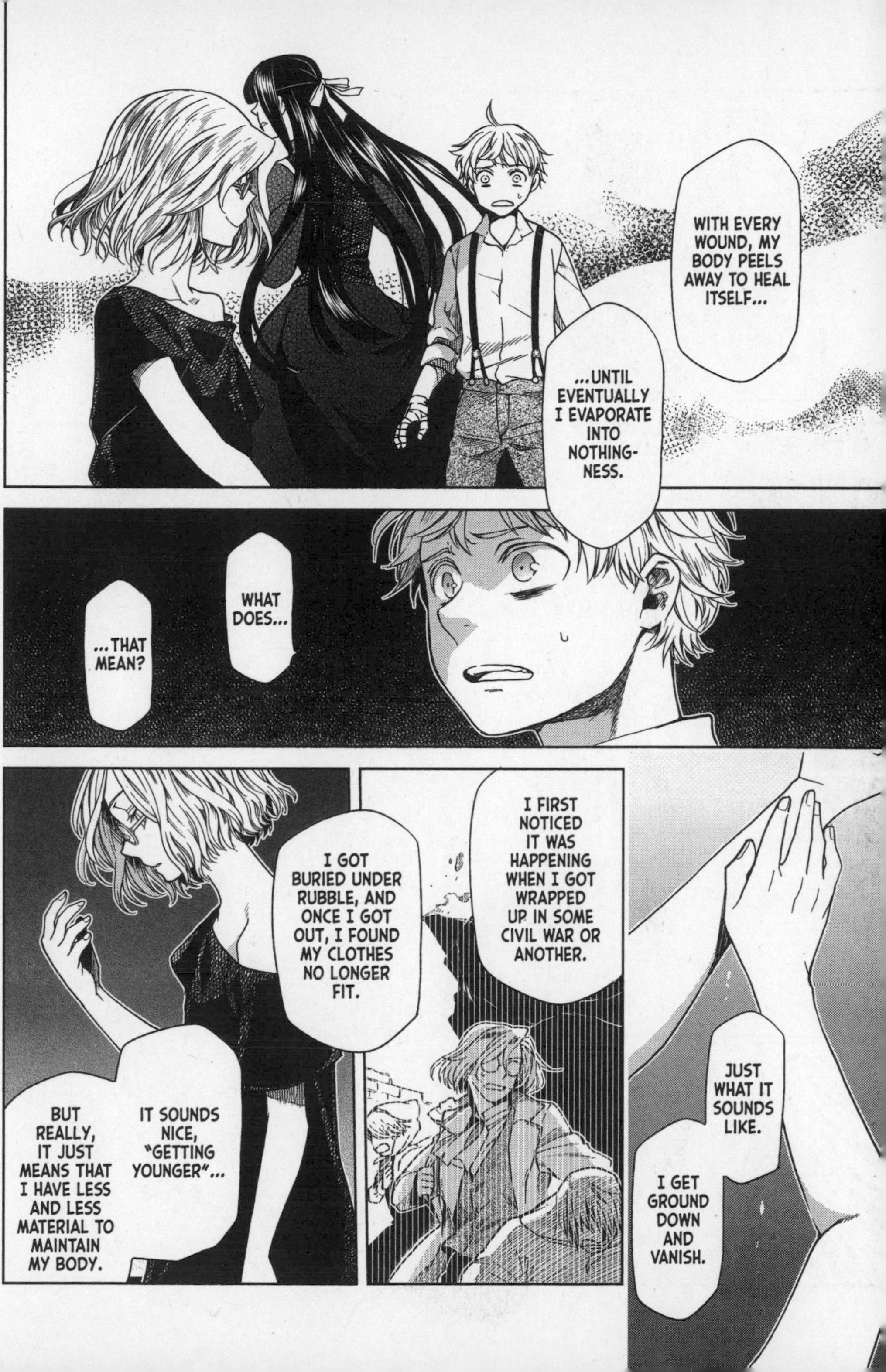
WITH EVERY WOUND, MY BODY PEELS AWAY TO HEAL ITSELF...
...UNTIL EVENTUALLY I EVAPORATE INTO NOTHING-NESS.
WHAT DOES...
...THAT MEAN?
JUST WHAT IT SOUNDS LIKE.
I GET GROUND DOWN AND VANISH.
I FIRST NOTICED IT WAS HAPPENING WHEN I GOT WRAPPED UP IN SOME CIVIL WAR OR ANOTHER.
I GOT BURIED UNDER RUBBLE, AND ONCE I GOT OUT, I FOUND MY CLOTHES NO LONGER FIT.
IT SOUNDS NICE, "GETTING YOUNGER"...
BUT REALLY, IT JUST MEANS THAT I HAVE LESS AND LESS MATERIAL TO MAINTAIN MY BODY.

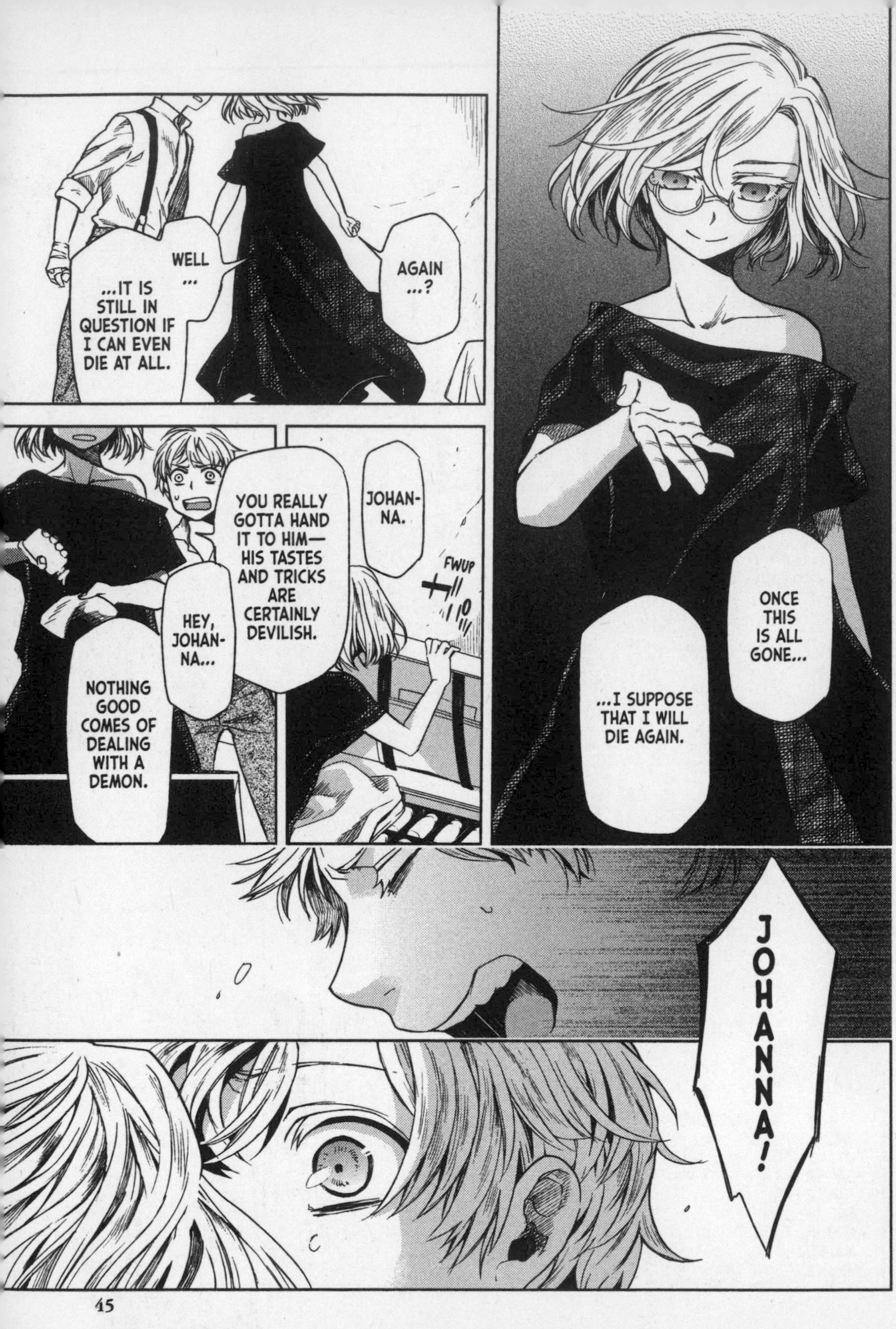

ONCE THIS IS ALL GONE...
...I SUPPOSE THAT I WILL DIE AGAIN.
AGAIN ...?
WELL ...
...IT IS STILL IN QUESTION IF I CAN EVEN DIE AT ALL.
JOHANNA.
FWUP
YOU REALLY GOTTA HAND IT TO HIM—HIS TASTES AND TRICKS ARE CERTAINLY DEVILISH.
HEY, JOHANNA...
NOTHING GOOD COMES OF DEALING WITH A DEMON.
JOHANNA!

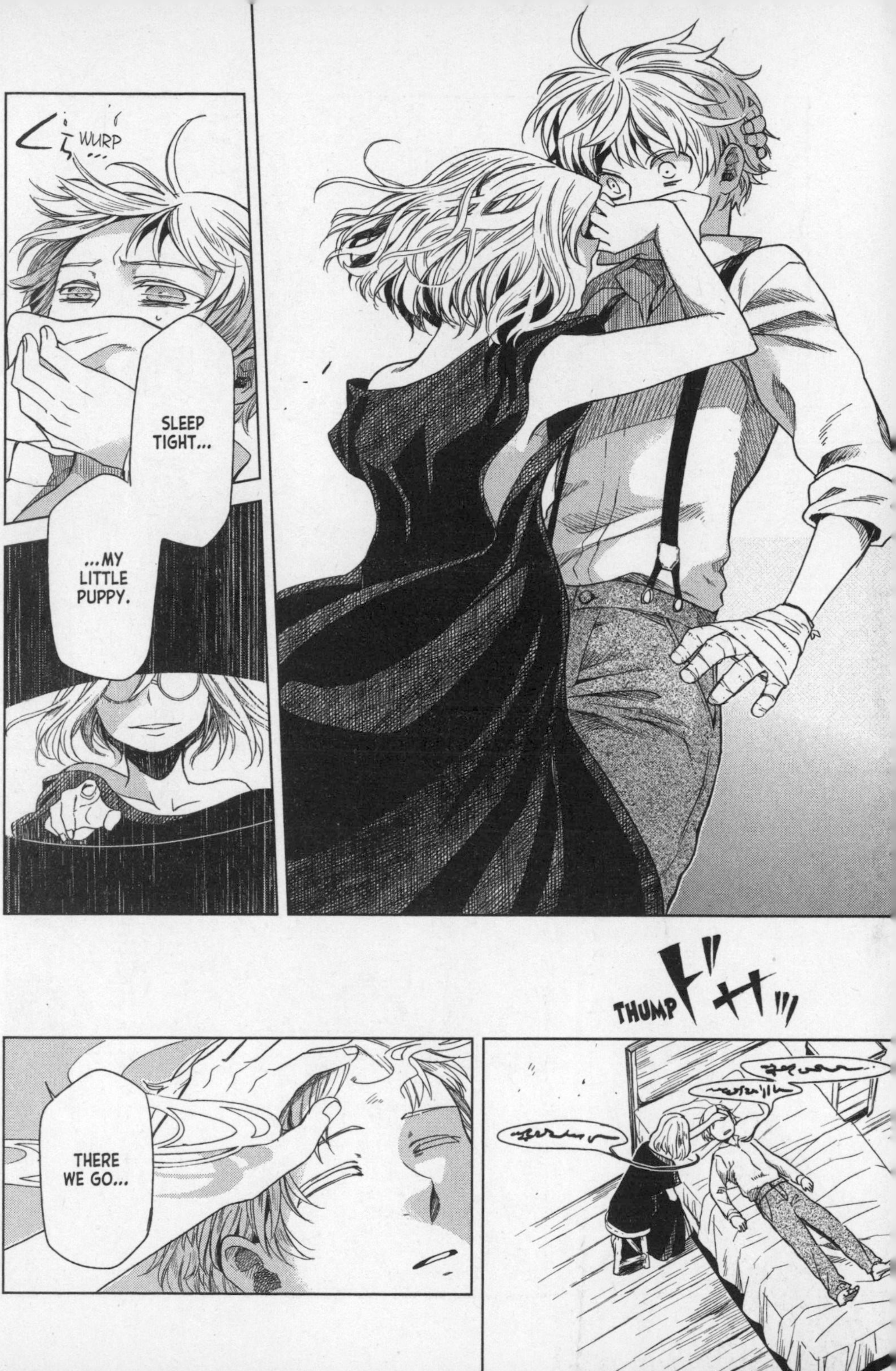
WURP
SLEEP TIGHT...
...MY LITTLE PUPPY.
THUMP
THERE WE GO...

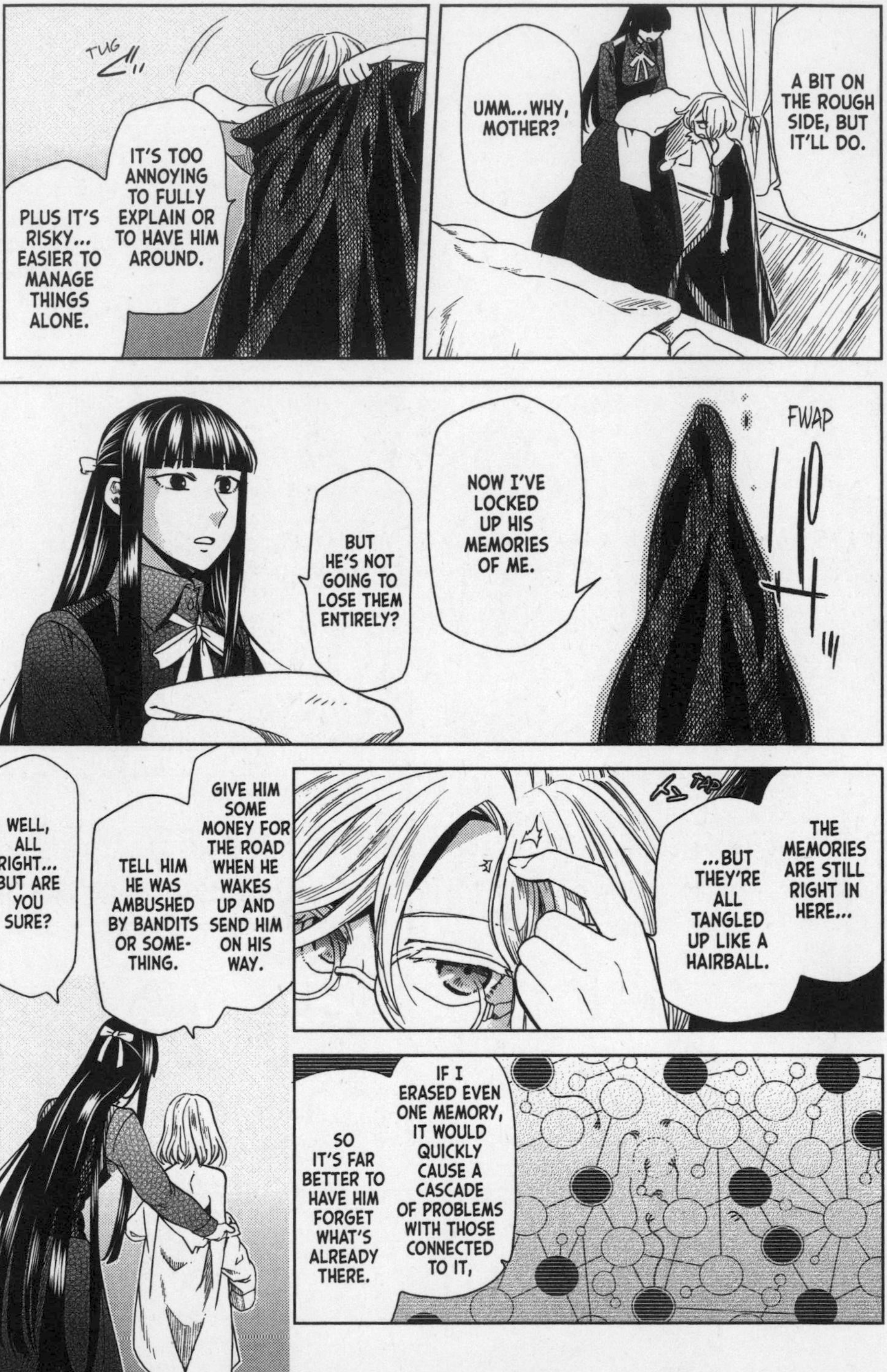
A BIT ON THE ROUGH SIDE, BUT IT'LL DO.
UMM...WHY, MOTHER?
TUG
IT'S TOO ANNOYING TO FULLY EXPLAIN OR TO HAVE HIM AROUND.
PLUS IT'S RISKY... EASIER TO MANAGE THINGS ALONE.
FWAP
NOW I'VE LOCKED UP HIS MEMORIES OF ME.
BUT HE'S NOT GOING TO LOSE THEM ENTIRELY?
TAP
THE MEMORIES ARE STILL RIGHT IN HERE...
...BUT THEY'RE ALL TANGLED UP LIKE A HAIRBALL.
IF I ERASED EVEN ONE MEMORY, IT WOULD QUICKLY CAUSE A CASCADE OF PROBLEMS WITH THOSE CONNECTED TO IT,
SO IT'S FAR BETTER TO HAVE HIM FORGET WHAT'S ALREADY THERE.
GIVE HIM SOME MONEY FOR THE ROAD WHEN HE WAKES UP AND SEND HIM ON HIS WAY.
TELL HIM HE WAS AMBUSHED BY BANDITS OR SOME-THING.
WELL, ALL RIGHT... BUT ARE YOU SURE?

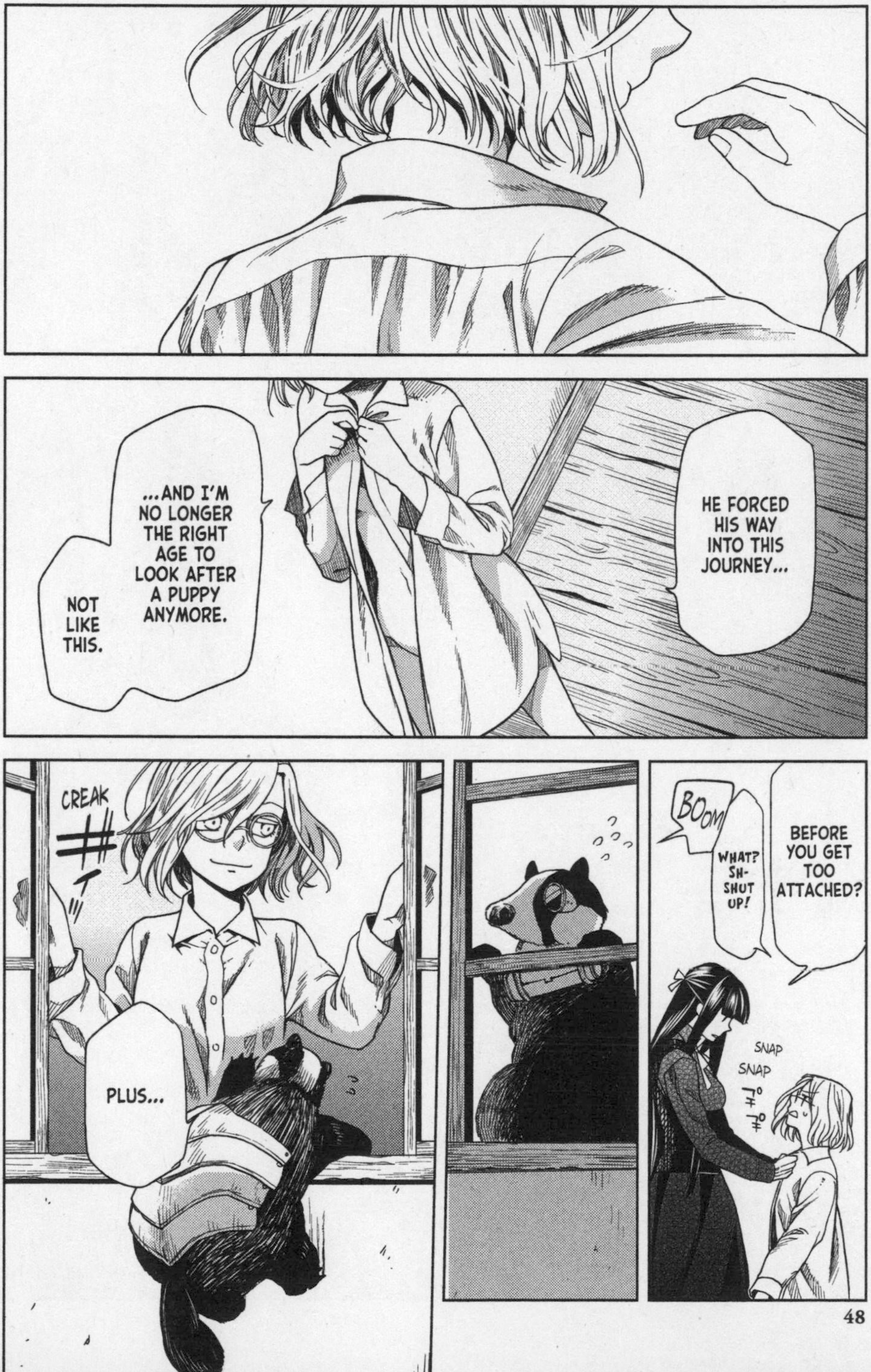
HE FORCED HIS WAY INTO THIS JOURNEY...
...AND I'M NO LONGER THE RIGHT AGE TO LOOK AFTER A PUPPY ANYMORE.
NOT LIKE THIS.
BEFORE YOU GET TOO ATTACHED?
BOOM
WHAT? SH-SHUT UP!
SNAP SNAP
CREAK
PLUS...

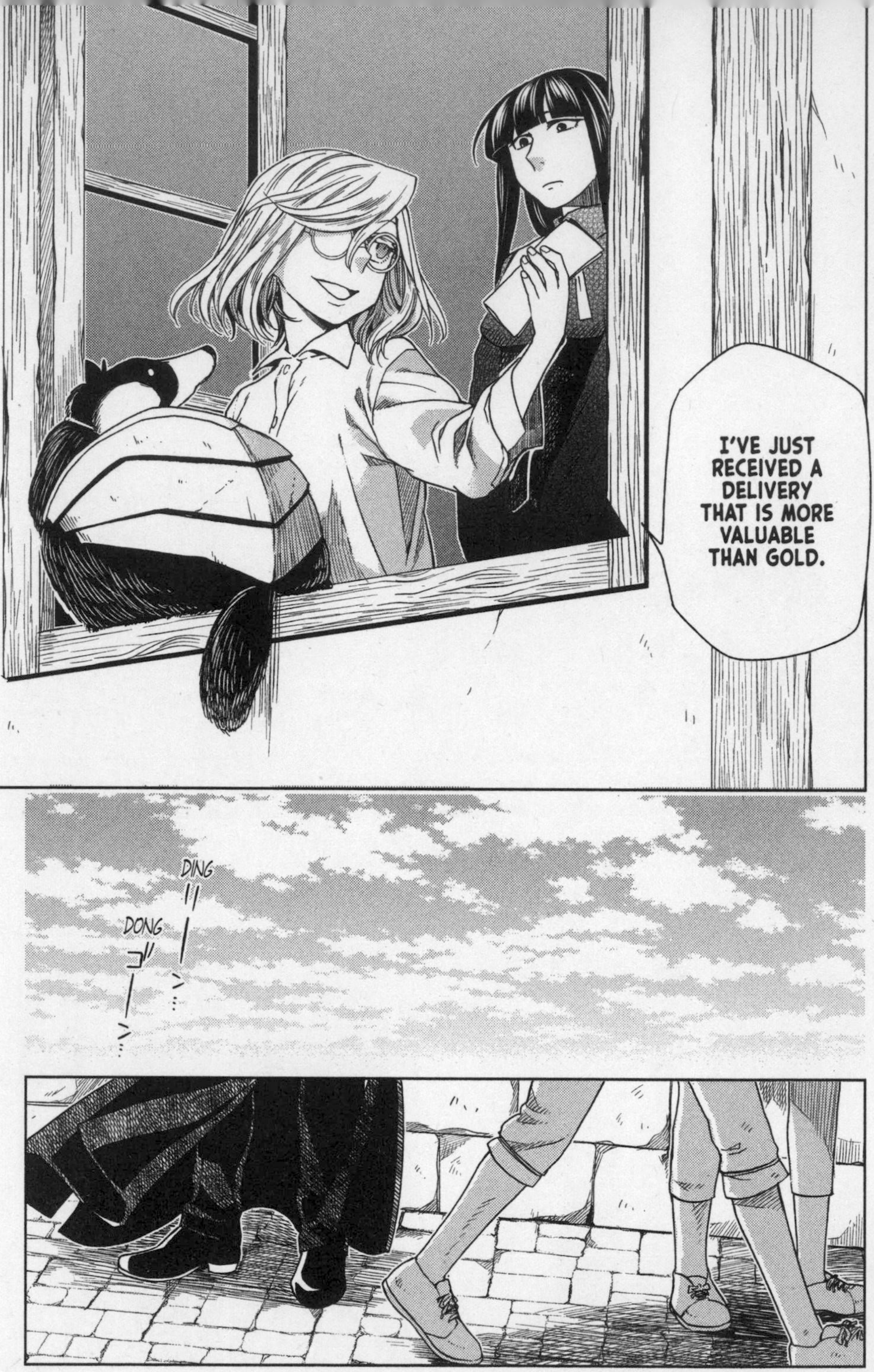
I'VE JUST RECEIVED A DELIVERY THAT IS MORE VALUABLE THAN GOLD.
DING
DONG

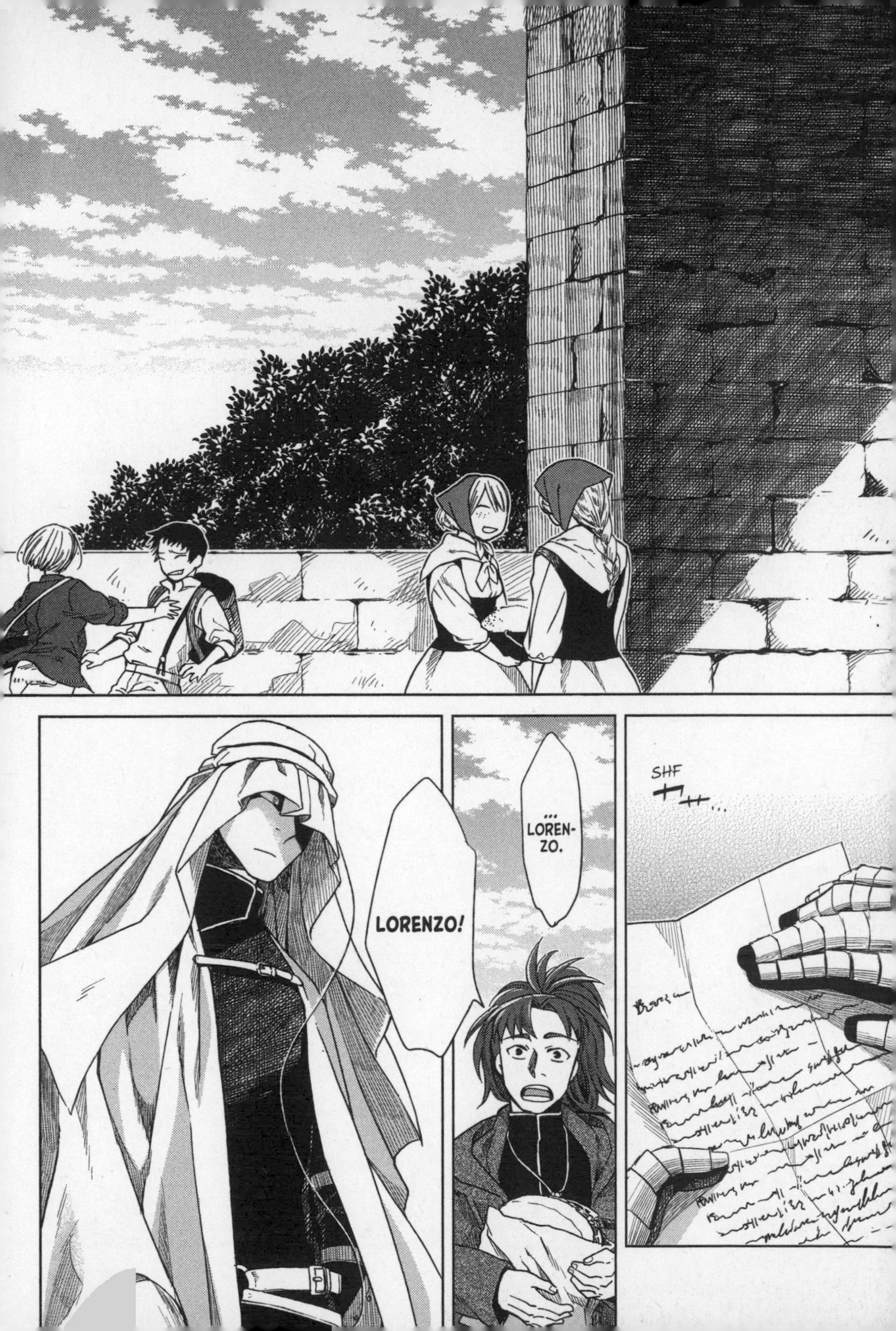
SHF
... LORENZO.
LORENZO!

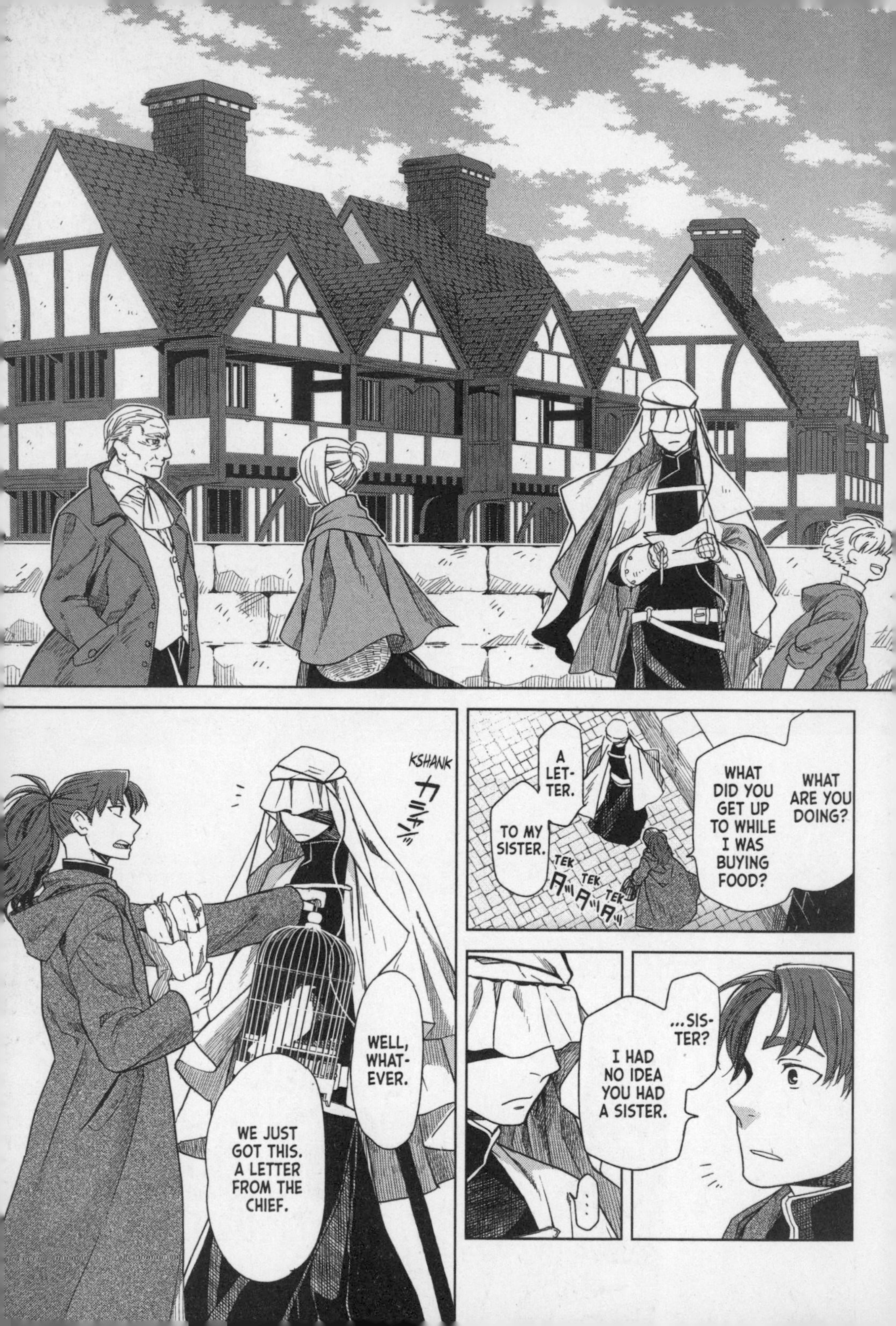
WHAT ARE YOU DOING?
WHAT DID YOU GET UP TO WHILE I WAS BUYING FOOD?
A LET- TER.
TO MY SISTER.
TEK TEK TEK
...SIS- TER?
I HAD NO IDEA YOU HAD A SISTER.
...
KSHANK
WELL, WHAT- EVER.
WE JUST GOT THIS. A LETTER FROM THE CHIEF.

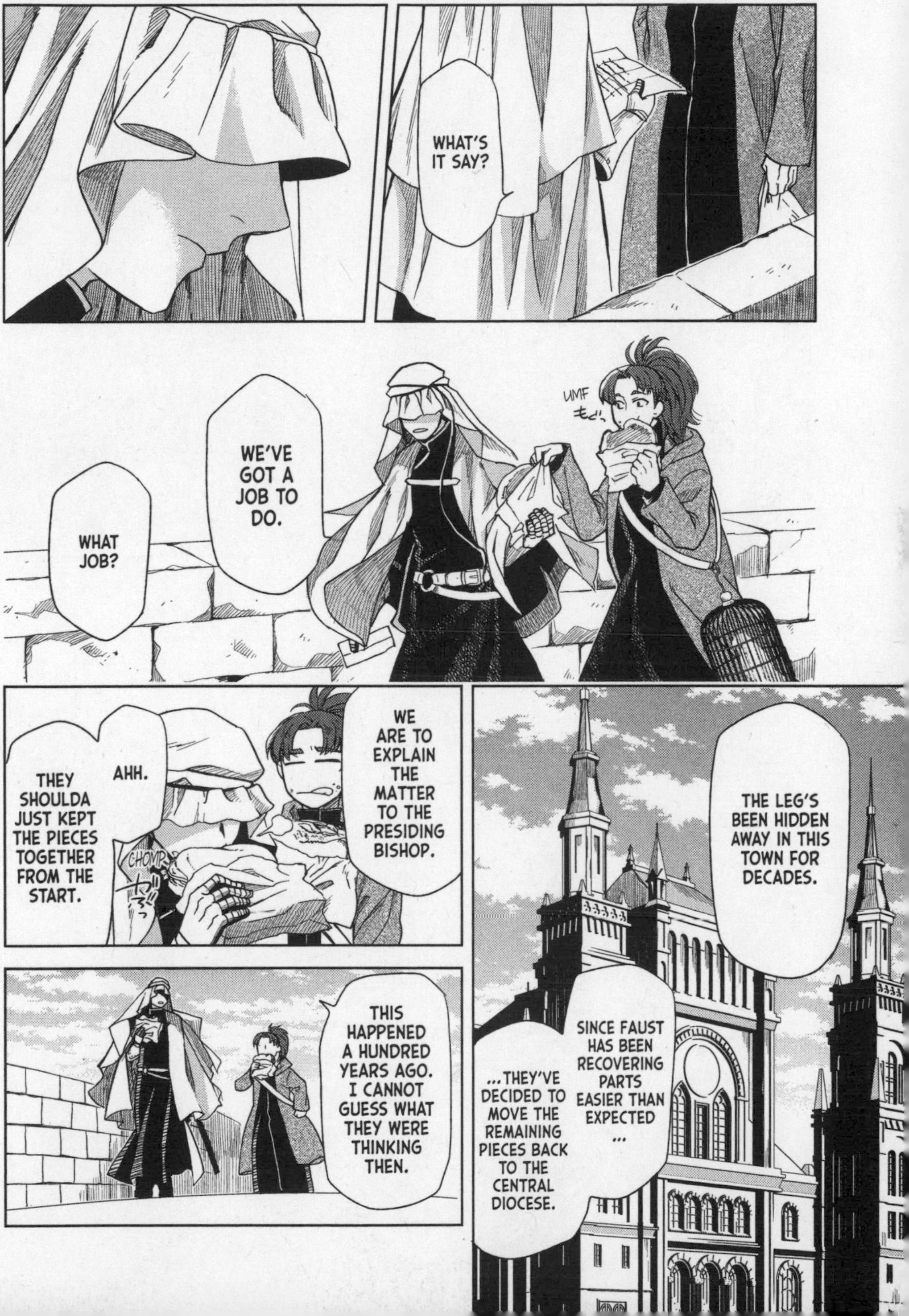
WHAT'S IT SAY?
UMF
もぐっ
WE'VE GOT A JOB TO DO.
WHAT JOB?
THE LEG'S BEEN HIDDEN AWAY IN THIS TOWN FOR DECADES.
SINCE FAUST HAS BEEN RECOVERING PARTS EASIER THAN EXPECTED ...
...THEY'VE DECIDED TO MOVE THE REMAINING PIECES BACK TO THE CENTRAL DIOCESE.
WE ARE TO EXPLAIN THE MATTER TO THE PRESIDING BISHOP.
AHH.
THEY SHOULDA JUST KEPT THE PIECES TOGETHER FROM THE START.
CHOMP
THIS HAPPENED A HUNDRED YEARS AGO. I CANNOT GUESS WHAT THEY WERE THINKING THEN.

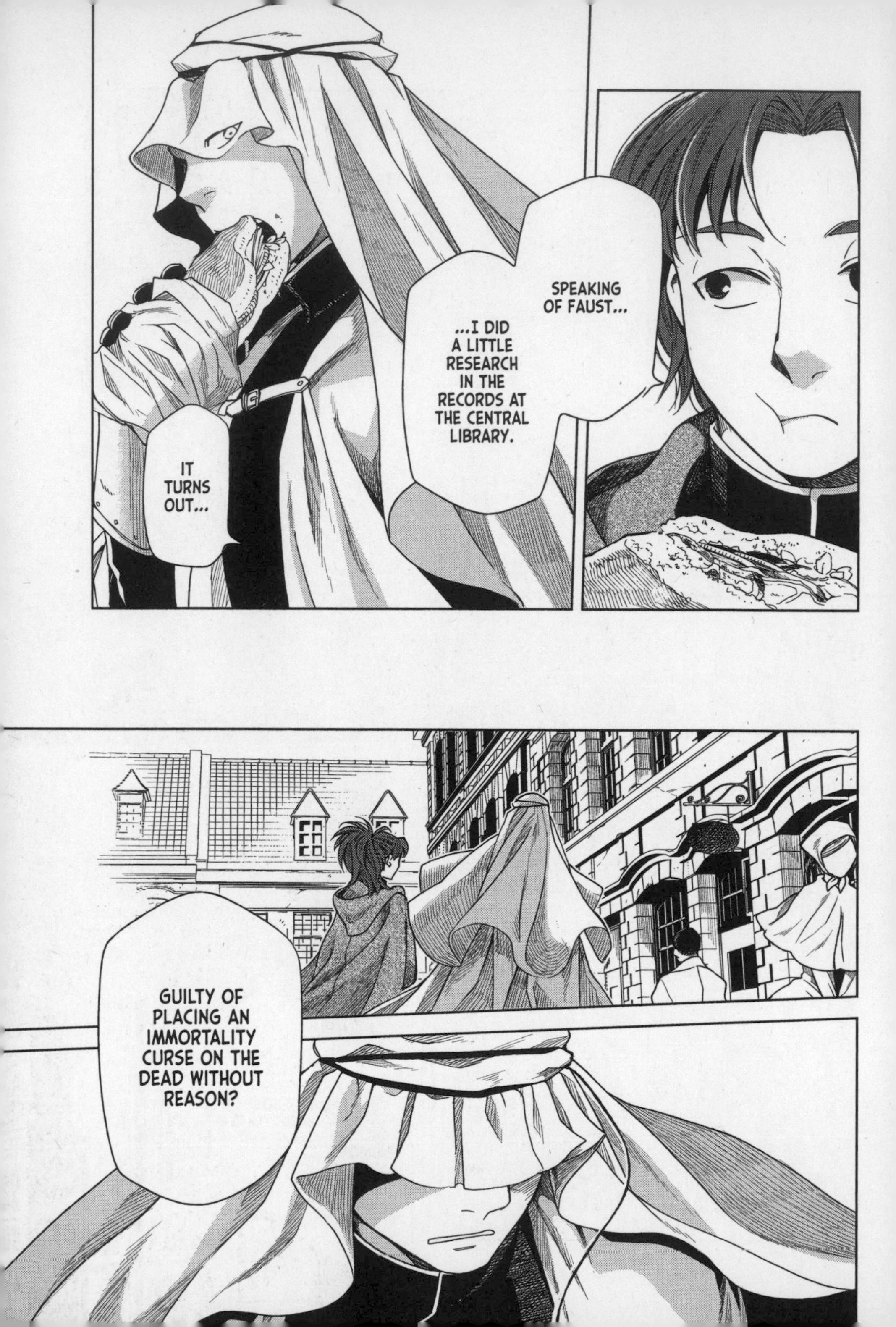
SPEAKING OF FAUST...
...I DID A LITTLE RESEARCH IN THE RECORDS AT THE CENTRAL LIBRARY.
IT TURNS OUT...
GUILTY OF PLACING AN IMMORTALITY CURSE ON THE DEAD WITHOUT REASON?

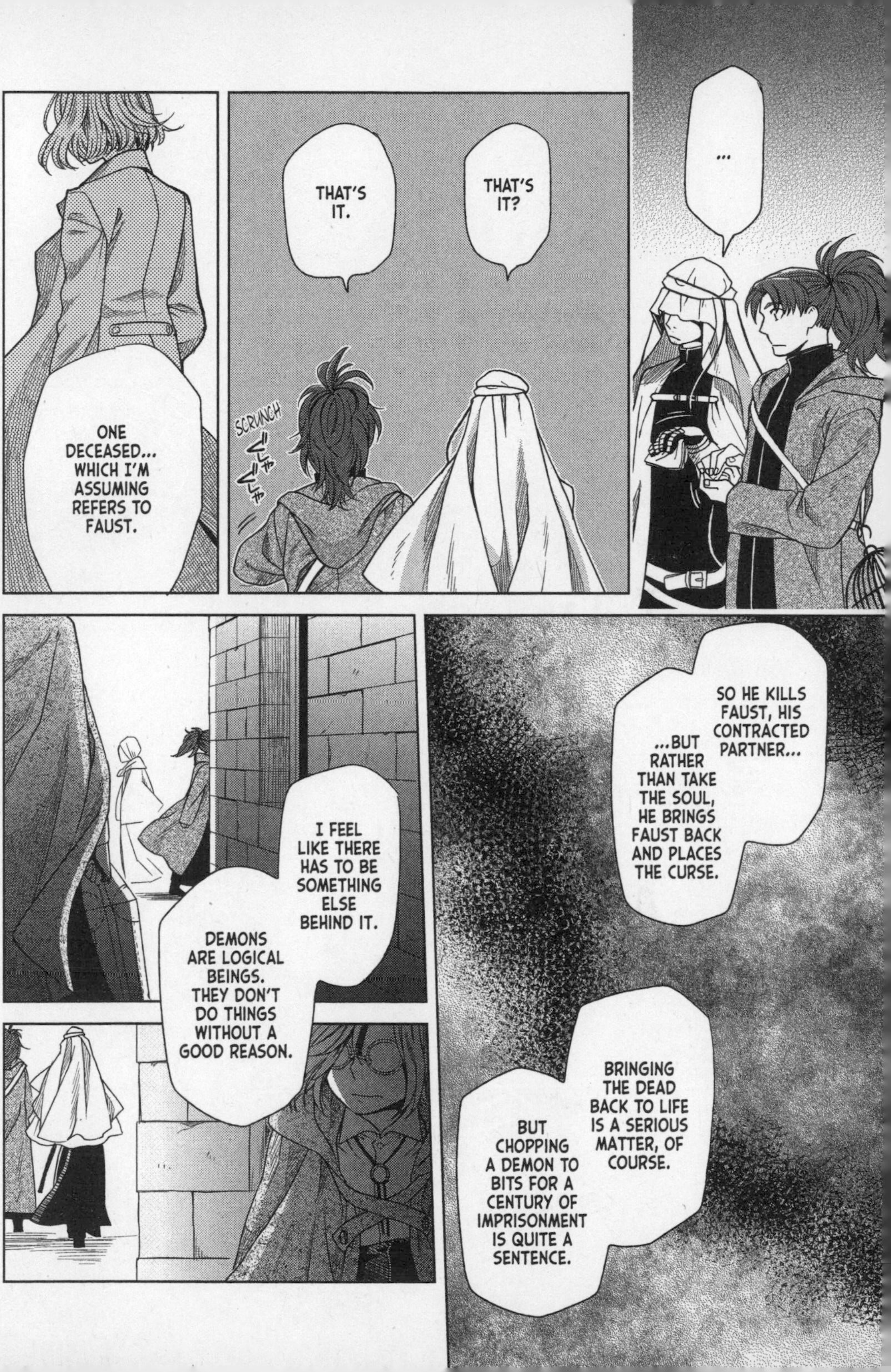
...
THAT'S IT?
THAT'S IT.
SCRUNCH
ONE DECEASED... WHICH I'M ASSUMING REFERS TO FAUST.
SO HE KILLS FAUST, HIS CONTRACTED PARTNER...
...BUT RATHER THAN TAKE THE SOUL, HE BRINGS FAUST BACK AND PLACES THE CURSE.
BRINGING THE DEAD BACK TO LIFE IS A SERIOUS MATTER, OF COURSE.
BUT CHOPPING A DEMON TO BITS FOR A CENTURY OF IMPRISONMENT IS QUITE A SENTENCE.
I FEEL LIKE THERE HAS TO BE SOMETHING ELSE BEHIND IT.
DEMONS ARE LOGICAL BEINGS. THEY DON'T DO THINGS WITHOUT A GOOD REASON.

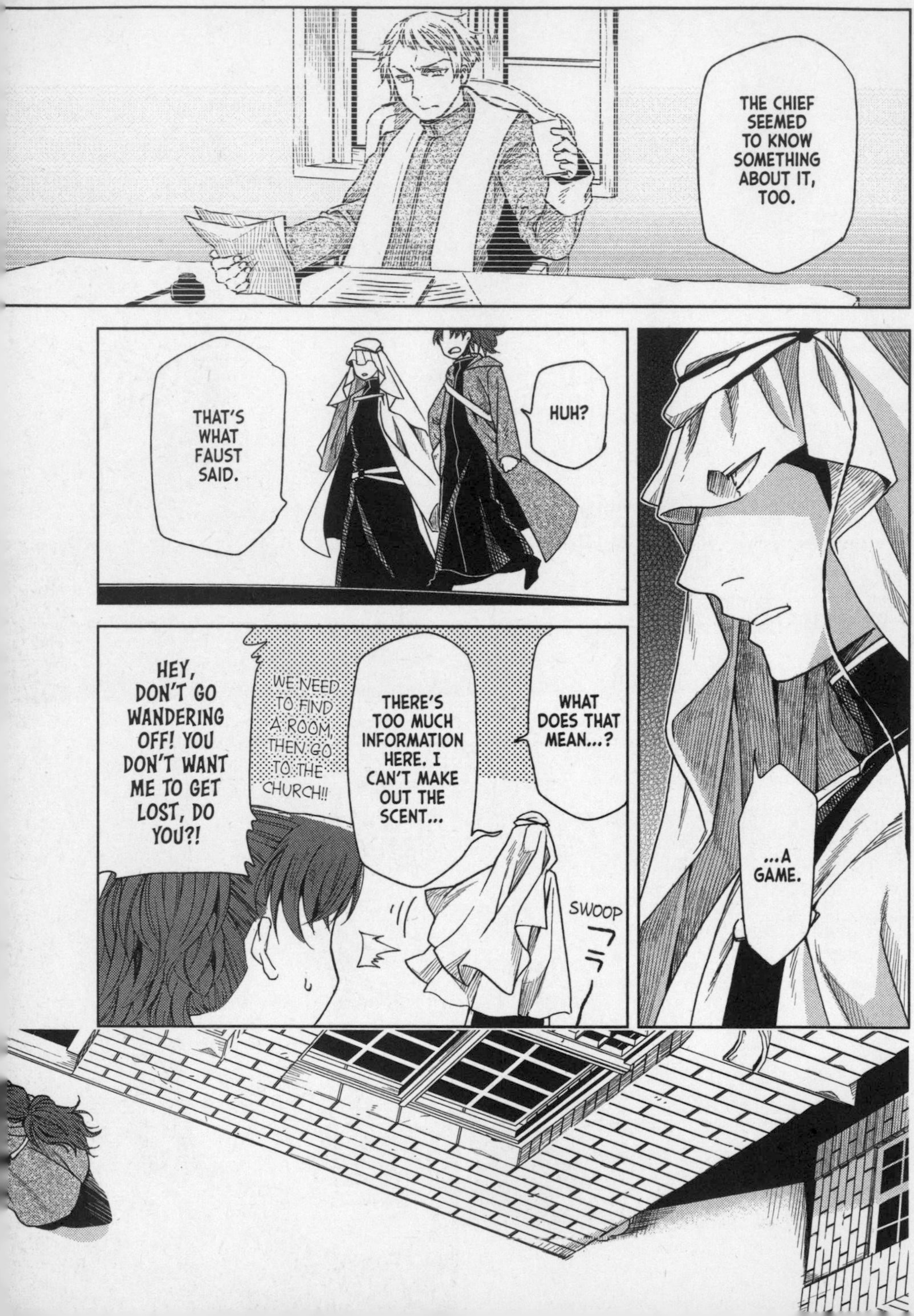
THE CHIEF SEEMED TO KNOW SOMETHING ABOUT IT, TOO.
...A GAME.
HUH?
THAT'S WHAT FAUST SAID.
WHAT DOES THAT MEAN...?
THERE'S TOO MUCH INFORMATION HERE. I CAN'T MAKE OUT THE SCENT...
WE NEED TO FIND A ROOM, THEN GO TO THE CHURCH!!
HEY, DON'T GO WANDERING OFF! YOU DON'T WANT ME TO GET LOST, DO YOU?!
SWOOP

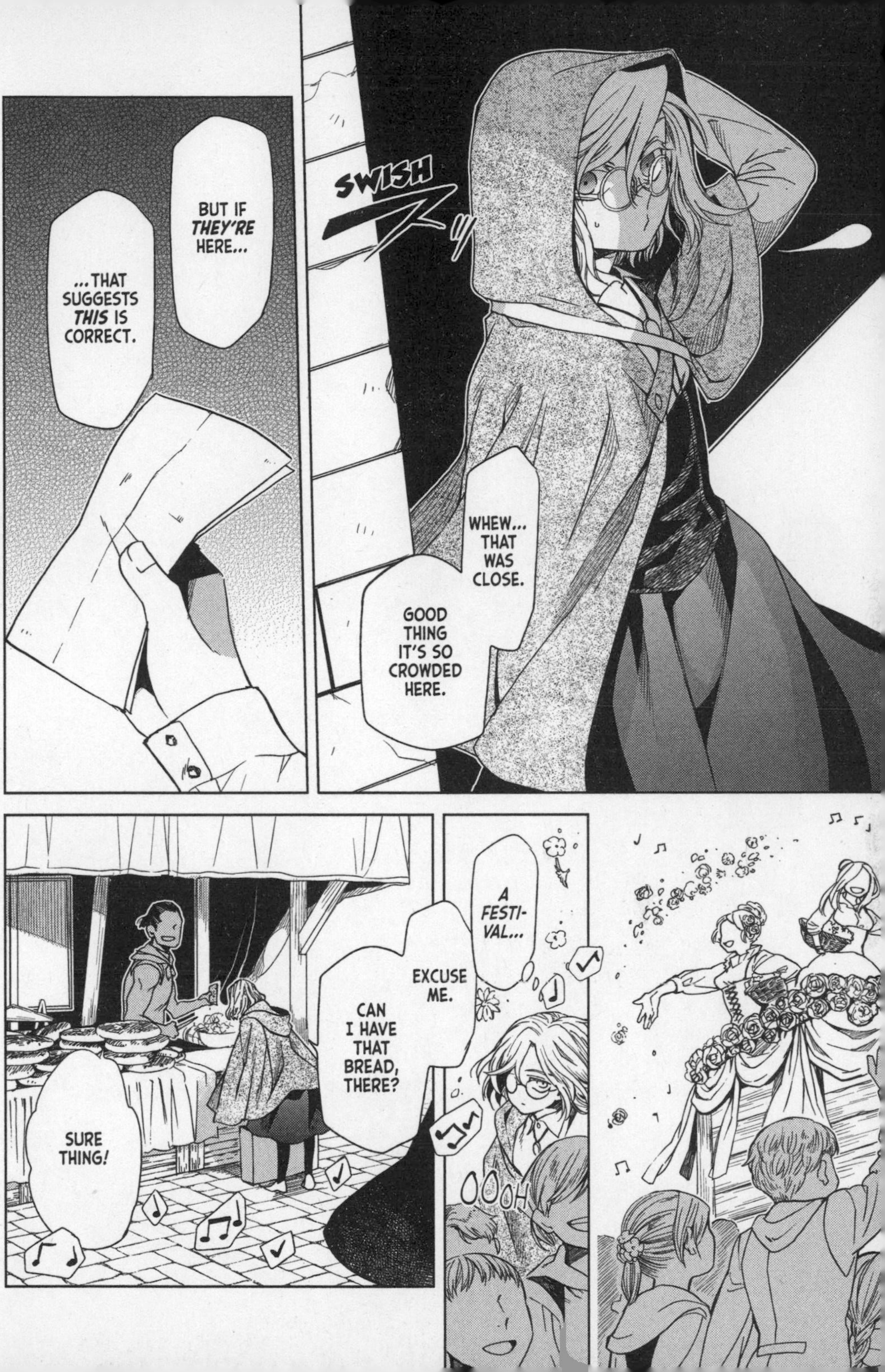
SWISH
WHEW... THAT WAS CLOSE.
GOOD THING IT'S SO CROWDED HERE.
BUT IF THEY'RE HERE...
...THAT SUGGESTS THIS IS CORRECT.
A FESTIVAL...
OOOH
EXCUSE ME.
CAN I HAVE THAT BREAD, THERE?
SURE THING!

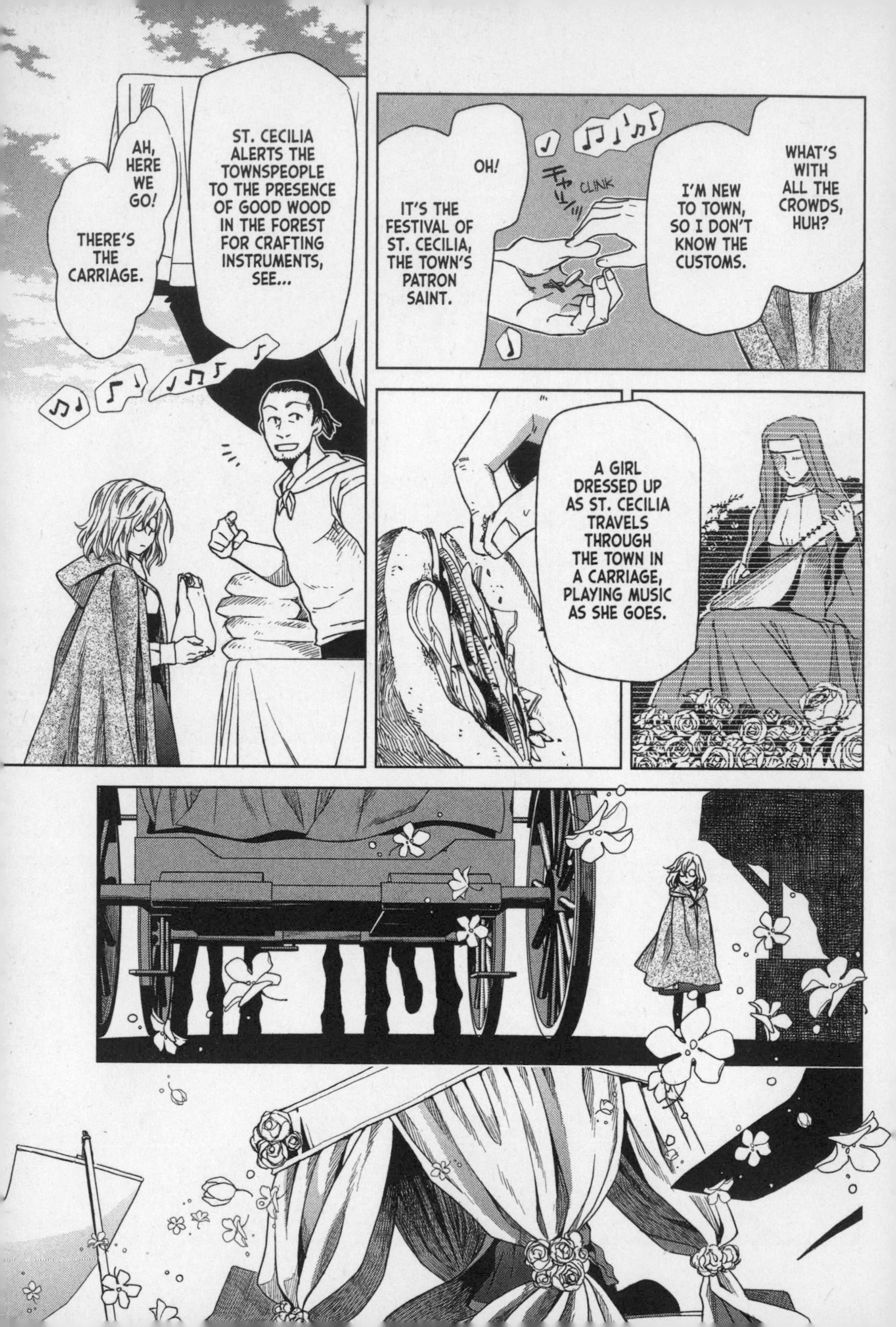
WHAT'S WITH ALL THE CROWDS, HUH?
I'M NEW TO TOWN, SO I DON'T KNOW THE CUSTOMS.
CLINK
OH!
IT'S THE FESTIVAL OF ST. CECILIA, THE TOWN'S PATRON SAINT.
A GIRL DRESSED UP AS ST. CECILIA TRAVELS THROUGH THE TOWN IN A CARRIAGE, PLAYING MUSIC AS SHE GOES.
ST. CECILIA ALERTS THE TOWNSPEOPLE TO THE PRESENCE OF GOOD WOOD IN THE FOREST FOR CRAFTING INSTRUMENTS, SEE...
AH, HERE WE GO!
THERE'S THE CARRIAGE.

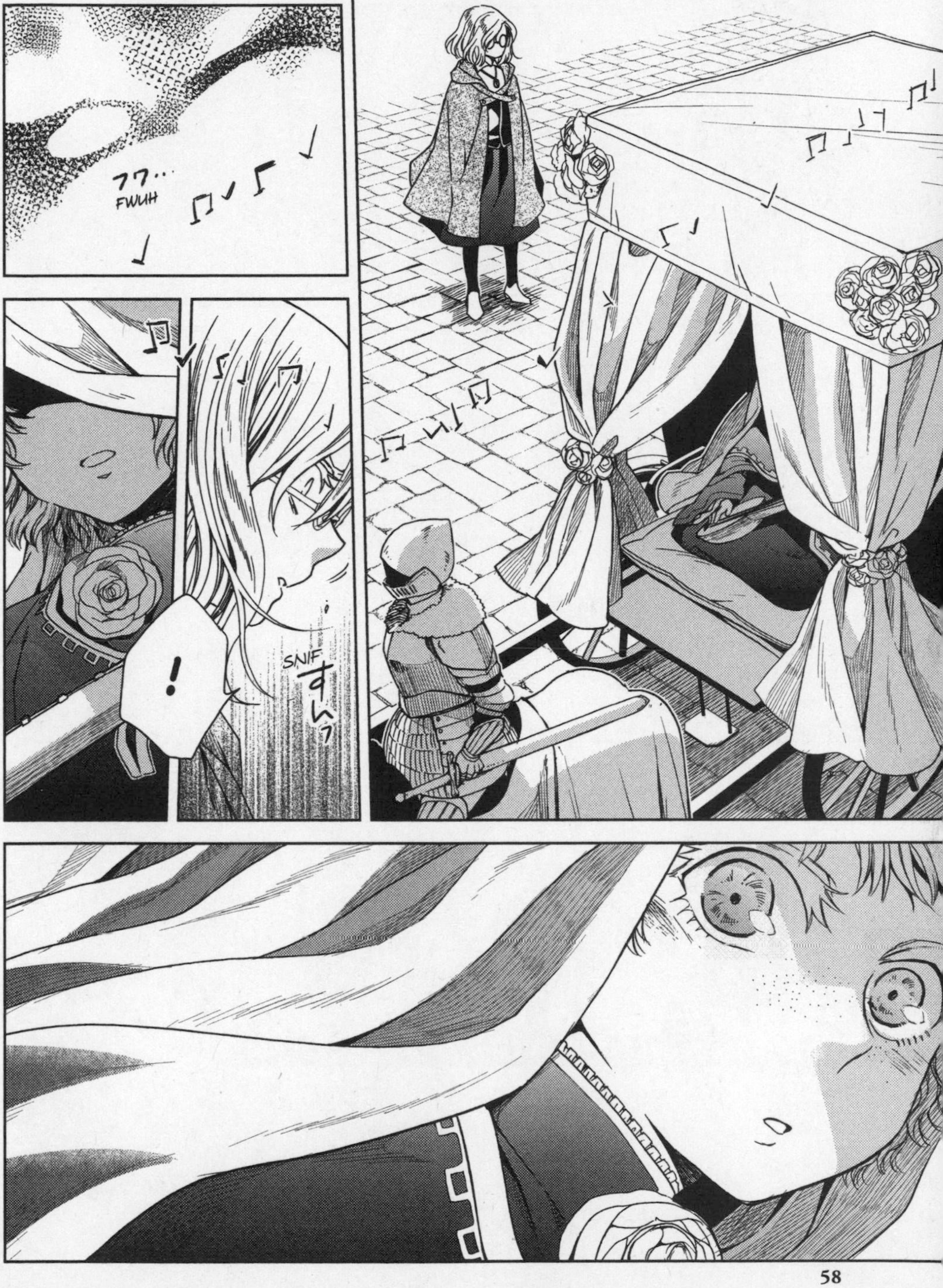
フフ…
FWUH
SNIF
すんっ
!

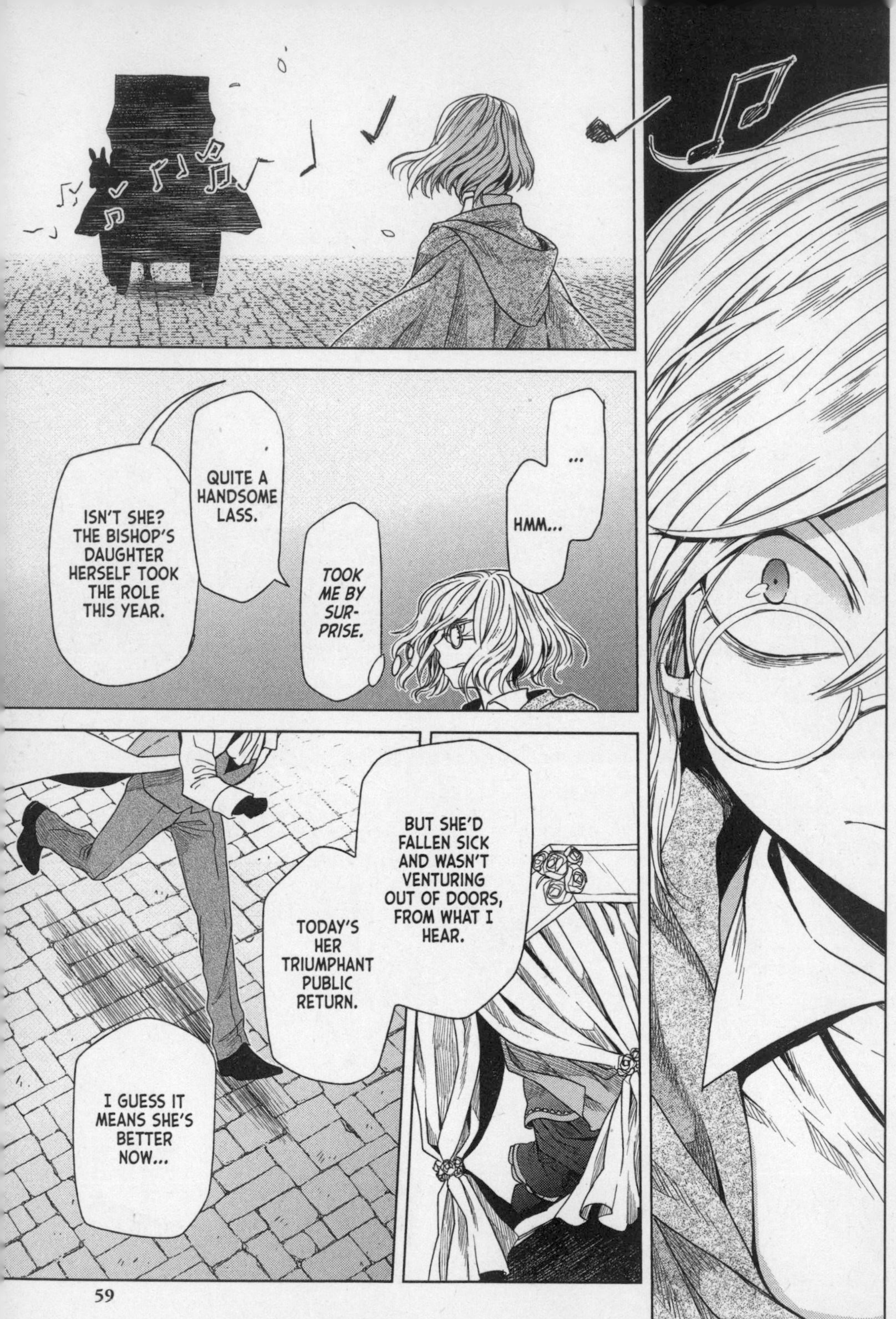
...
HMM...
TOOK ME BY SUR-PRISE.
QUITE A HANDSOME LASS.
ISN'T SHE? THE BISHOP'S DAUGHTER HERSELF TOOK THE ROLE THIS YEAR.
BUT SHE'D FALLEN SICK AND WASN'T VENTURING OUT OF DOORS, FROM WHAT I HEAR.
TODAY'S HER TRIUMPHANT PUBLIC RETURN.
I GUESS IT MEANS SHE'S BETTER NOW...

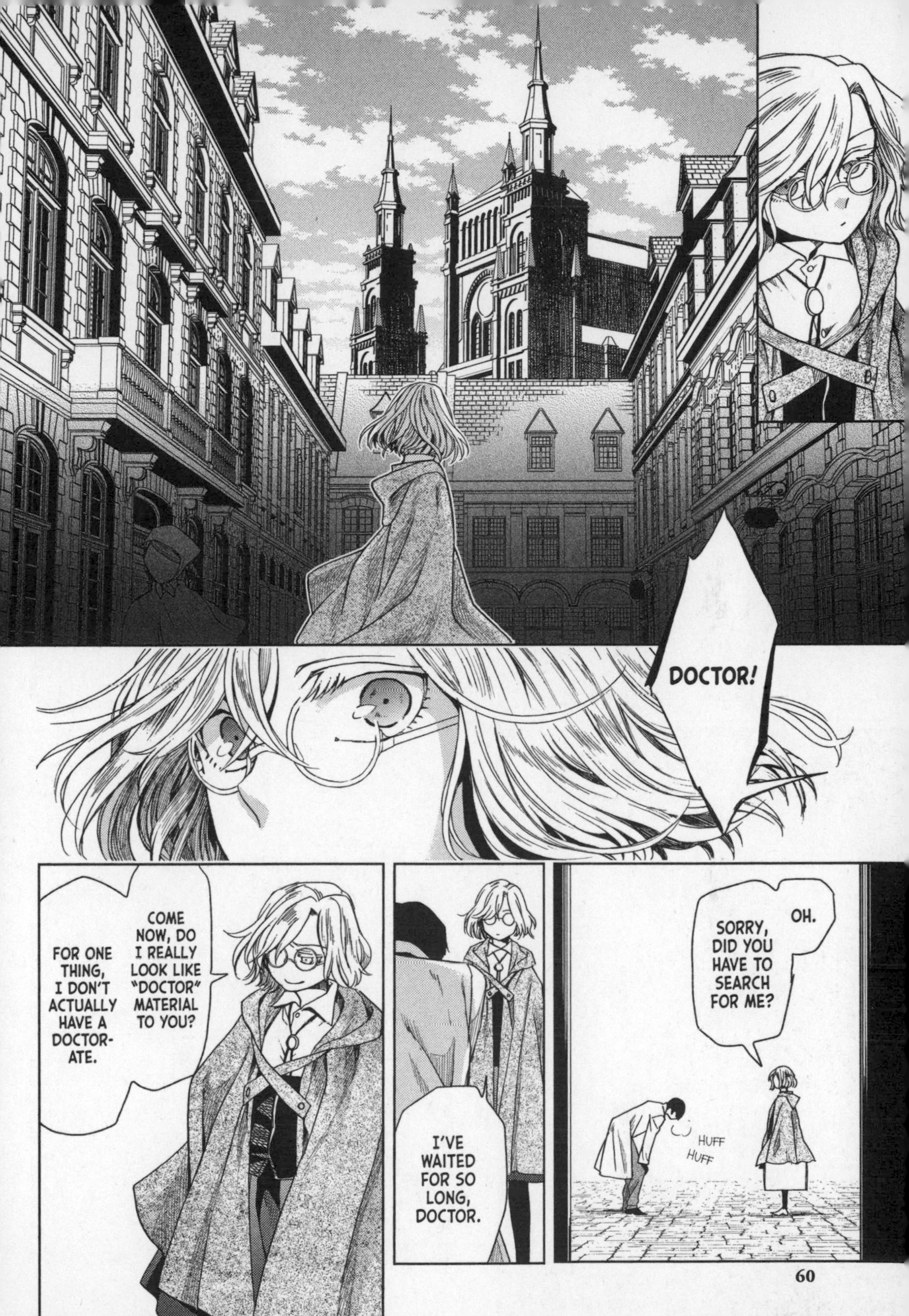
DOCTOR!
OH.
SORRY, DID YOU HAVE TO SEARCH FOR ME?
HUFF HUFF
I'VE WAITED FOR SO LONG, DOCTOR.
COME NOW, DO I REALLY LOOK LIKE "DOCTOR" MATERIAL TO YOU?
FOR ONE THING, I DON'T ACTUALLY HAVE A DOCTORATE.

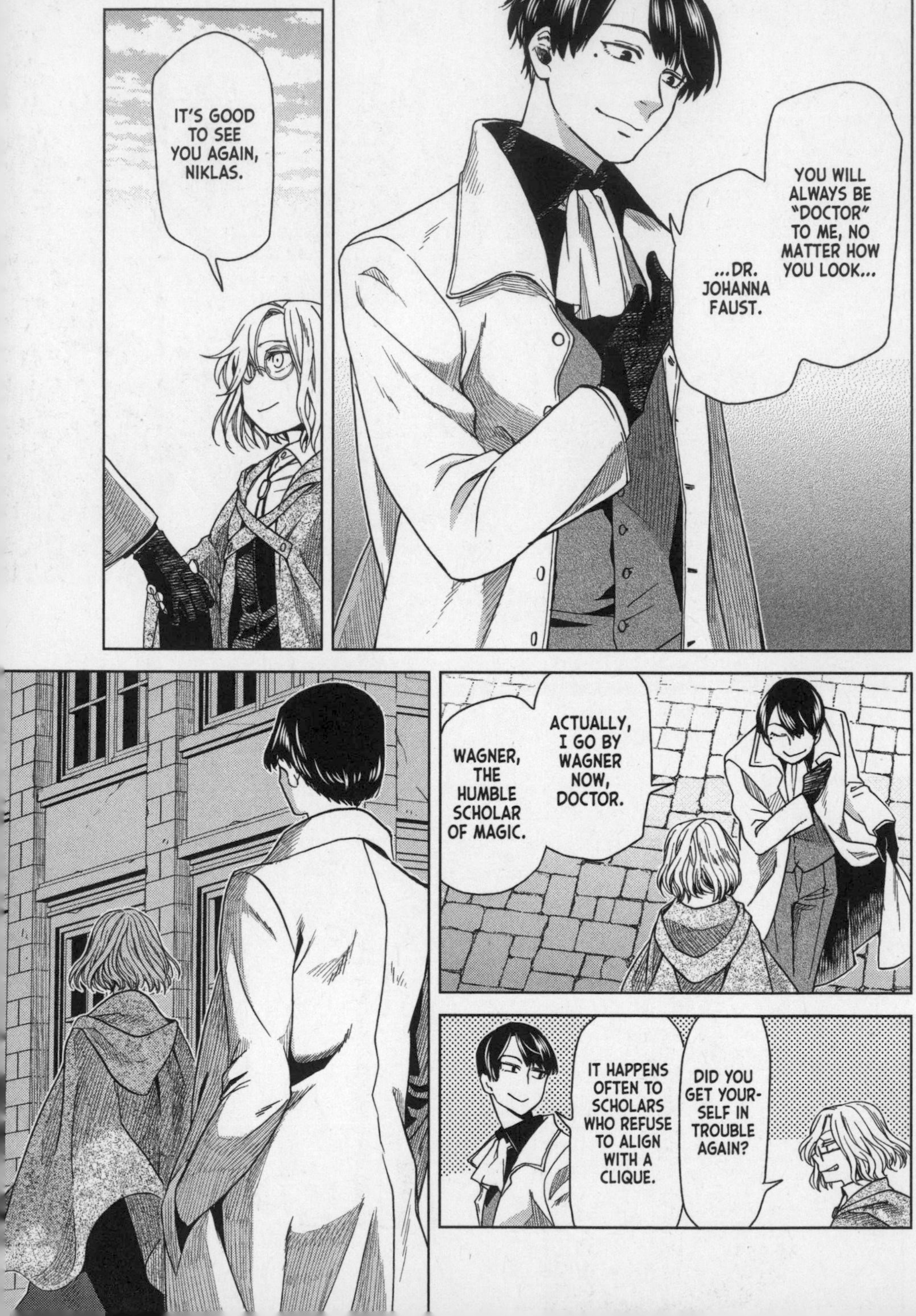
YOU WILL ALWAYS BE "DOCTOR" TO ME, NO MATTER HOW YOU LOOK...
...DR. JOHANNA FAUST.
IT'S GOOD TO SEE YOU AGAIN, NIKLAS.
ACTUALLY, I GO BY WAGNER NOW, DOCTOR.
WAGNER, THE HUMBLE SCHOLAR OF MAGIC.
DID YOU GET YOUR-SELF IN TROUBLE AGAIN?
IT HAPPENS OFTEN TO SCHOLARS WHO REFUSE TO ALIGN WITH A CLIQUE.

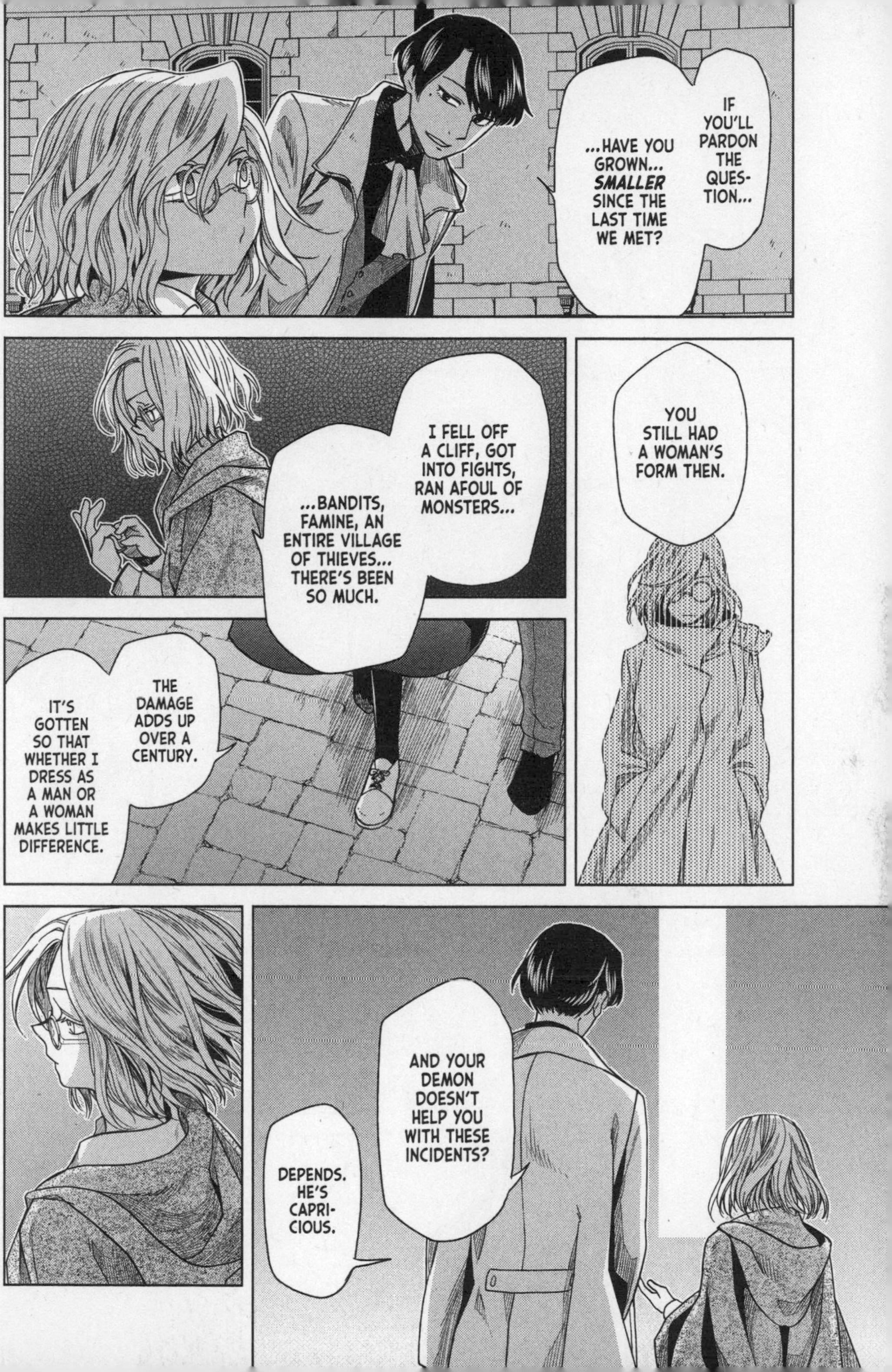
IF YOU'LL PARDON THE QUES-TION...
...HAVE YOU GROWN... ***SMALLER*** SINCE THE LAST TIME WE MET?
YOU STILL HAD A WOMAN'S FORM THEN.
I FELL OFF A CLIFF, GOT INTO FIGHTS, RAN AFOUL OF MONSTERS...
...BANDITS, FAMINE, AN ENTIRE VILLAGE OF THIEVES... THERE'S BEEN SO MUCH.
THE DAMAGE ADDS UP OVER A CENTURY.
IT'S GOTTEN SO THAT WHETHER I DRESS AS A MAN OR A WOMAN MAKES LITTLE DIFFERENCE.
AND YOUR DEMON DOESN'T HELP YOU WITH THESE INCIDENTS?
DEPENDS. HE'S CAPRI-CIOUS.

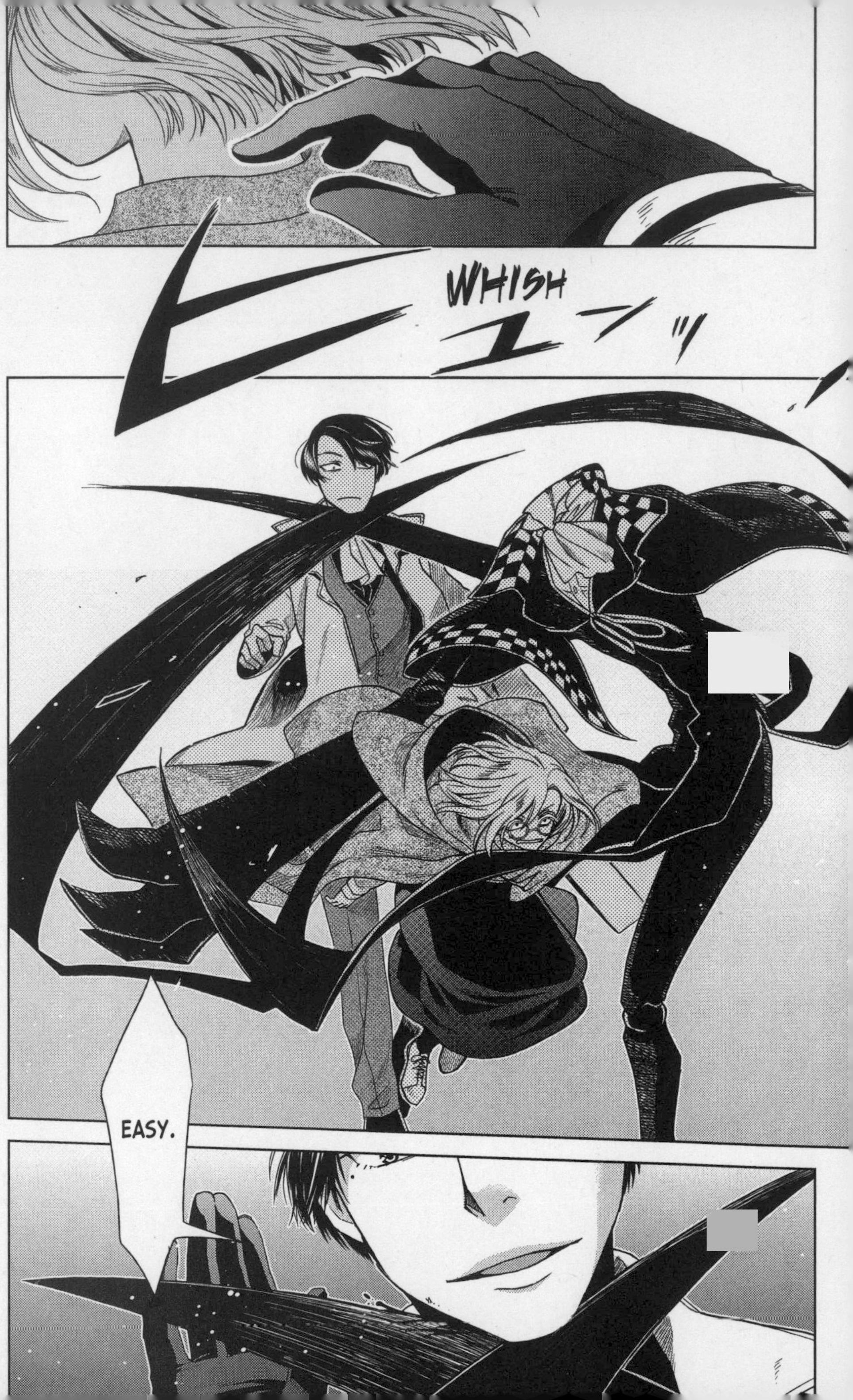
WHISH
ヒュンッ
EASY.

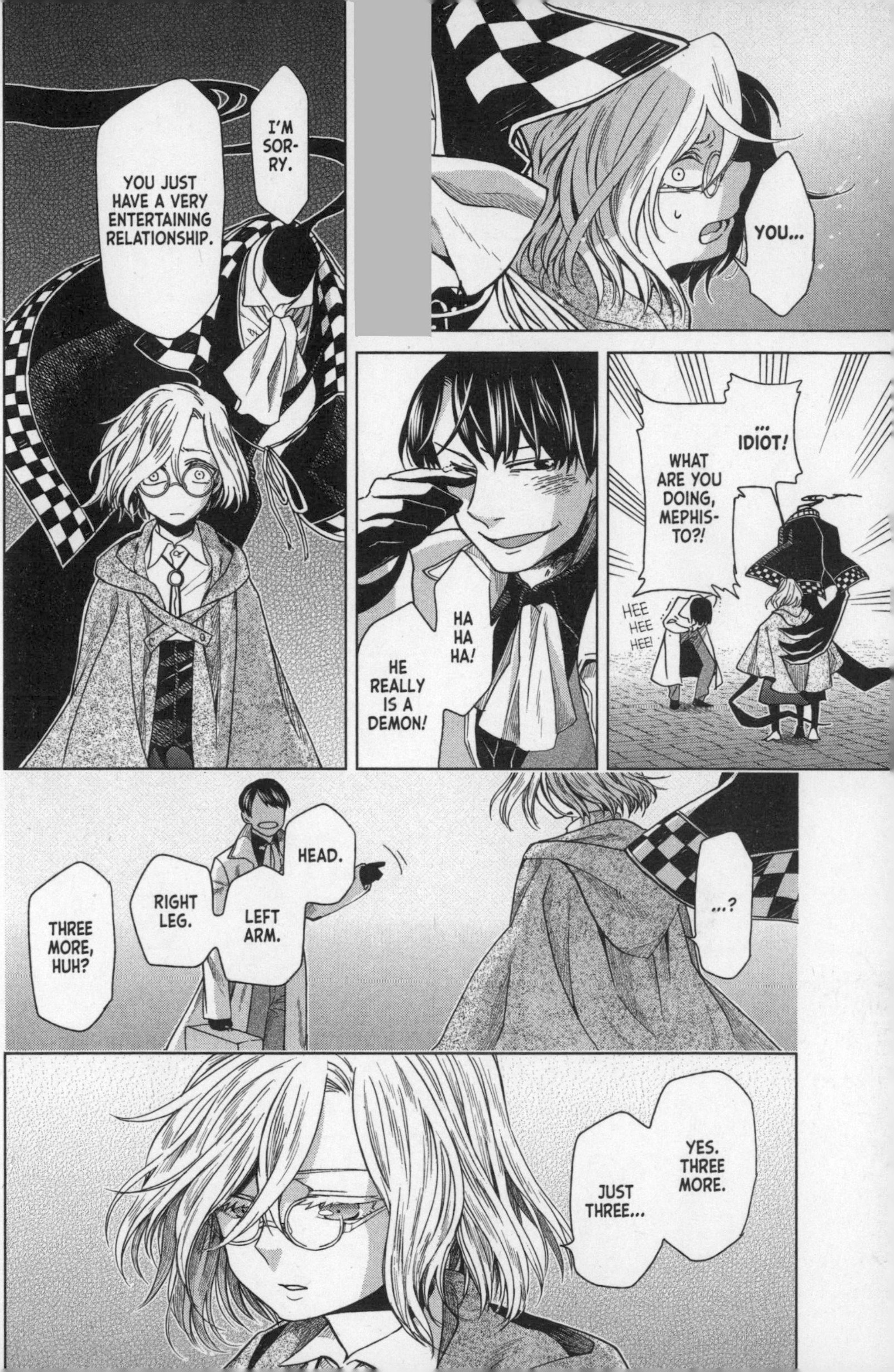
YOU...
...IDIOT!
WHAT ARE YOU DOING, MEPHISTO?!
HEE HEE HEE!
HA HA HA!
HE REALLY IS A DEMON!
I'M SORRY.
YOU JUST HAVE A VERY ENTERTAINING RELATIONSHIP.
...?
HEAD.
LEFT ARM.
RIGHT LEG.
THREE MORE, HUH?
YES. THREE MORE.
JUST THREE...

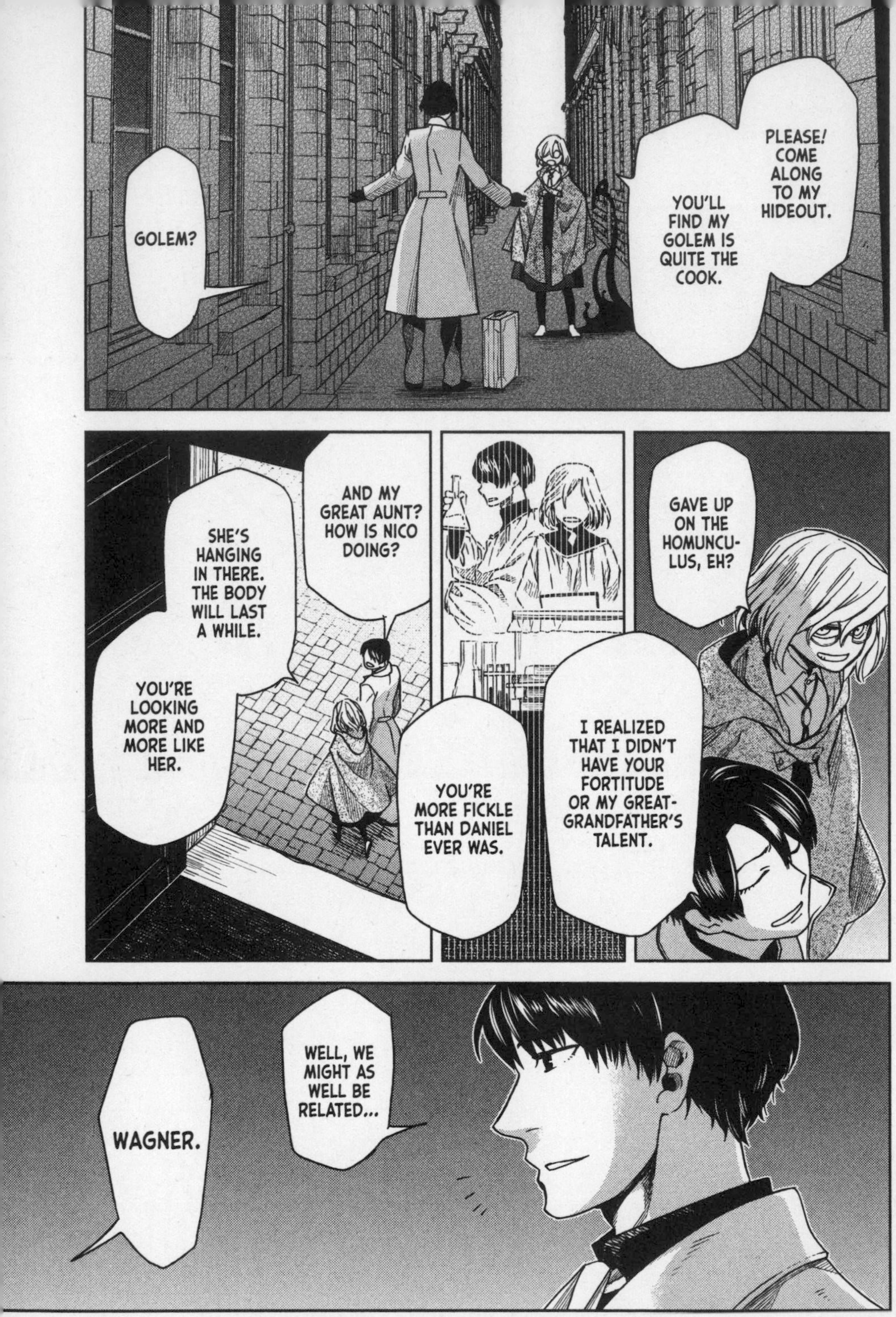
PLEASE! COME ALONG TO MY HIDEOUT.
YOU'LL FIND MY GOLEM IS QUITE THE COOK.
GOLEM?
GAVE UP ON THE HOMUNCU-LUS, EH?
I REALIZED THAT I DIDN'T HAVE YOUR FORTITUDE OR MY GREAT-GRANDFATHER'S TALENT.
YOU'RE MORE FICKLE THAN DANIEL EVER WAS.
AND MY GREAT AUNT? HOW IS NICO DOING?
SHE'S HANGING IN THERE. THE BODY WILL LAST A WHILE.
YOU'RE LOOKING MORE AND MORE LIKE HER.
WELL, WE MIGHT AS WELL BE RELATED...
WAGNER.

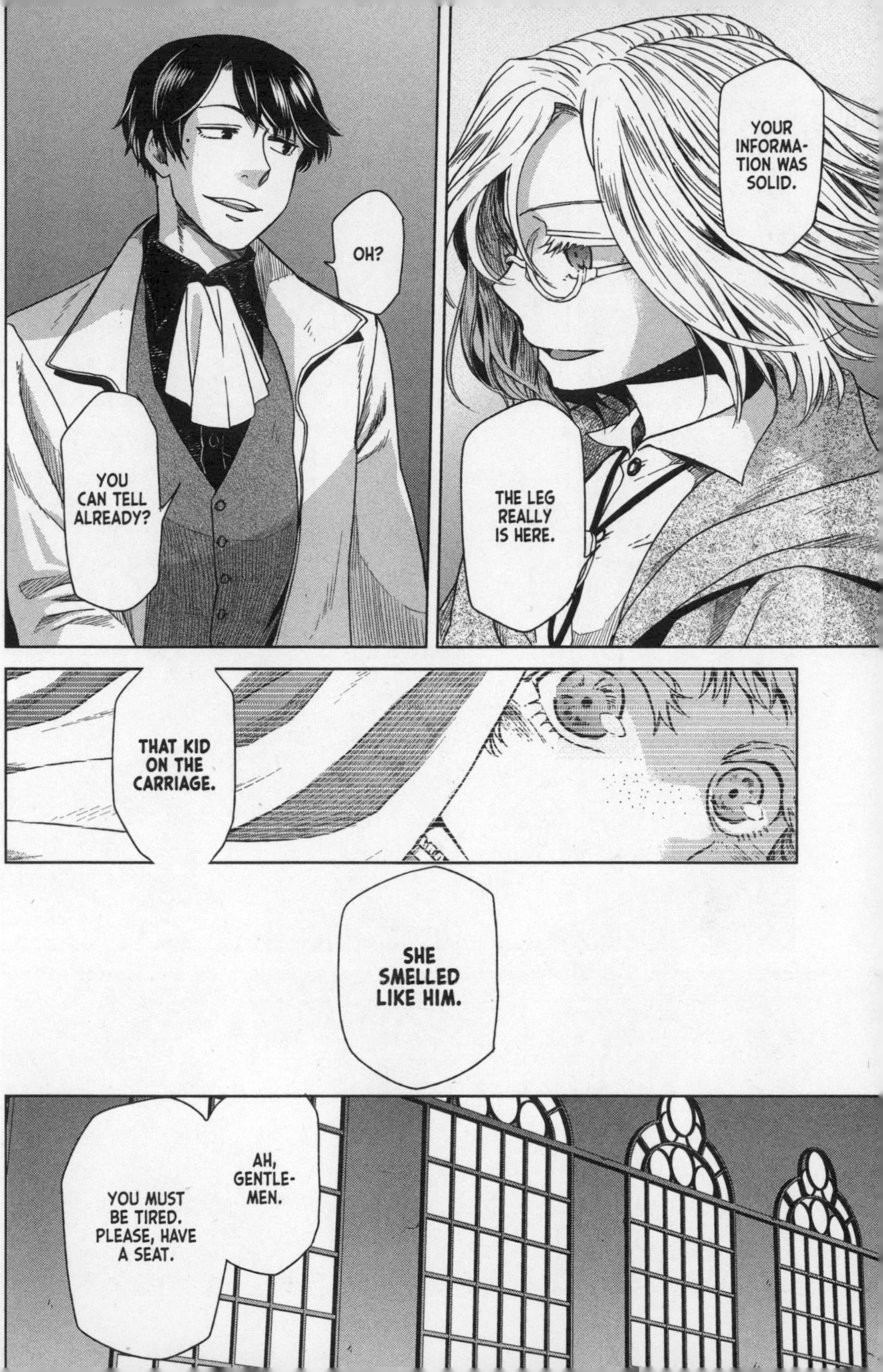
YOUR INFORMATION WAS SOLID.
THE LEG REALLY IS HERE.
OH?
YOU CAN TELL ALREADY?
THAT KID ON THE CARRIAGE.
SHE SMELLED LIKE HIM.
AH, GENTLEMEN.
YOU MUST BE TIRED. PLEASE, HAVE A SEAT.

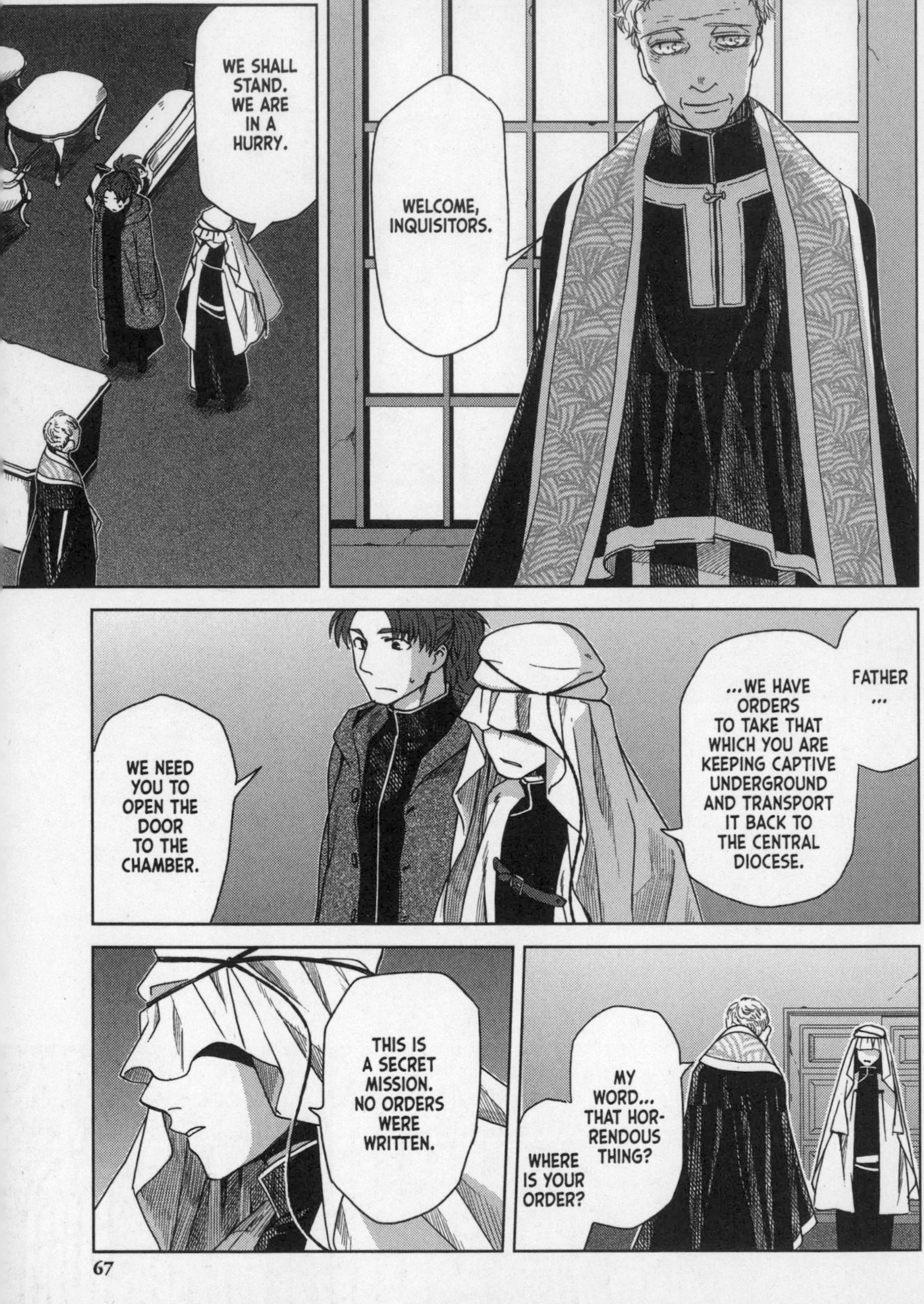
WELCOME, INQUISITORS.
WE SHALL STAND. WE ARE IN A HURRY.
FATHER...
...WE HAVE ORDERS TO TAKE THAT WHICH YOU ARE KEEPING CAPTIVE UNDERGROUND AND TRANSPORT IT BACK TO THE CENTRAL DIOCESE.
WE NEED YOU TO OPEN THE DOOR TO THE CHAMBER.
MY WORD... THAT HORRENDOUS THING?
WHERE IS YOUR ORDER?
THIS IS A SECRET MISSION. NO ORDERS WERE WRITTEN.

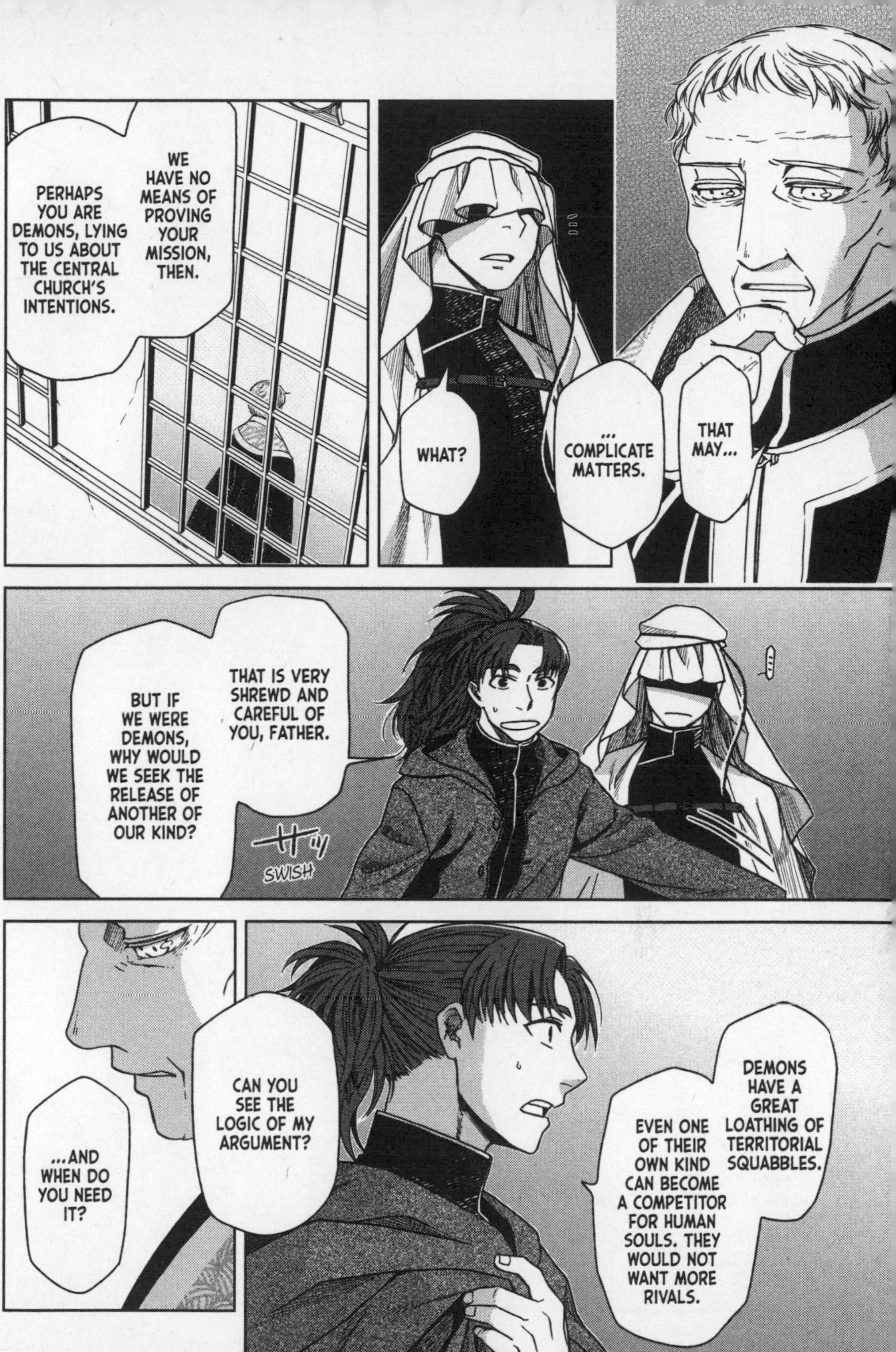
THAT MAY...
... COMPLICATE MATTERS.
WHAT?
WE HAVE NO MEANS OF PROVING YOUR MISSION, THEN.
PERHAPS YOU ARE DEMONS, LYING TO US ABOUT THE CENTRAL CHURCH'S INTENTIONS.
THAT IS VERY SHREWD AND CAREFUL OF YOU, FATHER.
BUT IF WE WERE DEMONS, WHY WOULD WE SEEK THE RELEASE OF ANOTHER OF OUR KIND?
SWISH
DEMONS HAVE A GREAT LOATHING OF TERRITORIAL SQUABBLES.
EVEN ONE OF THEIR OWN KIND CAN BECOME A COMPETITOR FOR HUMAN SOULS. THEY WOULD NOT WANT MORE RIVALS.
CAN YOU SEE THE LOGIC OF MY ARGUMENT?
...AND WHEN DO YOU NEED IT?

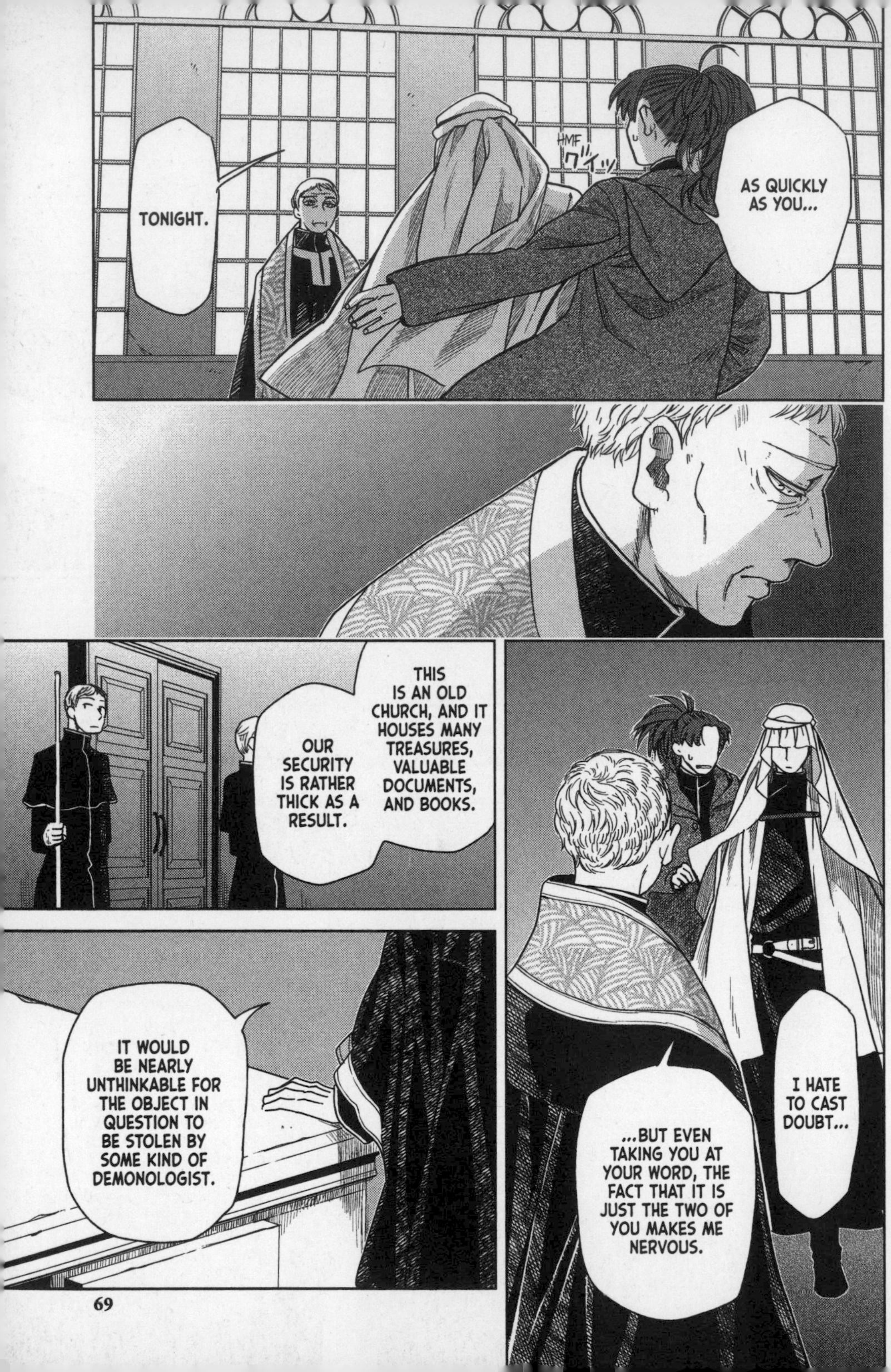
AS QUICKLY AS YOU...
HMF
グイッ
TONIGHT.
I HATE TO CAST DOUBT...
...BUT EVEN TAKING YOU AT YOUR WORD, THE FACT THAT IT IS JUST THE TWO OF YOU MAKES ME NERVOUS.
THIS IS AN OLD CHURCH, AND IT HOUSES MANY TREASURES, VALUABLE DOCUMENTS, AND BOOKS.
OUR SECURITY IS RATHER THICK AS A RESULT.
IT WOULD BE NEARLY UNTHINKABLE FOR THE OBJECT IN QUESTION TO BE STOLEN BY SOME KIND OF DEMONOLOGIST.

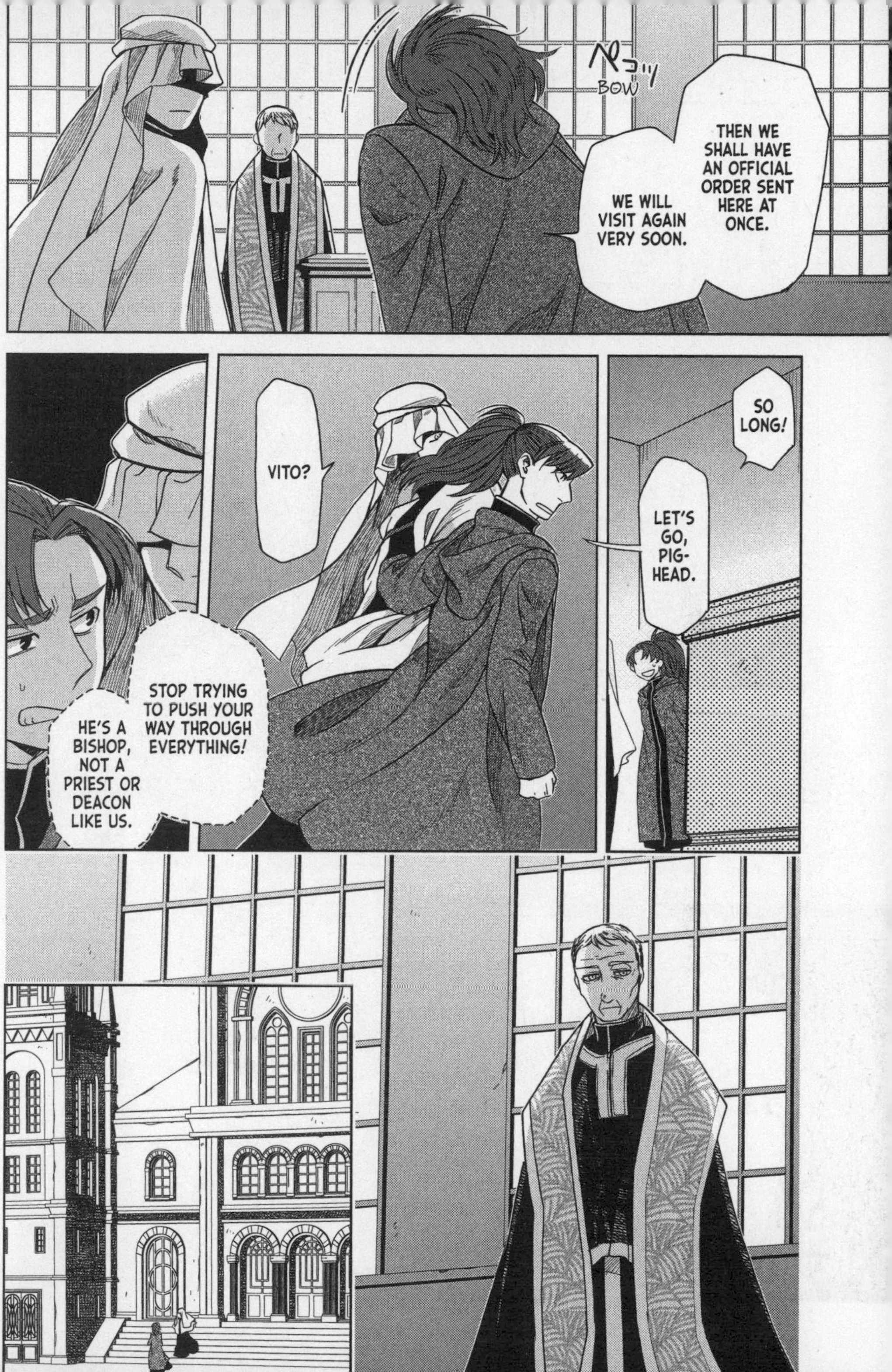
ペコッ
BOW
THEN WE SHALL HAVE AN OFFICIAL ORDER SENT HERE AT ONCE.
WE WILL VISIT AGAIN VERY SOON.
SO LONG!
LET'S GO, PIG-HEAD.
VITO?
STOP TRYING TO PUSH YOUR WAY THROUGH EVERYTHING!
HE'S A BISHOP, NOT A PRIEST OR DEACON LIKE US.

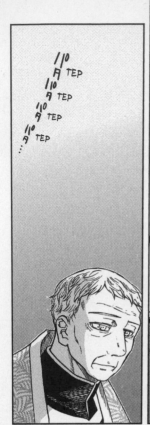

PA TEP
PA TEP
PA TEP
PA TEP
PA...

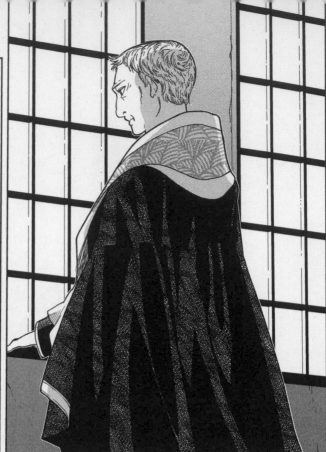

CLICK

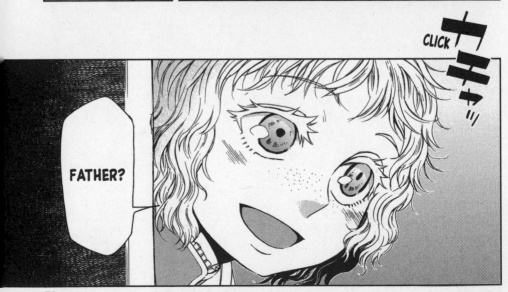

FATHER?

71

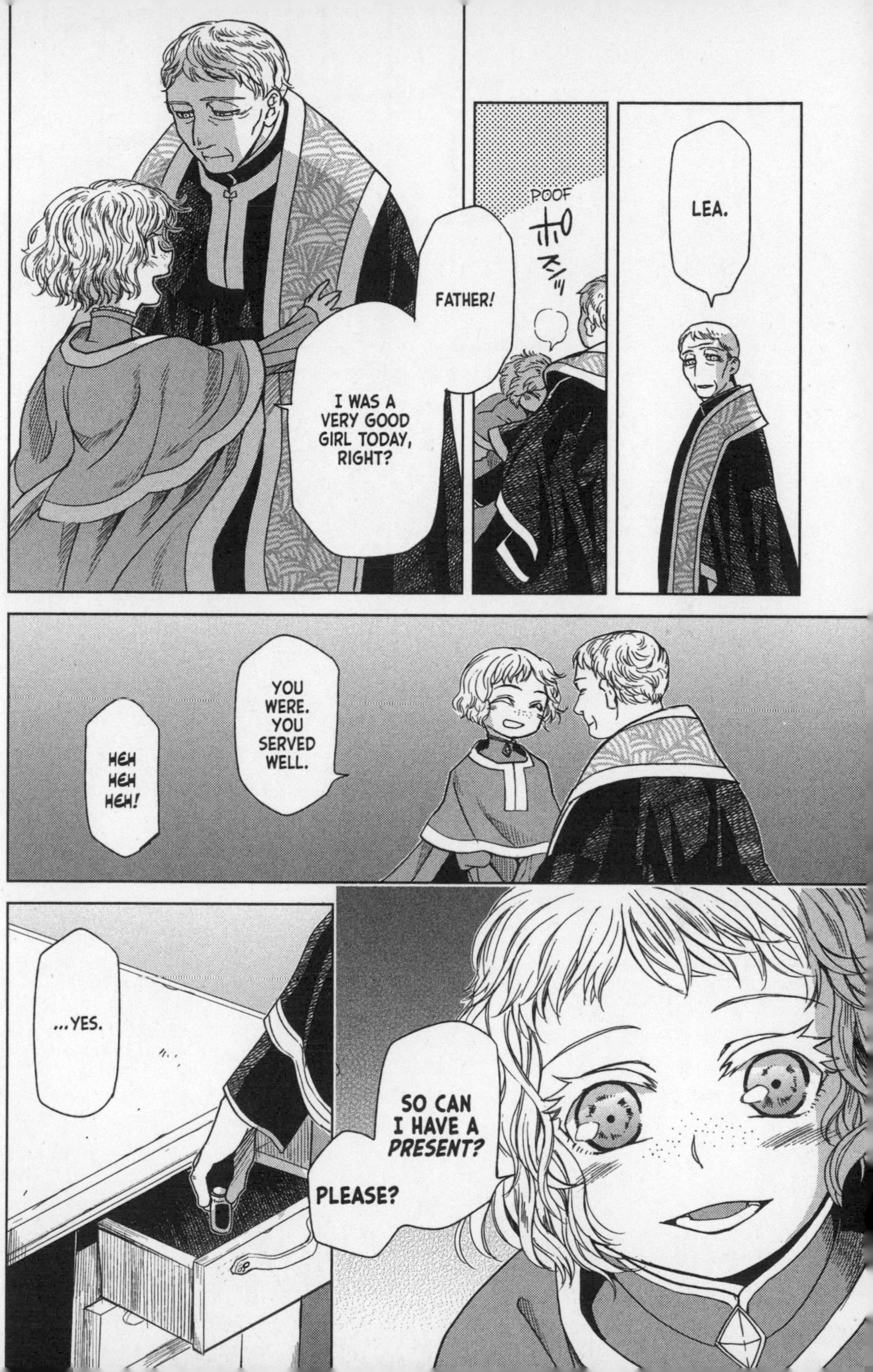
LEA.
POOF
FATHER!
I WAS A VERY GOOD GIRL TODAY, RIGHT?
YOU WERE. YOU SERVED WELL.
HEH HEH HEH!
SO CAN I HAVE A *PRESENT*?
PLEASE?
...YES.

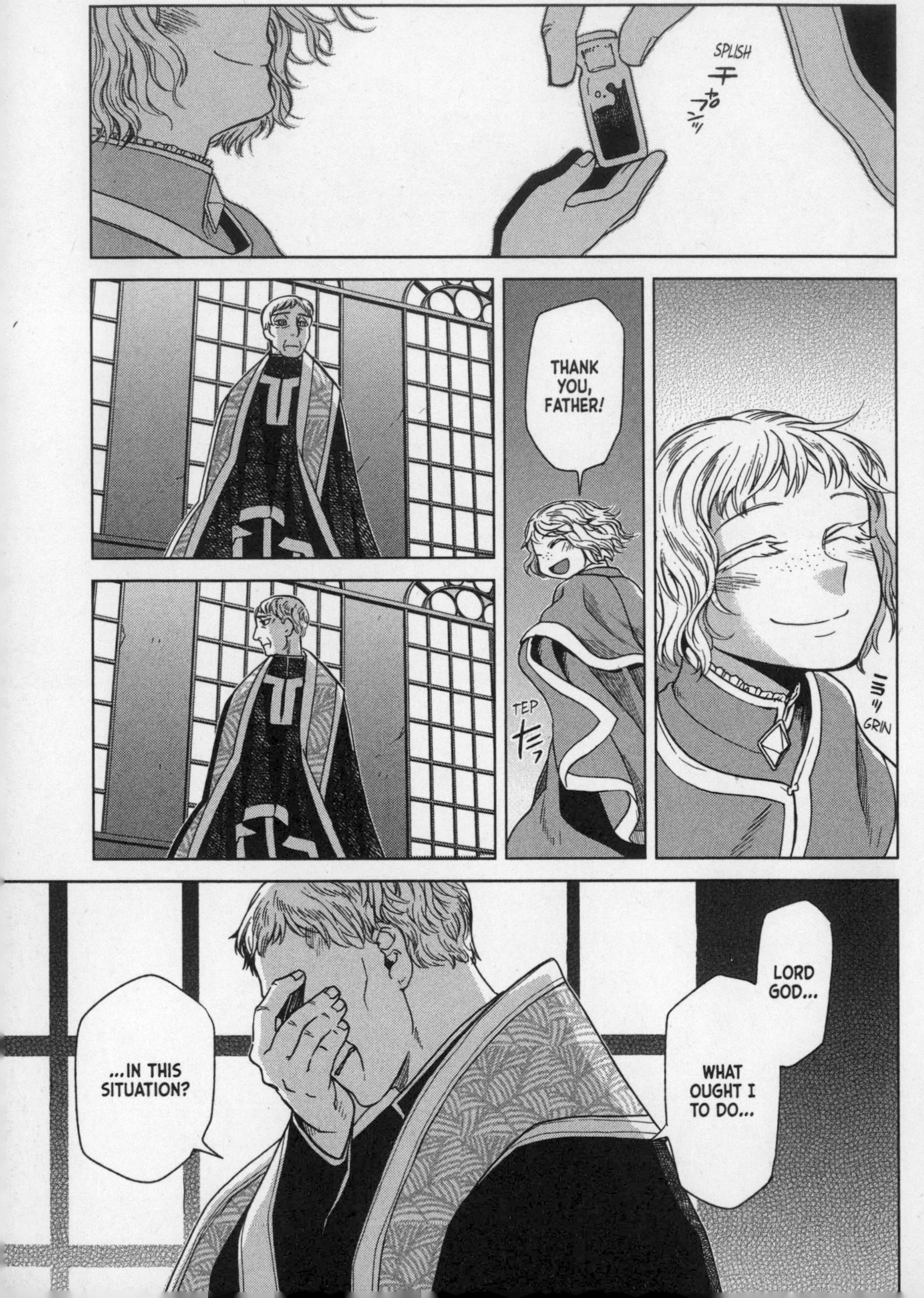
SPLISH
GRIN
THANK YOU, FATHER!
TEP
LORD GOD...
WHAT OUGHT I TO DO...
...IN THIS SITUATION?

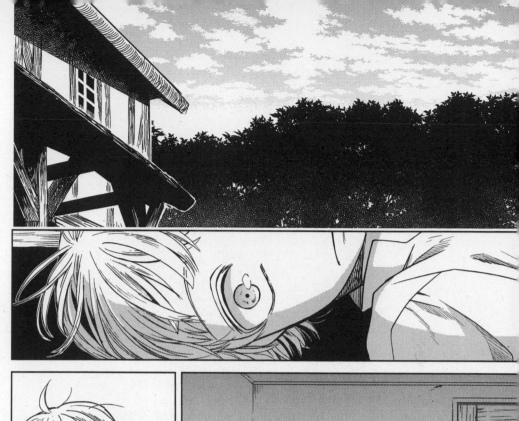

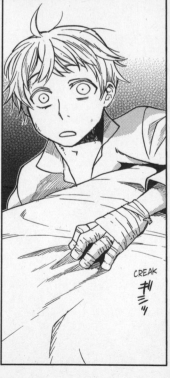

CREAK
サ｜｜｜

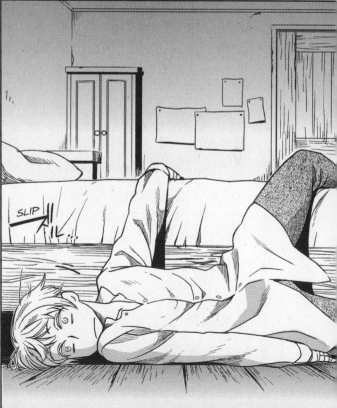

SLIP
スル…

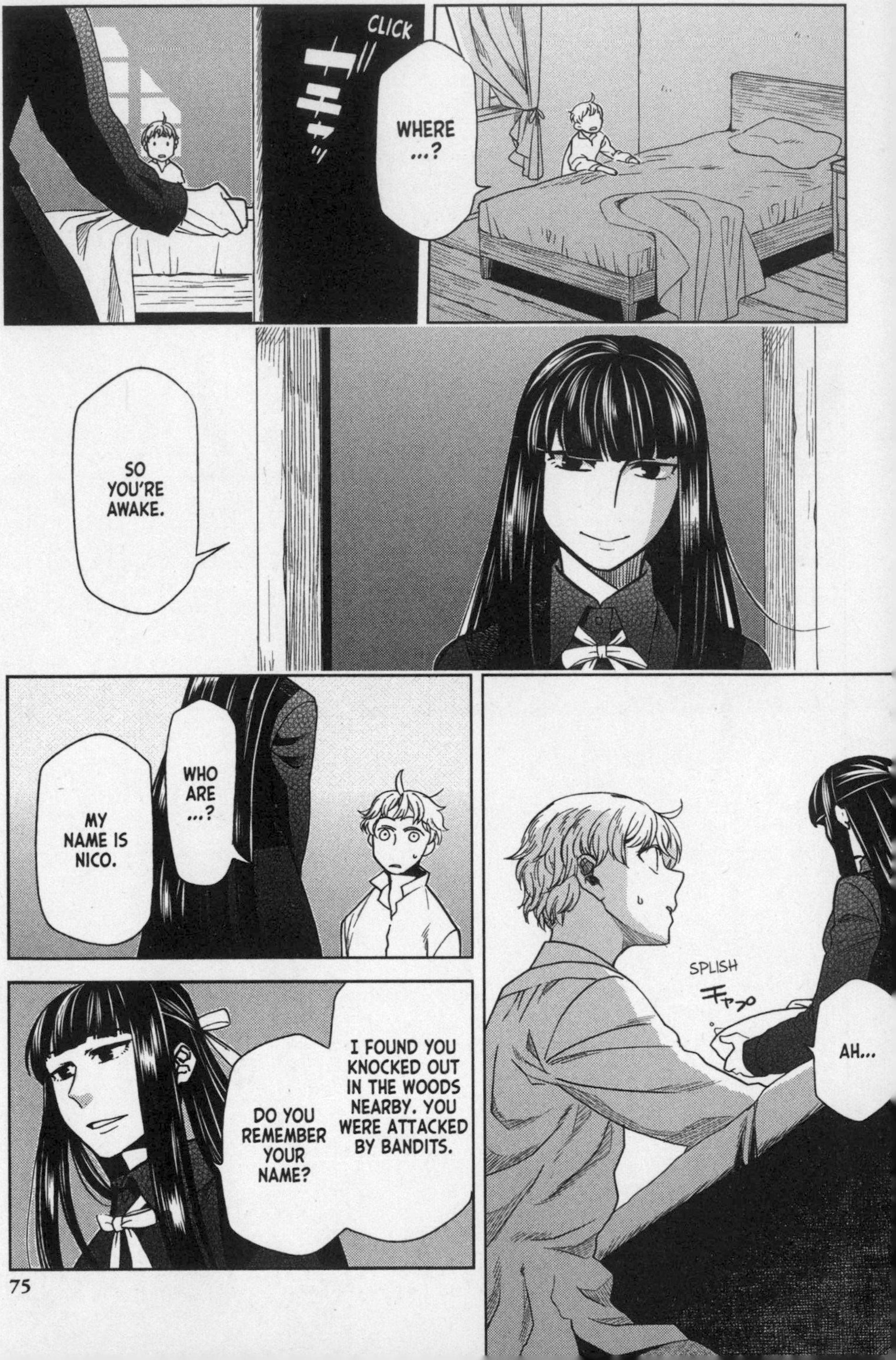
WHERE ...?
CLICK
SO YOU'RE AWAKE.
SPLISH
AH...
WHO ARE ...?
MY NAME IS NICO.
I FOUND YOU KNOCKED OUT IN THE WOODS NEARBY. YOU WERE ATTACKED BY BANDITS.
DO YOU REMEMBER YOUR NAME?

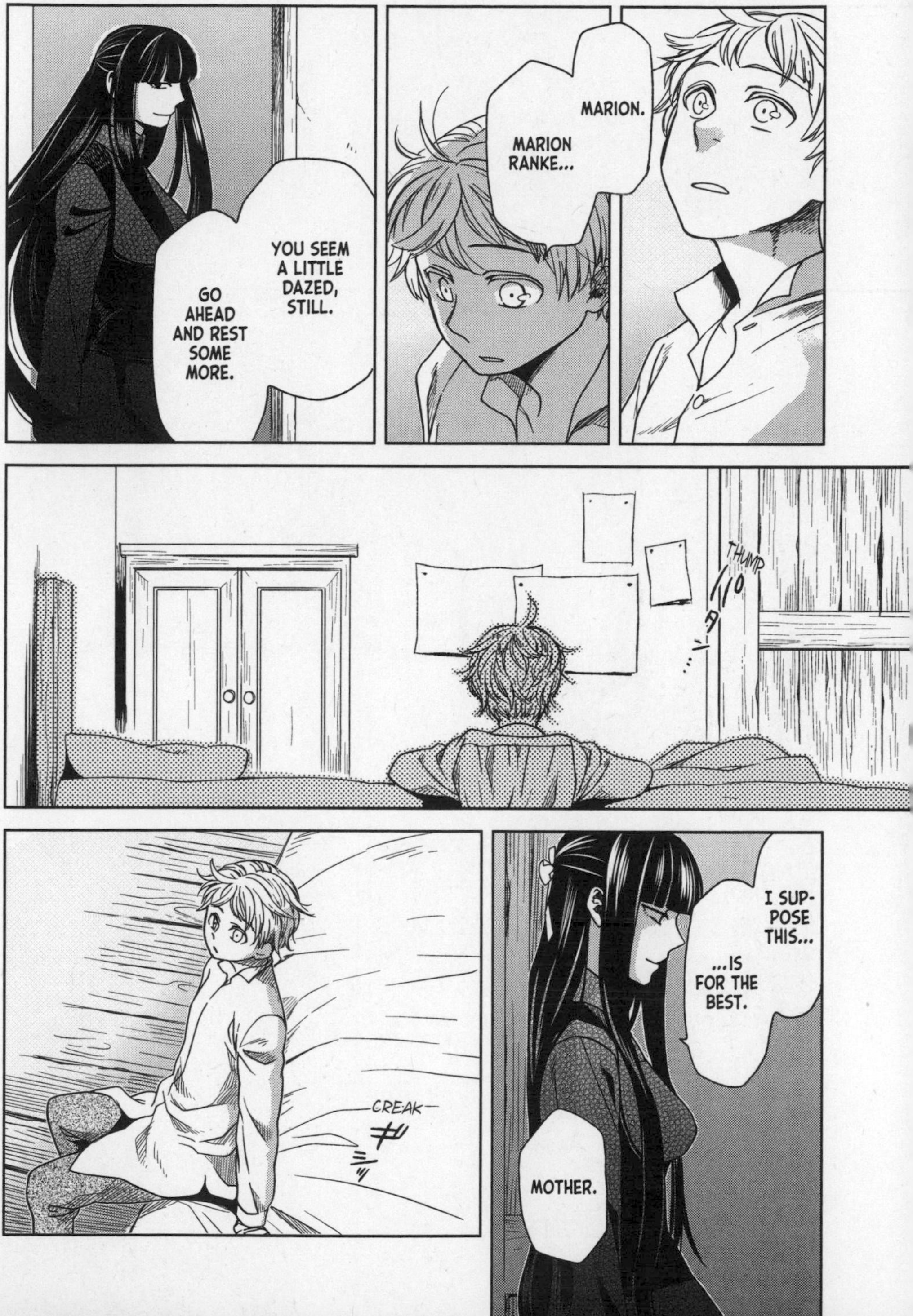
MARION.
MARION RANKE...
YOU SEEM A LITTLE DAZED, STILL.
GO AHEAD AND REST SOME MORE.
THUMP
I SUP-POSE THIS...
...IS FOR THE BEST.
MOTHER.
CREAK

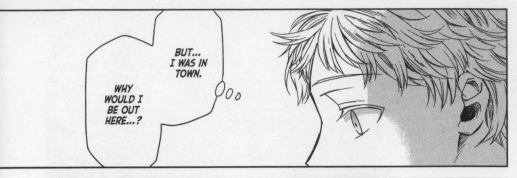

BUT... I WAS IN TOWN.
WHY WOULD I BE OUT HERE...?
MY MIND FEELS FOGGY...
PLUS...
...I'M INJURED...
SHLIP
シュル...
FWUP
INFLAMED SKIN...?
SHE SAID I WAS ATTACKED BY BANDITS...
...BUT THE ONLY PLACE I'M HURT IS ON MY PALMS.

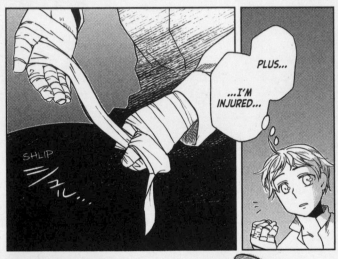

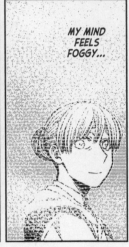

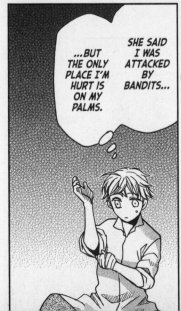

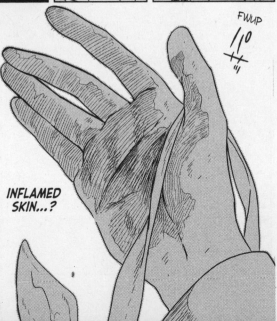

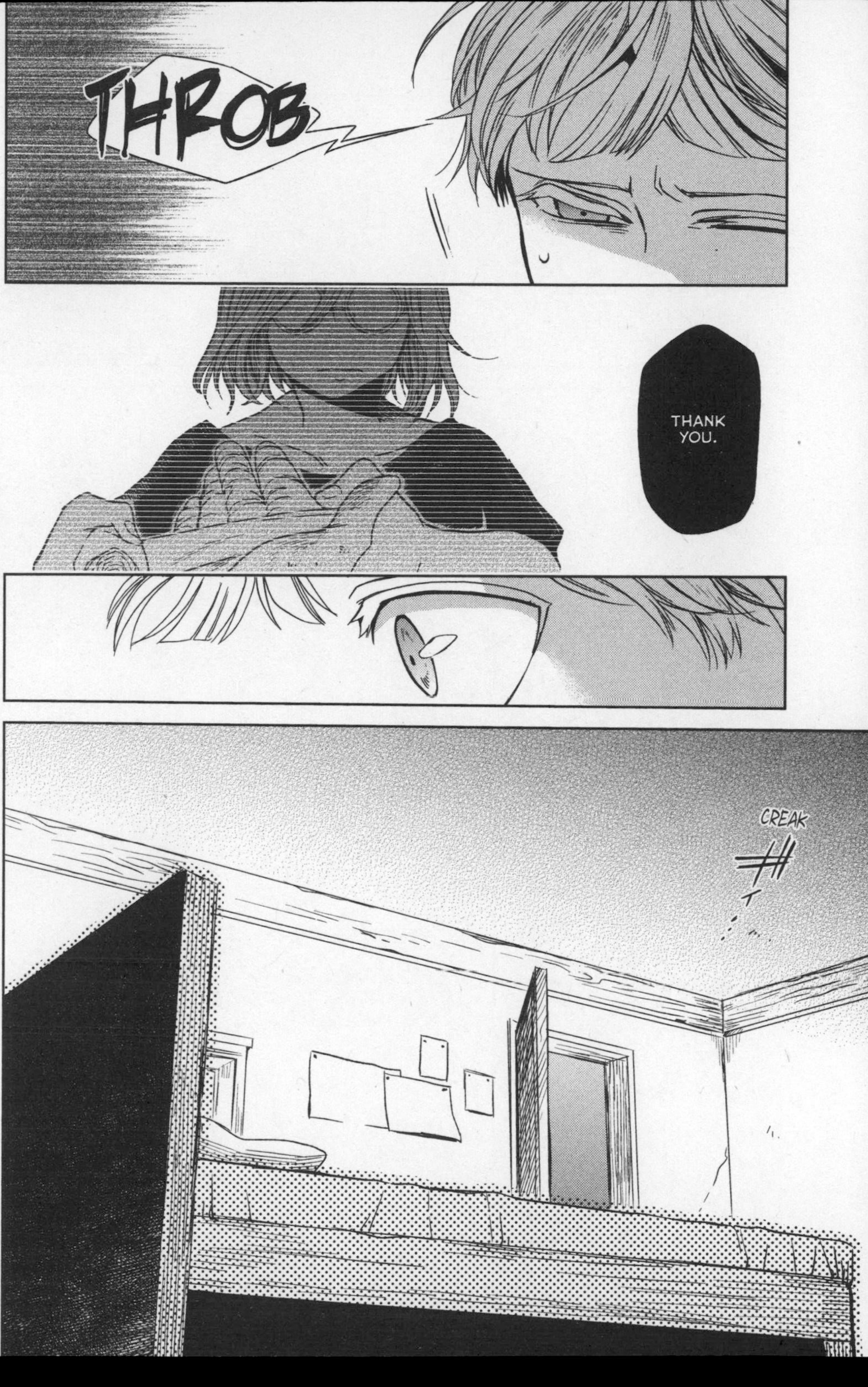
THROB
THANK YOU.
CREAK

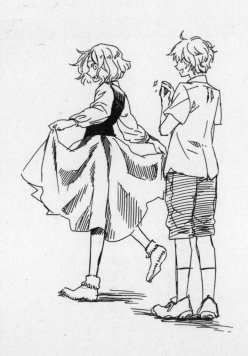

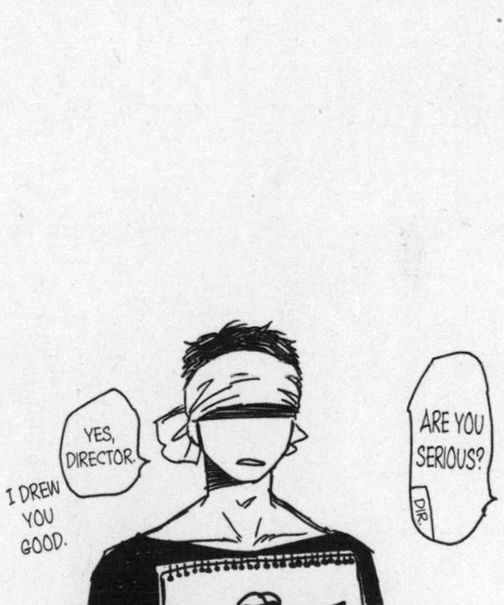
ARE YOU SERIOUS?
DIR.
YES, DIRECTOR.
I DREW YOU GOOD.

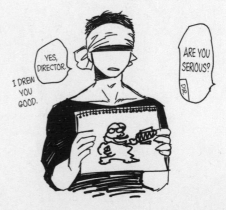

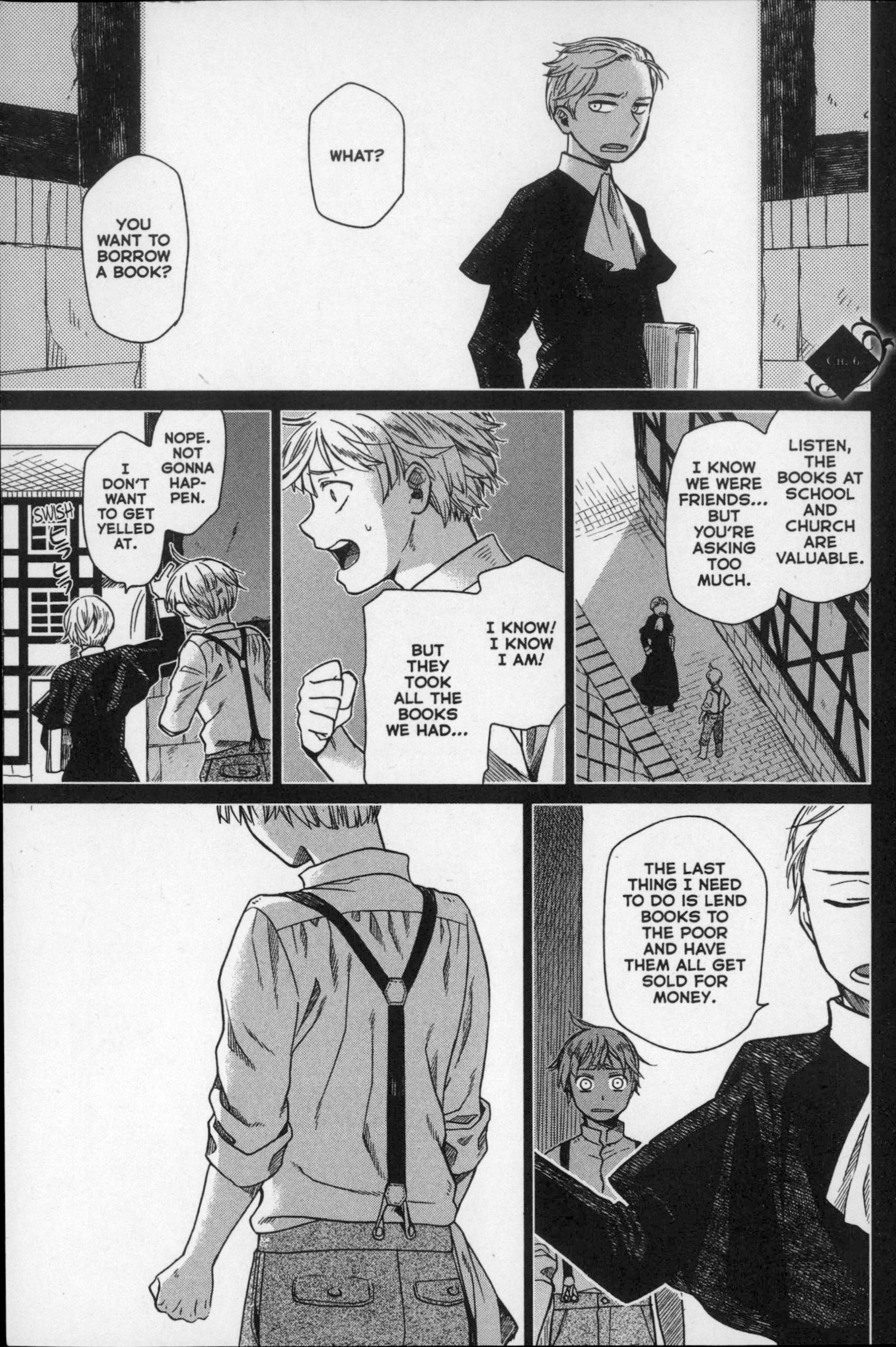
WHAT?
YOU WANT TO BORROW A BOOK?
Ch. 6
LISTEN, THE BOOKS AT SCHOOL AND CHURCH ARE VALUABLE.
I KNOW WE WERE FRIENDS... BUT YOU'RE ASKING TOO MUCH.
I KNOW! I KNOW I AM!
BUT THEY TOOK ALL THE BOOKS WE HAD...
NOPE. NOT GONNA HAP-PEN.
I DON'T WANT TO GET YELLED AT.
SWISH
THE LAST THING I NEED TO DO IS LEND BOOKS TO THE POOR AND HAVE THEM ALL GET SOLD FOR MONEY.

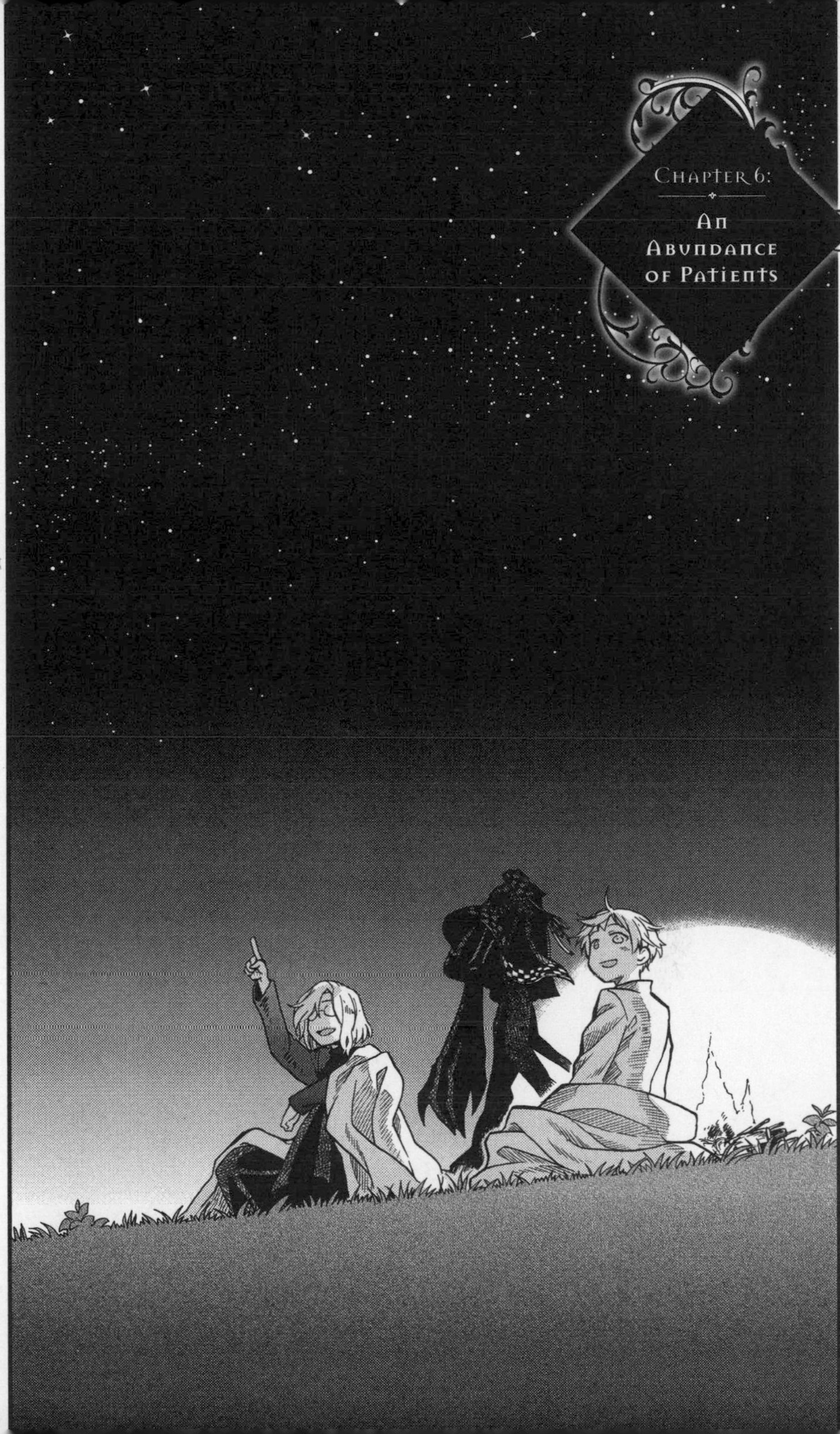
Chapter 6:
An Abundance of Patients

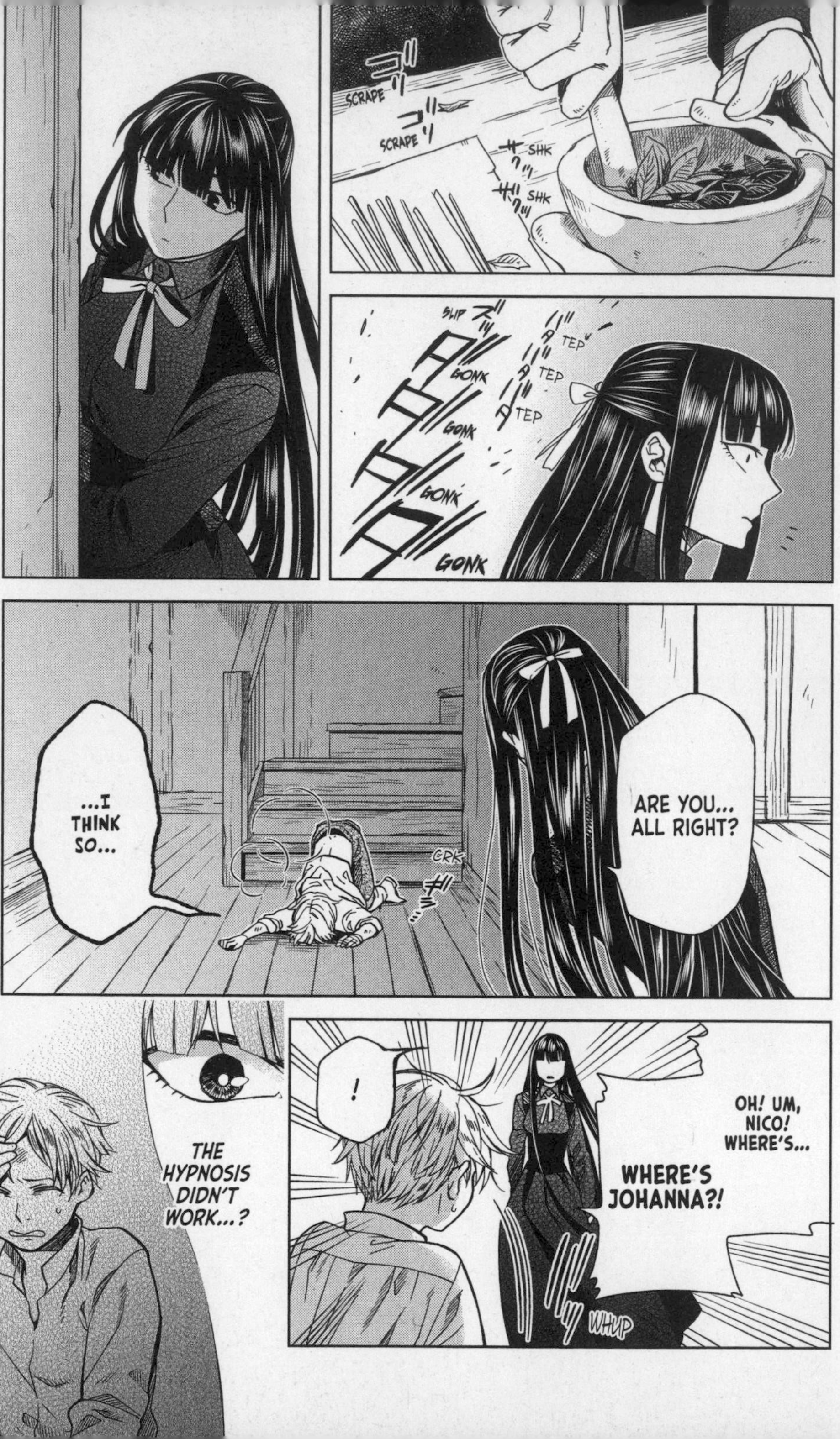
SCRAPE
SCRAPE
SHK
SHK
SLIP
TEP
TEP
TEP
GONK
GONK
GONK
GONK
ARE YOU... ALL RIGHT?
GRK
...I THINK SO...
!
OH! UM, NICO! WHERE'S...
WHERE'S JOHANNA?!
WHUP
THE HYPNOSIS DIDN'T WORK...?

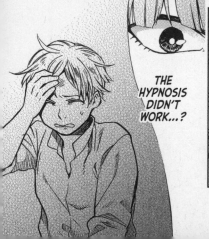

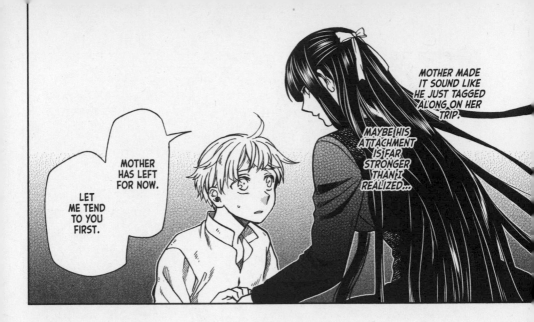

MOTHER MADE IT SOUND LIKE HE JUST TAGGED ALONG ON HER TRIP.

MAYBE HIS ATTACHMENT IS FAR STRONGER THAN I REALIZED...

MOTHER HAS LEFT FOR NOW.

LET ME TEND TO YOU FIRST.

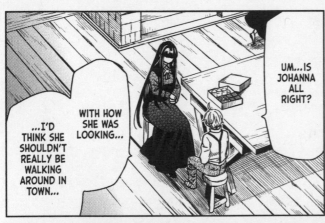

UM...IS JOHANNA ALL RIGHT?

WITH HOW SHE WAS LOOKING...

...I'D THINK SHE SHOULDN'T REALLY BE WALKING AROUND IN TOWN...

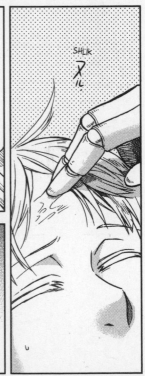

SHLIK

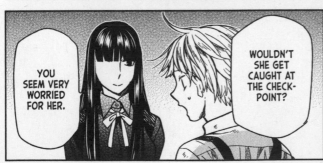

WOULDN'T SHE GET CAUGHT AT THE CHECK-POINT?

YOU SEEM VERY WORRIED FOR HER.

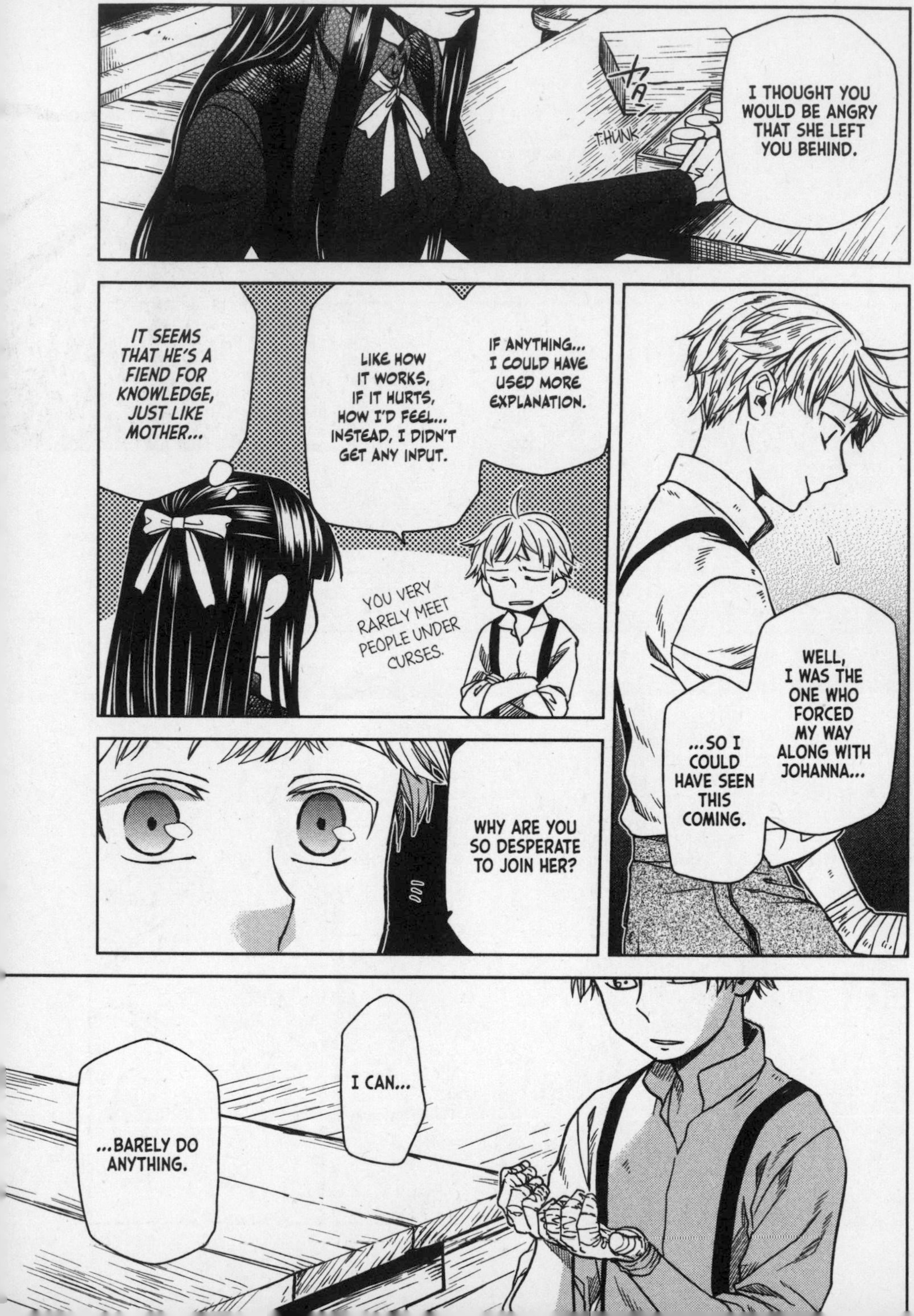
T-HUNK
I THOUGHT YOU WOULD BE ANGRY THAT SHE LEFT YOU BEHIND.
WELL, I WAS THE ONE WHO FORCED MY WAY ALONG WITH JOHANNA...
...SO I COULD HAVE SEEN THIS COMING.
IF ANYTHING... I COULD HAVE USED MORE EXPLANATION.
LIKE HOW IT WORKS, IF IT HURTS, HOW I'D FEEL... INSTEAD, I DIDN'T GET ANY INPUT.
YOU VERY RARELY MEET PEOPLE UNDER CURSES.
IT SEEMS THAT HE'S A FIEND FOR KNOWLEDGE, JUST LIKE MOTHER...
WHY ARE YOU SO DESPERATE TO JOIN HER?
I CAN...
...BARELY DO ANYTHING.

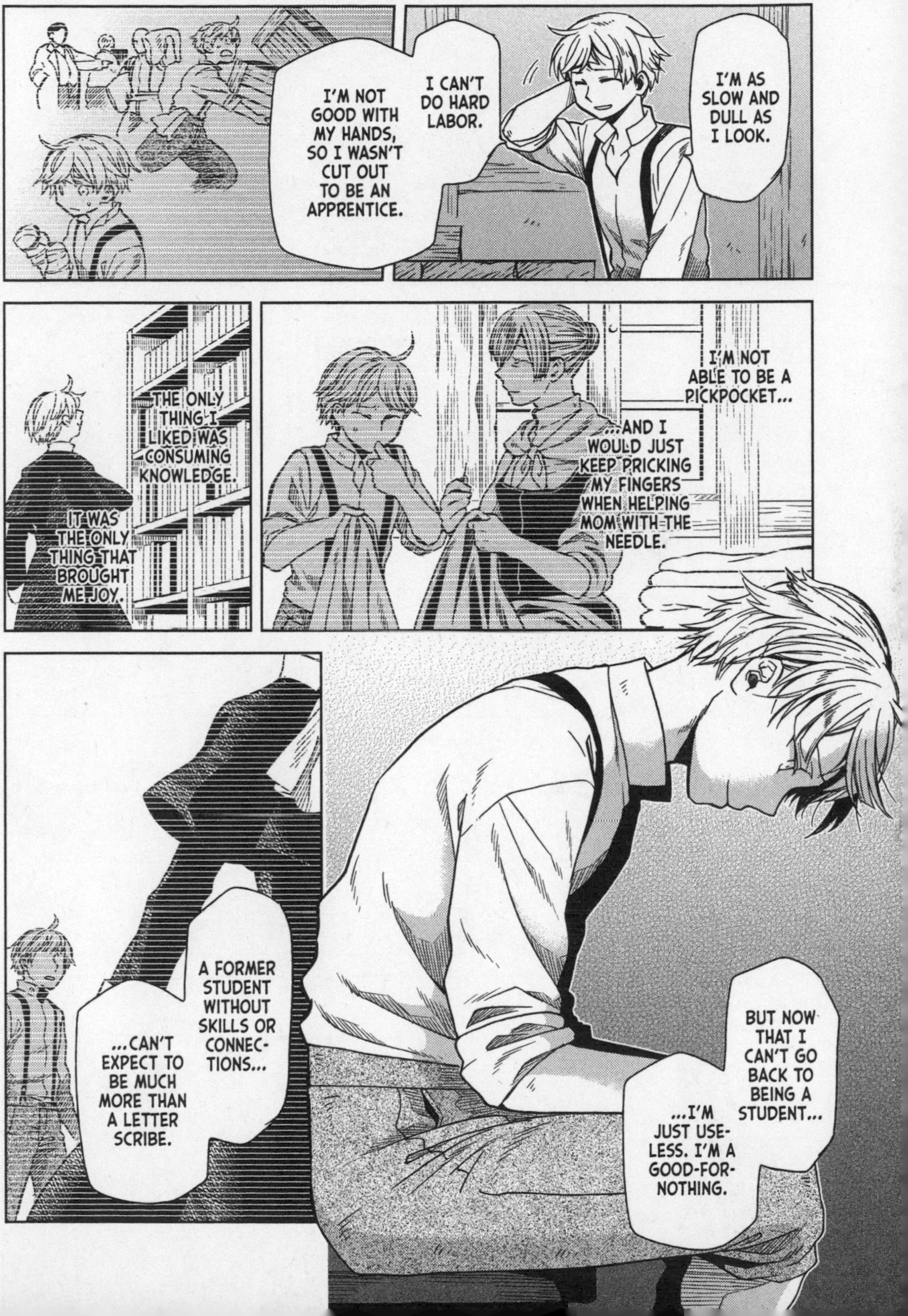
I'M AS SLOW AND DULL AS I LOOK.
I CAN'T DO HARD LABOR.
I'M NOT GOOD WITH MY HANDS, SO I WASN'T CUT OUT TO BE AN APPRENTICE.
I'M NOT ABLE TO BE A PICKPOCKET...
...AND I WOULD JUST KEEP PRICKING MY FINGERS WHEN HELPING MOM WITH THE NEEDLE.
THE ONLY THING I LIKED WAS CONSUMING KNOWLEDGE.
IT WAS THE ONLY THING THAT BROUGHT ME JOY.
BUT NOW THAT I CAN'T GO BACK TO BEING A STUDENT...
...I'M JUST USELESS. I'M A GOOD-FOR-NOTHING.
A FORMER STUDENT WITHOUT SKILLS OR CONNECTIONS...
...CAN'T EXPECT TO BE MUCH MORE THAN A LETTER SCRIBE.

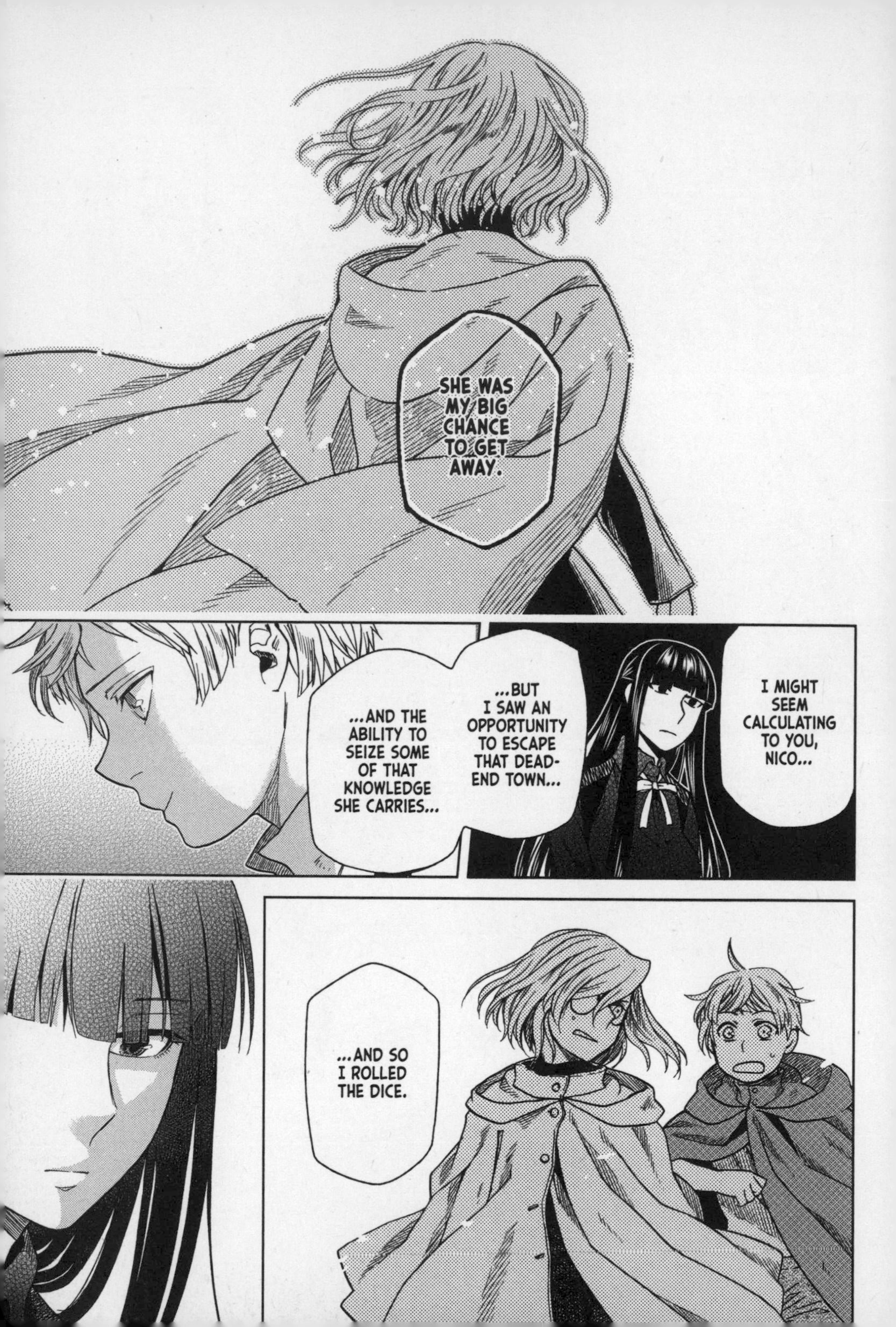
SHE WAS MY BIG CHANCE TO GET AWAY.
I MIGHT SEEM CALCULATING TO YOU, NICO...
...BUT I SAW AN OPPORTUNITY TO ESCAPE THAT DEAD-END TOWN...
...AND THE ABILITY TO SEIZE SOME OF THAT KNOWLEDGE SHE CARRIES...
...AND SO I ROLLED THE DICE.

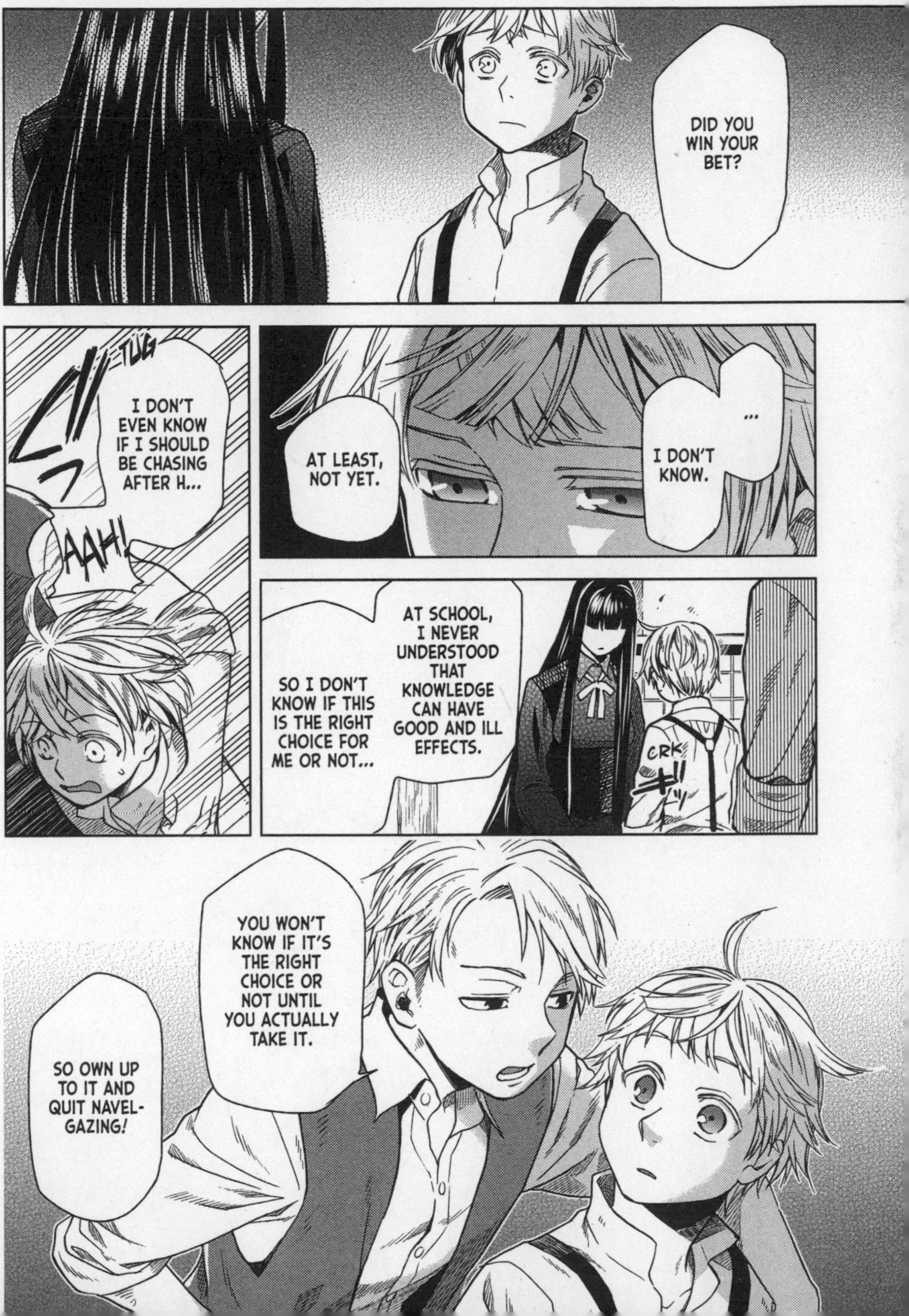
DID YOU WIN YOUR BET?
...
I DON'T KNOW.
AT LEAST, NOT YET.
AT SCHOOL, I NEVER UNDERSTOOD THAT KNOWLEDGE CAN HAVE GOOD AND ILL EFFECTS.
SO I DON'T KNOW IF THIS IS THE RIGHT CHOICE FOR ME OR NOT...
CRK
TUG
I DON'T EVEN KNOW IF I SHOULD BE CHASING AFTER H...
AAH!
YOU WON'T KNOW IF IT'S THE RIGHT CHOICE OR NOT UNTIL YOU ACTUALLY TAKE IT.
SO OWN UP TO IT AND QUIT NAVEL-GAZING!

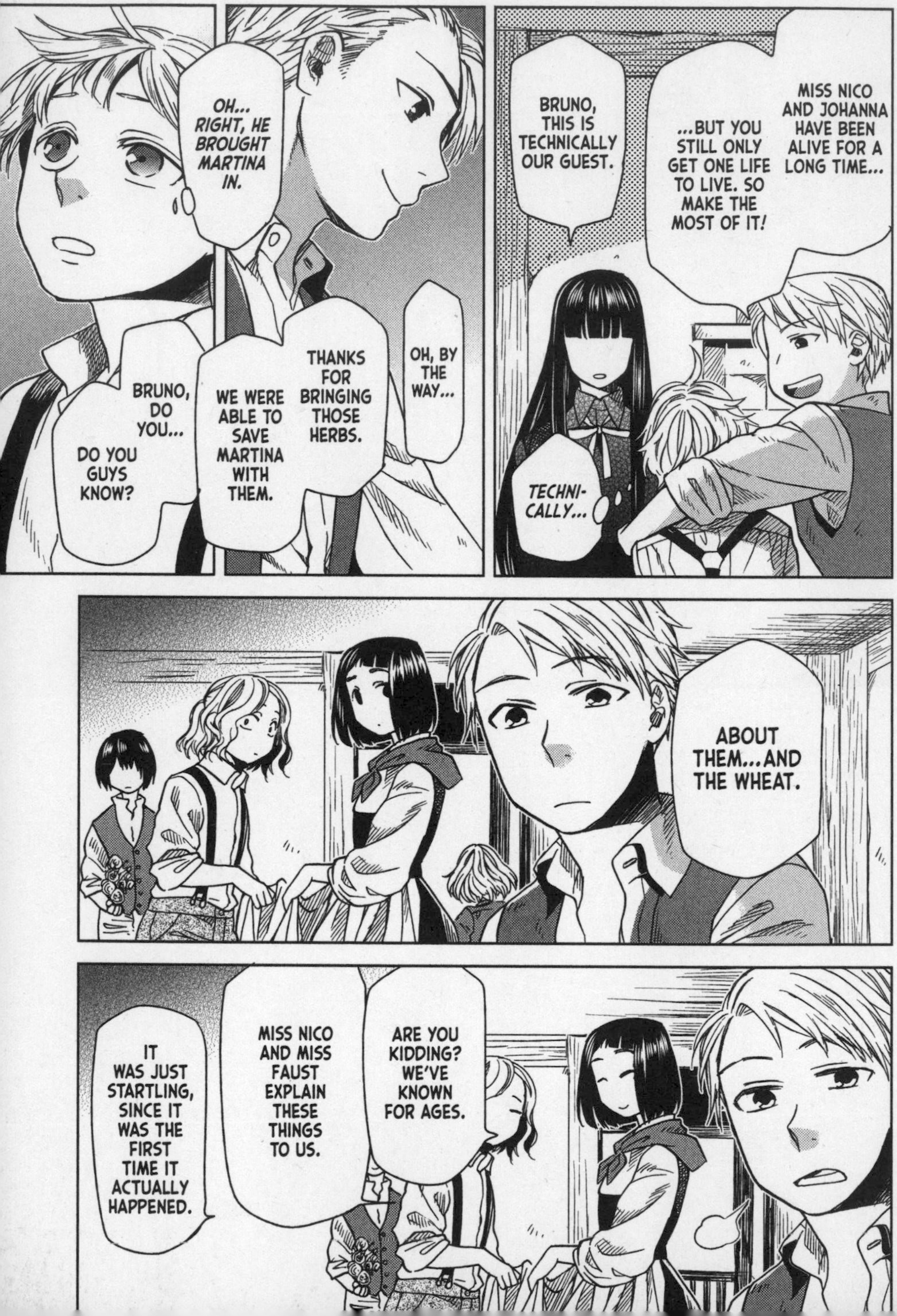
MISS NICO AND JOHANNA HAVE BEEN ALIVE FOR A LONG TIME...
...BUT YOU STILL ONLY GET ONE LIFE TO LIVE. SO MAKE THE MOST OF IT!
BRUNO, THIS IS TECHNICALLY OUR GUEST.
TECHNICALLY...
OH, BY THE WAY...
THANKS FOR BRINGING THOSE HERBS.
WE WERE ABLE TO SAVE MARTINA WITH THEM.
OH... RIGHT, HE BROUGHT MARTINA IN.
BRUNO, DO YOU...
DO YOU GUYS KNOW?
ABOUT THEM...AND THE WHEAT.
ARE YOU KIDDING? WE'VE KNOWN FOR AGES.
MISS NICO AND MISS FAUST EXPLAIN THESE THINGS TO US.
IT WAS JUST STARTLING, SINCE IT WAS THE FIRST TIME IT ACTUALLY HAPPENED.

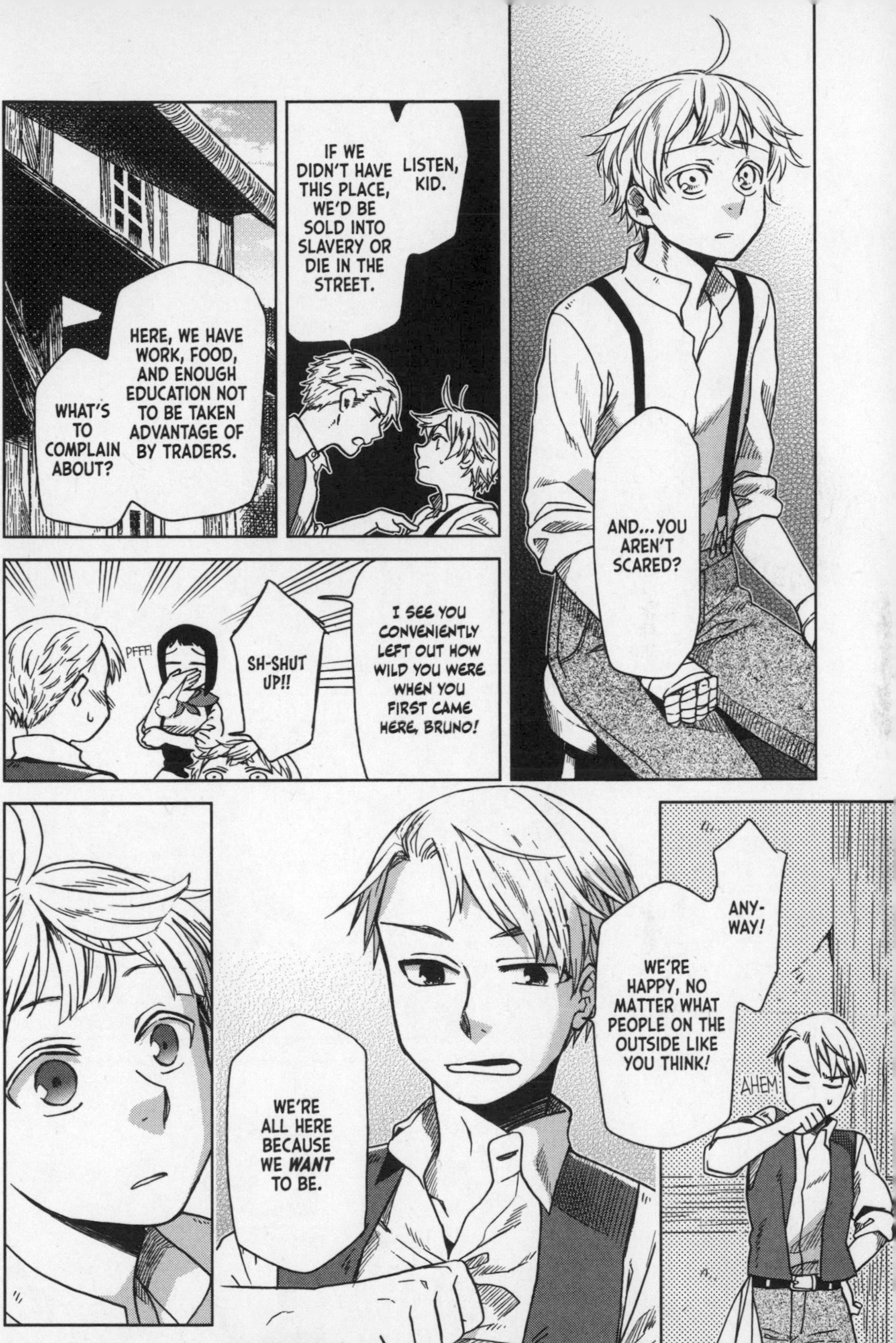
AND...YOU AREN'T SCARED?
LISTEN, KID.
IF WE DIDN'T HAVE THIS PLACE, WE'D BE SOLD INTO SLAVERY OR DIE IN THE STREET.
HERE, WE HAVE WORK, FOOD, AND ENOUGH EDUCATION NOT TO BE TAKEN ADVANTAGE OF BY TRADERS.
WHAT'S TO COMPLAIN ABOUT?
I SEE YOU CONVENIENTLY LEFT OUT HOW WILD YOU WERE WHEN YOU FIRST CAME HERE, BRUNO!
SH-SHUT UP!!
PFFF!
ANY-WAY!
WE'RE HAPPY, NO MATTER WHAT PEOPLE ON THE OUTSIDE LIKE YOU THINK!
AHEM
WE'RE ALL HERE BECAUSE WE *WANT* TO BE.

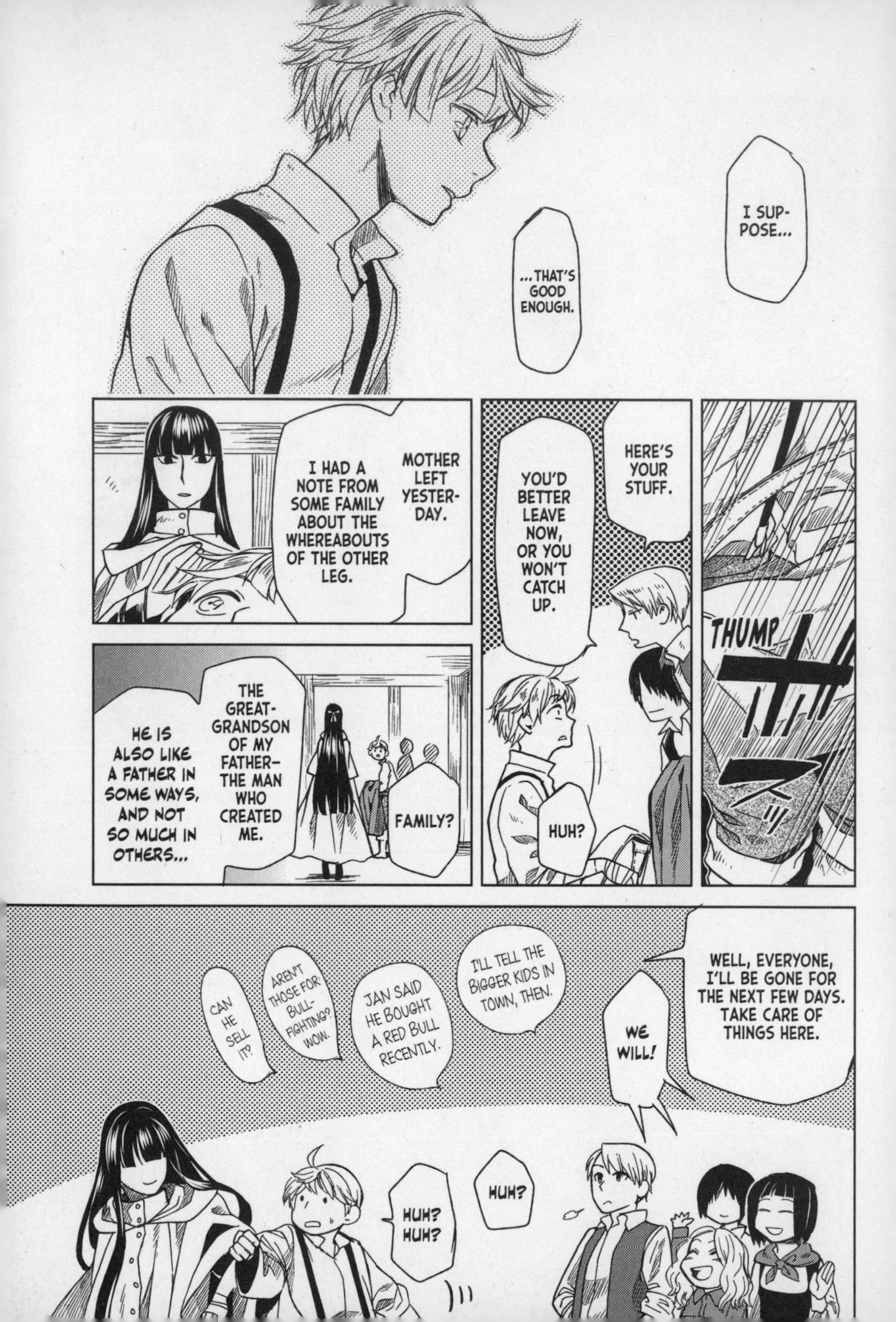
I SUP-POSE...
...THAT'S GOOD ENOUGH.
THUMP
HERE'S YOUR STUFF.
YOU'D BETTER LEAVE NOW, OR YOU WON'T CATCH UP.
HUH?
MOTHER LEFT YESTER-DAY.
I HAD A NOTE FROM SOME FAMILY ABOUT THE WHEREABOUTS OF THE OTHER LEG.
FAMILY?
THE GREAT-GRANDSON OF MY FATHER—THE MAN WHO CREATED ME.
HE IS ALSO LIKE A FATHER IN SOME WAYS, AND NOT SO MUCH IN OTHERS...
WELL, EVERYONE, I'LL BE GONE FOR THE NEXT FEW DAYS. TAKE CARE OF THINGS HERE.
WE WILL!
I'LL TELL THE BIGGER KIDS IN TOWN, THEN.
JAN SAID HE BOUGHT A RED BULL RECENTLY.
AREN'T THOSE FOR BULL-FIGHTING? WOW.
CAN HE SELL IT?
HUH?
HUH? HUH?

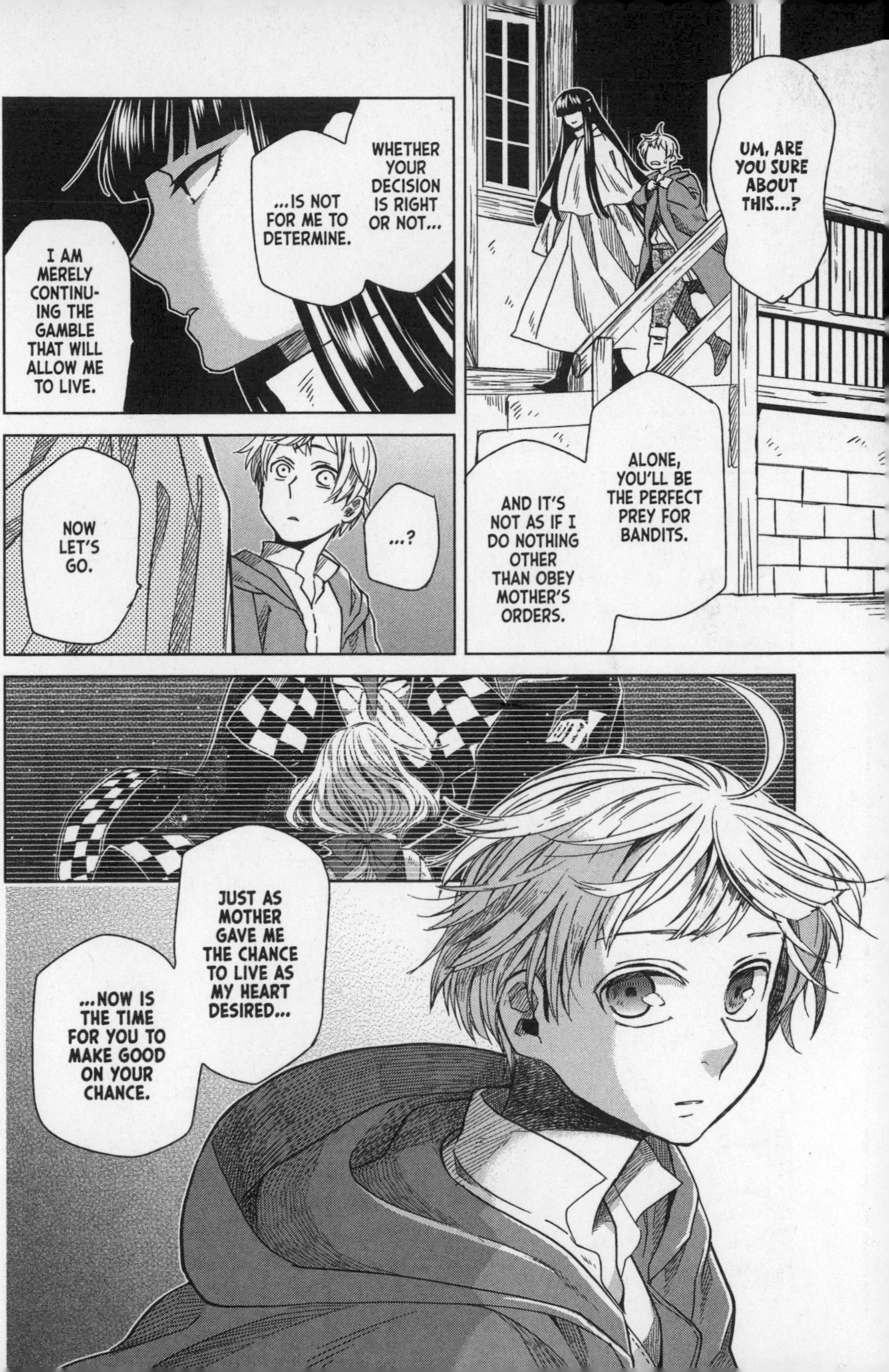

UM, ARE YOU SURE ABOUT THIS...?
ALONE, YOU'LL BE THE PERFECT PREY FOR BANDITS.
AND IT'S NOT AS IF I DO NOTHING OTHER THAN OBEY MOTHER'S ORDERS.
WHETHER YOUR DECISION IS RIGHT OR NOT...
...IS NOT FOR ME TO DETERMINE.
I AM MERELY CONTINUING THE GAMBLE THAT WILL ALLOW ME TO LIVE.
...?
NOW LET'S GO.
JUST AS MOTHER GAVE ME THE CHANCE TO LIVE AS MY HEART DESIRED...
...NOW IS THE TIME FOR YOU TO MAKE GOOD ON YOUR CHANCE.

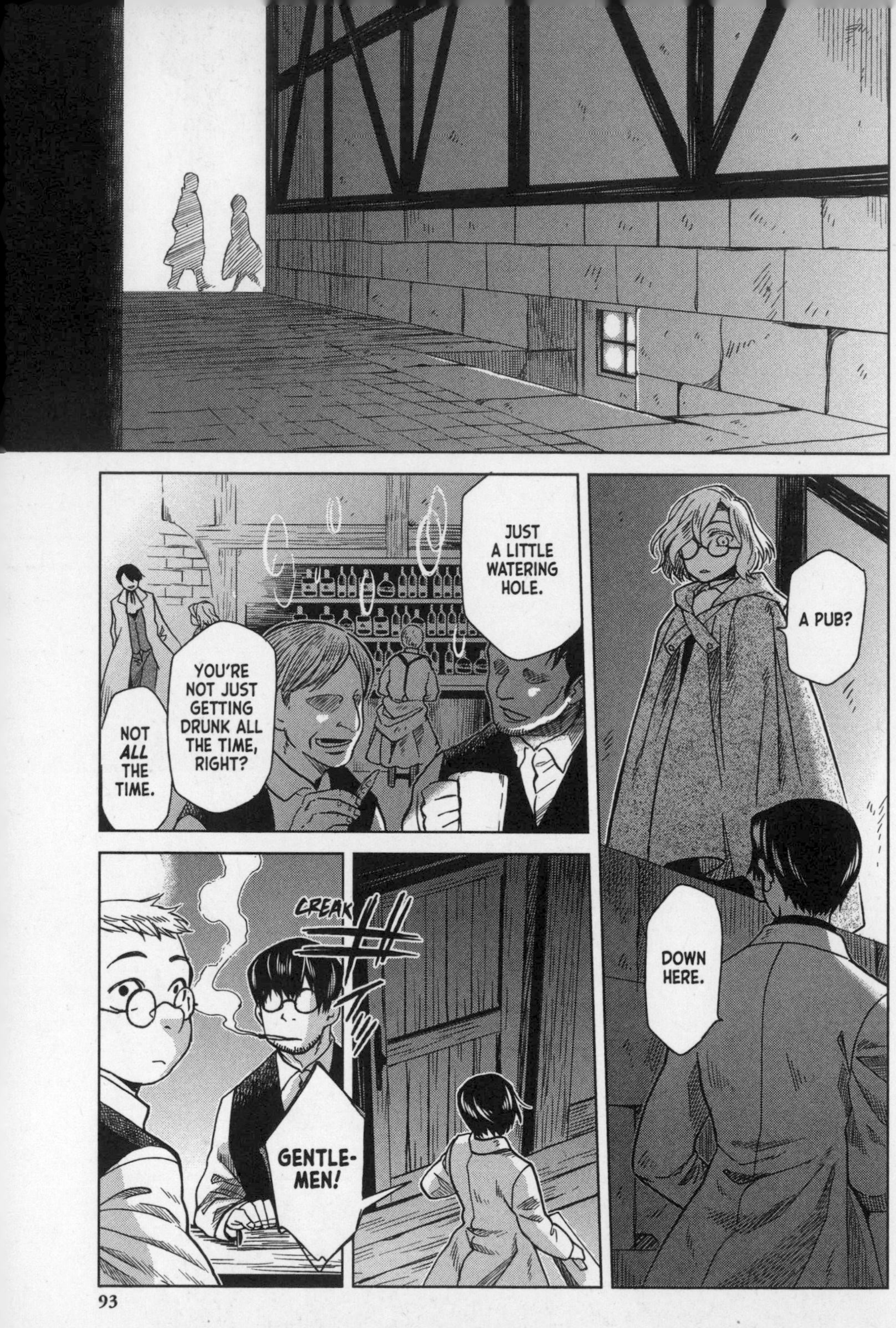
A PUB?
DOWN HERE.
JUST A LITTLE WATERING HOLE.
YOU'RE NOT JUST GETTING DRUNK ALL THE TIME, RIGHT?
NOT *ALL* THE TIME.
CREAK
GENTLE-MEN!

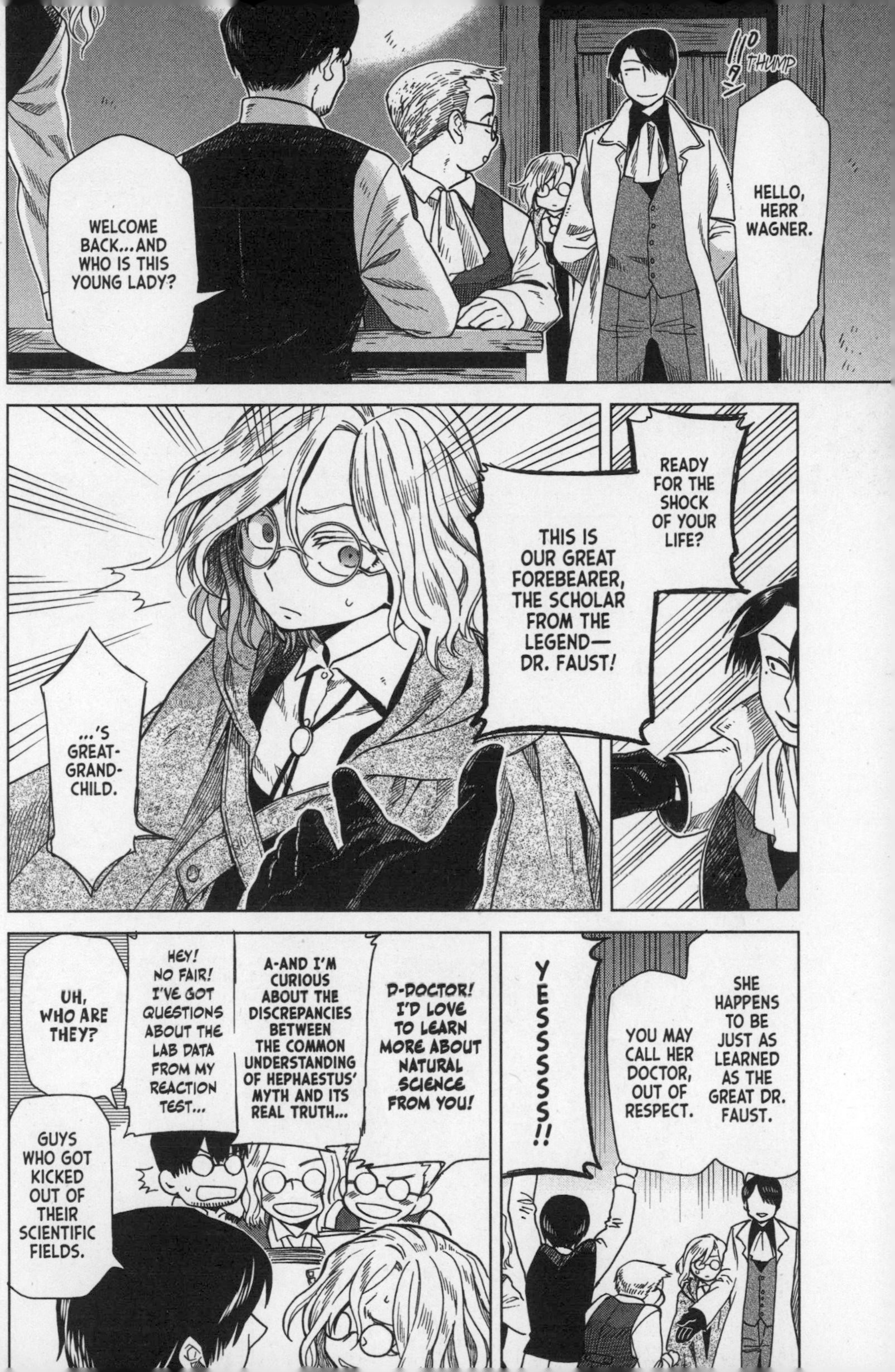
THUMP
HELLO, HERR WAGNER.
WELCOME BACK...AND WHO IS THIS YOUNG LADY?
READY FOR THE SHOCK OF YOUR LIFE?
THIS IS OUR GREAT FOREBEARER, THE SCHOLAR FROM THE LEGEND— DR. FAUST!
...'S GREAT-GRAND-CHILD.
SHE HAPPENS TO BE JUST AS LEARNED AS THE GREAT DR. FAUST.
YOU MAY CALL HER DOCTOR, OUT OF RESPECT.
YESSSSS!!
D-DOCTOR! I'D LOVE TO LEARN MORE ABOUT NATURAL SCIENCE FROM YOU!
A-AND I'M CURIOUS ABOUT THE DISCREPANCIES BETWEEN THE COMMON UNDERSTANDING OF HEPHAESTUS' MYTH AND ITS REAL TRUTH...
HEY! NO FAIR! I'VE GOT QUESTIONS ABOUT THE LAB DATA FROM MY REACTION TEST...
UH, WHO ARE THEY?
GUYS WHO GOT KICKED OUT OF THEIR SCIENTIFIC FIELDS.

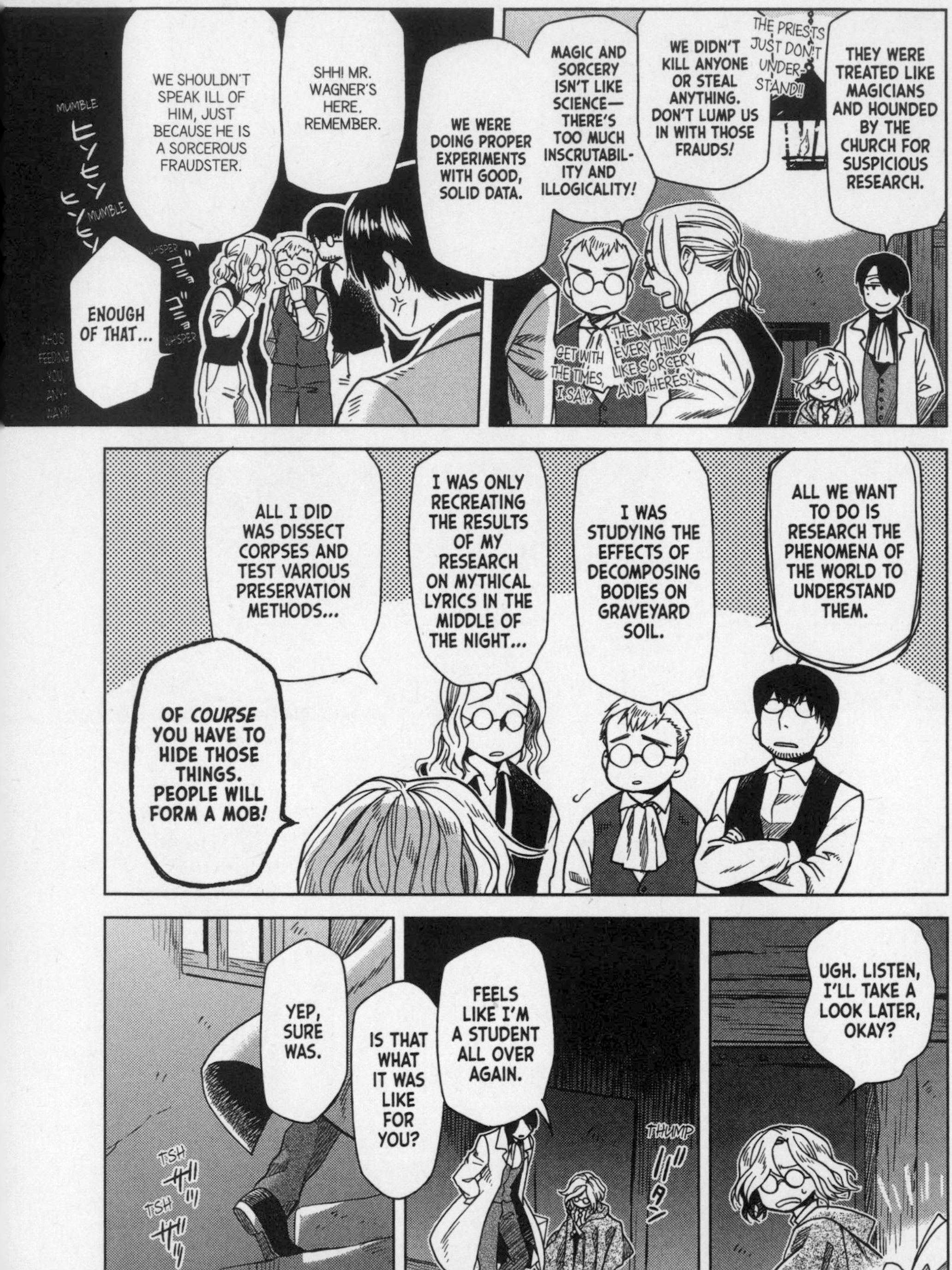
THEY WERE TREATED LIKE MAGICIANS AND HOUNDED BY THE CHURCH FOR SUSPICIOUS RESEARCH.
THE PRIESTS JUST DON'T UNDERSTAND!!
WE DIDN'T KILL ANYONE OR STEAL ANYTHING. DON'T LUMP US IN WITH THOSE FRAUDS!
MAGIC AND SORCERY ISN'T LIKE SCIENCE—THERE'S TOO MUCH INSCRUTABILITY AND ILLOGICALITY!
THEY TREAT EVERYTHING LIKE SORCERY AND HERESY!
GET WITH THE TIMES, I SAY.
WE WERE DOING PROPER EXPERIMENTS WITH GOOD, SOLID DATA.
SHH! MR. WAGNER'S HERE, REMEMBER.
WE SHOULDN'T SPEAK ILL OF HIM, JUST BECAUSE HE IS A SORCEROUS FRAUDSTER.
MUMBLE
MUMBLE
WHISPER
WHISPER
ENOUGH OF THAT...
WHO'S FEEDING YOU, ANYWAY?!
ALL WE WANT TO DO IS RESEARCH THE PHENOMENA OF THE WORLD TO UNDERSTAND THEM.
I WAS STUDYING THE EFFECTS OF DECOMPOSING BODIES ON GRAVEYARD SOIL.
I WAS ONLY RECREATING THE RESULTS OF MY RESEARCH ON MYTHICAL LYRICS IN THE MIDDLE OF THE NIGHT...
ALL I DID WAS DISSECT CORPSES AND TEST VARIOUS PRESERVATION METHODS...
OF COURSE YOU HAVE TO HIDE THOSE THINGS. PEOPLE WILL FORM A MOB!
UGH. LISTEN, I'LL TAKE A LOOK LATER, OKAY?
THUMP
FEELS LIKE I'M A STUDENT ALL OVER AGAIN.
IS THAT WHAT IT WAS LIKE FOR YOU?
YEP, SURE WAS.
TSH
TSH

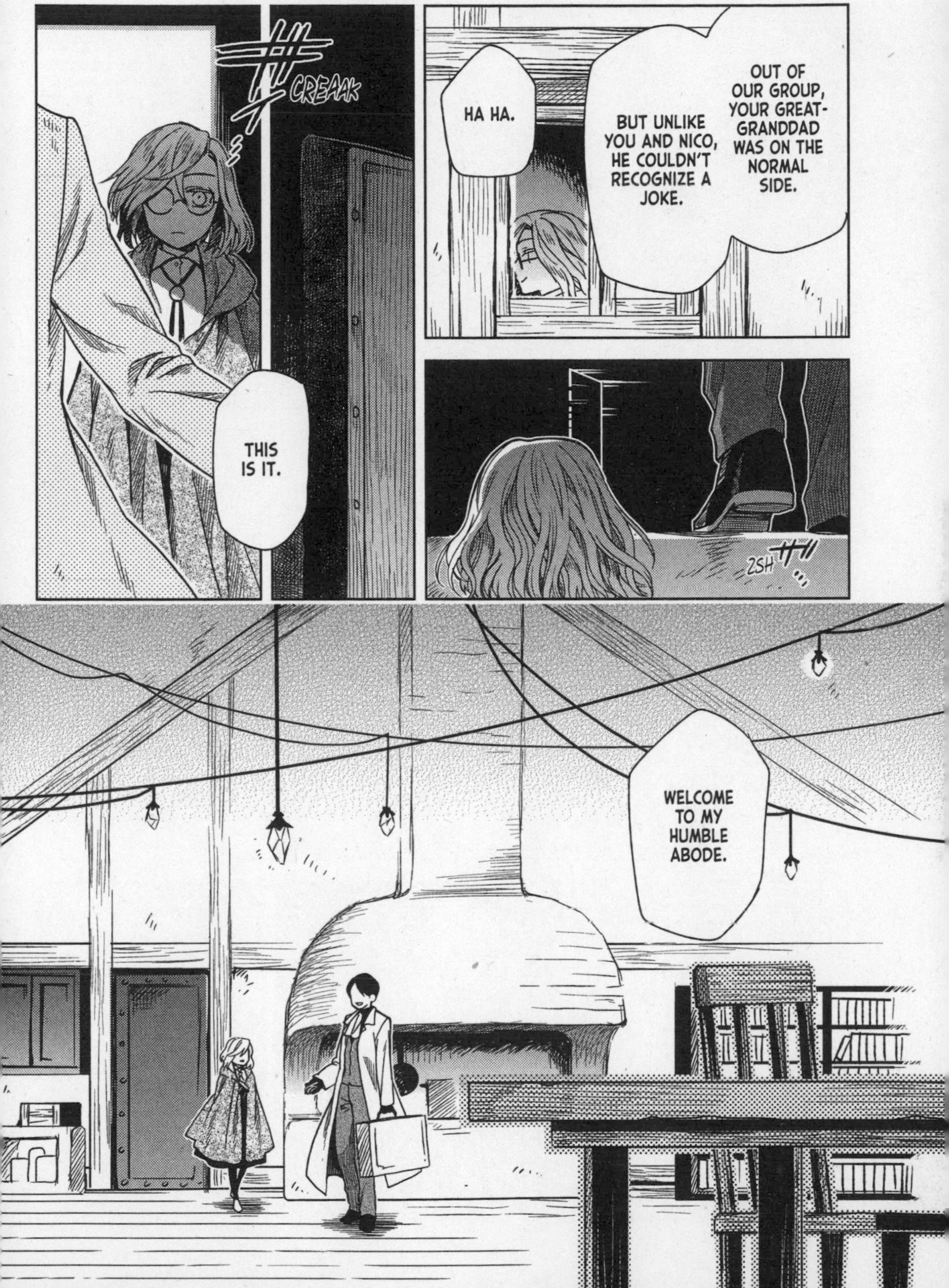
OUT OF OUR GROUP, YOUR GREAT-GRANDDAD WAS ON THE NORMAL SIDE.
BUT UNLIKE YOU AND NICO, HE COULDN'T RECOGNIZE A JOKE.
HA HA.
ZSH
CREAAK
THIS IS IT.
WELCOME TO MY HUMBLE ABODE.

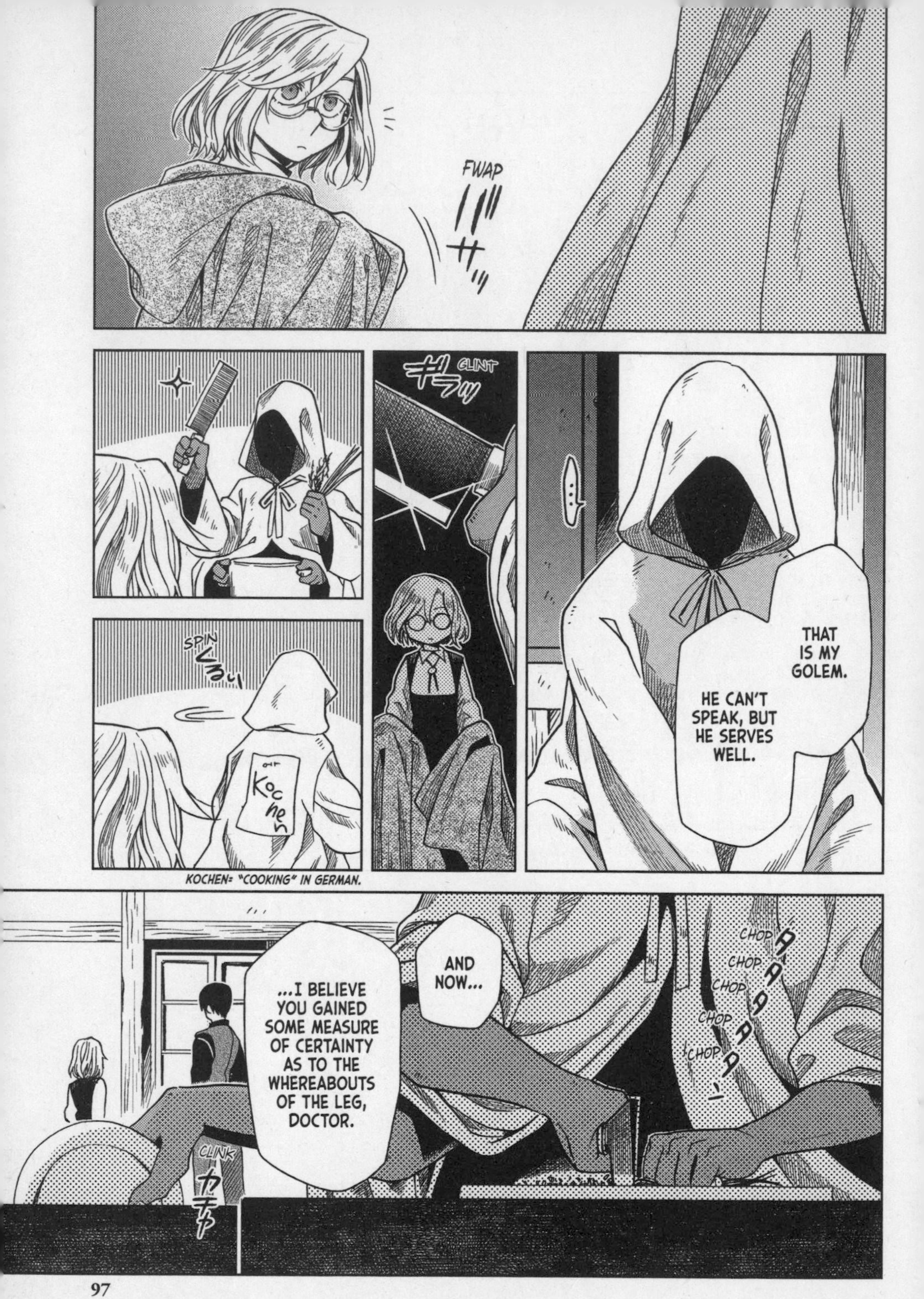
FWAP
...
THAT IS MY GOLEM.
HE CAN'T SPEAK, BUT HE SERVES WELL.
GLINT
SPIN
Kochen
KOCHEN= "COOKING" IN GERMAN.
CHOP CHOP CHOP CHOP CHOP
AND NOW...
...I BELIEVE YOU GAINED SOME MEASURE OF CERTAINTY AS TO THE WHEREABOUTS OF THE LEG, DOCTOR.
CLINK

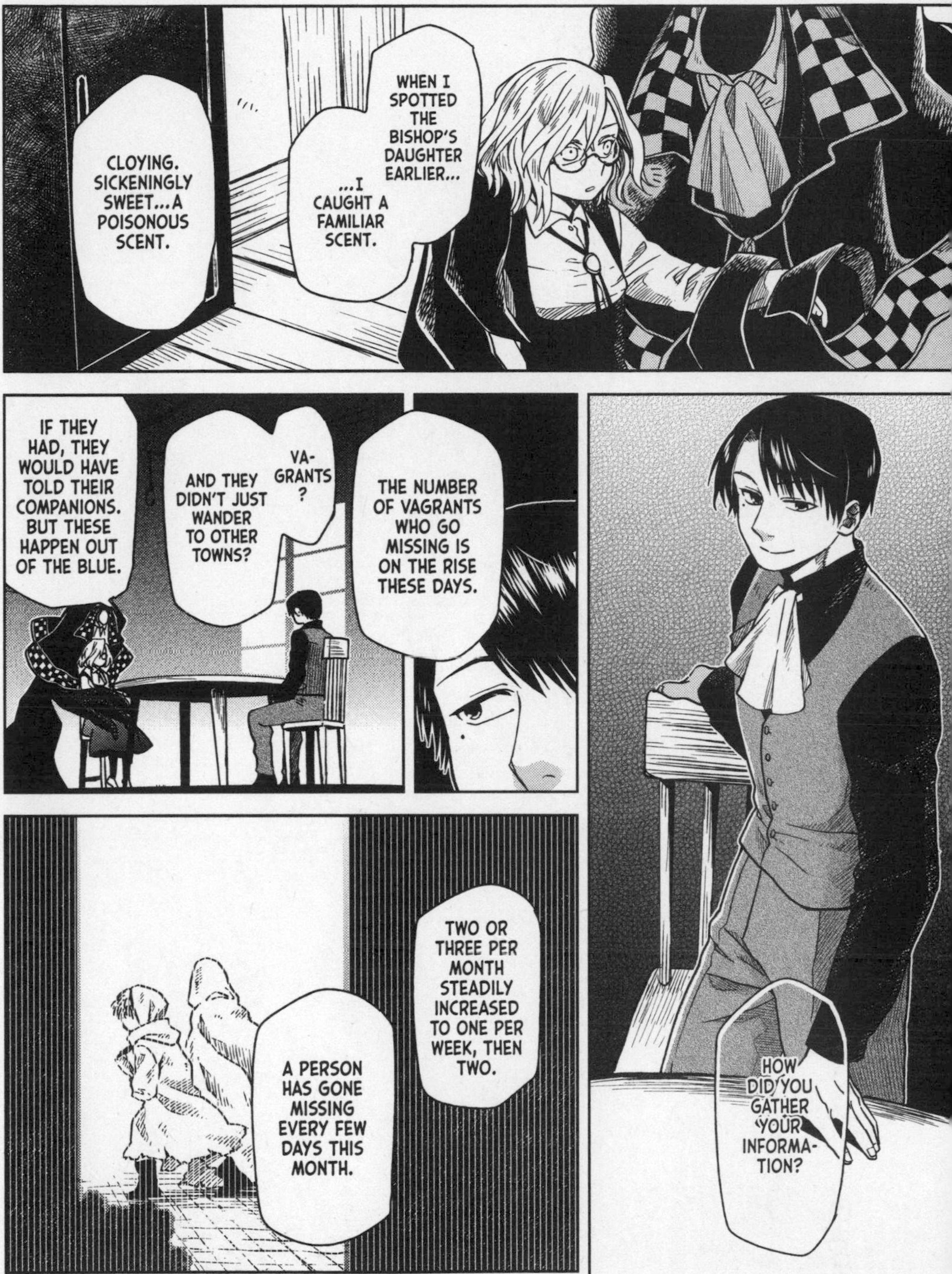
WHEN I SPOTTED THE BISHOP'S DAUGHTER EARLIER...
...I CAUGHT A FAMILIAR SCENT.
CLOYING. SICKENINGLY SWEET...A POISONOUS SCENT.
HOW DID YOU GATHER YOUR INFORMATION?
THE NUMBER OF VAGRANTS WHO GO MISSING IS ON THE RISE THESE DAYS.
VA-GRANTS?
AND THEY DIDN'T JUST WANDER TO OTHER TOWNS?
IF THEY HAD, THEY WOULD HAVE TOLD THEIR COMPANIONS. BUT THESE HAPPEN OUT OF THE BLUE.
TWO OR THREE PER MONTH STEADILY INCREASED TO ONE PER WEEK, THEN TWO.
A PERSON HAS GONE MISSING EVERY FEW DAYS THIS MONTH.

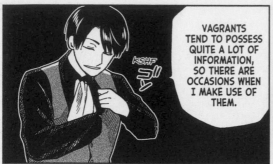

VAGRANTS TEND TO POSSESS QUITE A LOT OF INFORMATION, SO THERE ARE OCCASIONS WHEN I MAKE USE OF THEM.

KSHF コリ

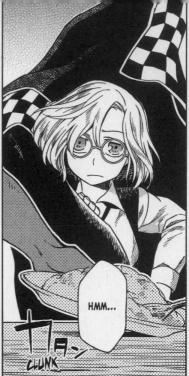

HMM...

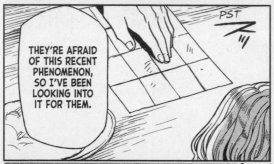

PST

THEY'RE AFRAID OF THIS RECENT PHENOMENON, SO I'VE BEEN LOOKING INTO IT FOR THEM.

カターン
CLUNK

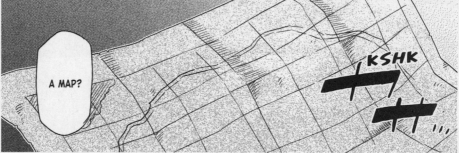

A MAP?

KSHK

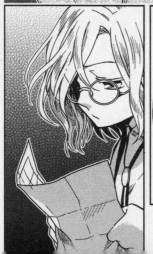

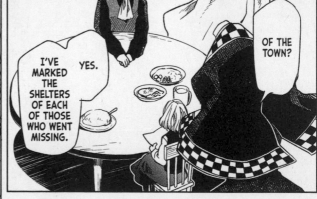

YES.

I'VE MARKED THE SHELTERS OF EACH OF THOSE WHO WENT MISSING.

OF THE TOWN?

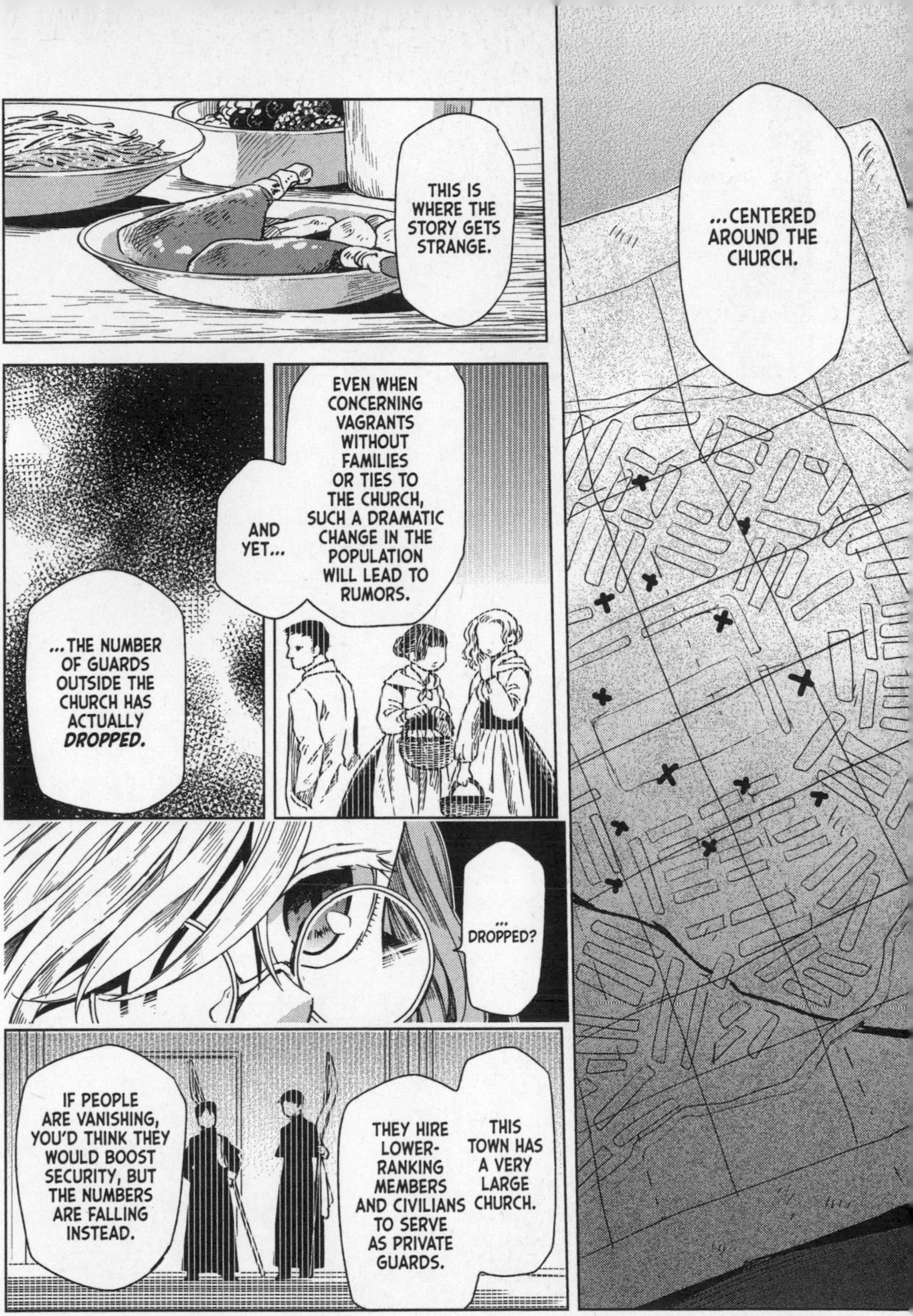
...CENTERED AROUND THE CHURCH.
THIS IS WHERE THE STORY GETS STRANGE.
EVEN WHEN CONCERNING VAGRANTS WITHOUT FAMILIES OR TIES TO THE CHURCH, SUCH A DRAMATIC CHANGE IN THE POPULATION WILL LEAD TO RUMORS.
AND YET...
...THE NUMBER OF GUARDS OUTSIDE THE CHURCH HAS ACTUALLY *DROPPED.*
...DROPPED?
THIS TOWN HAS A VERY LARGE CHURCH.
THEY HIRE LOWER-RANKING MEMBERS AND CIVILIANS TO SERVE AS PRIVATE GUARDS.
IF PEOPLE ARE VANISHING, YOU'D THINK THEY WOULD BOOST SECURITY, BUT THE NUMBERS ARE FALLING INSTEAD.

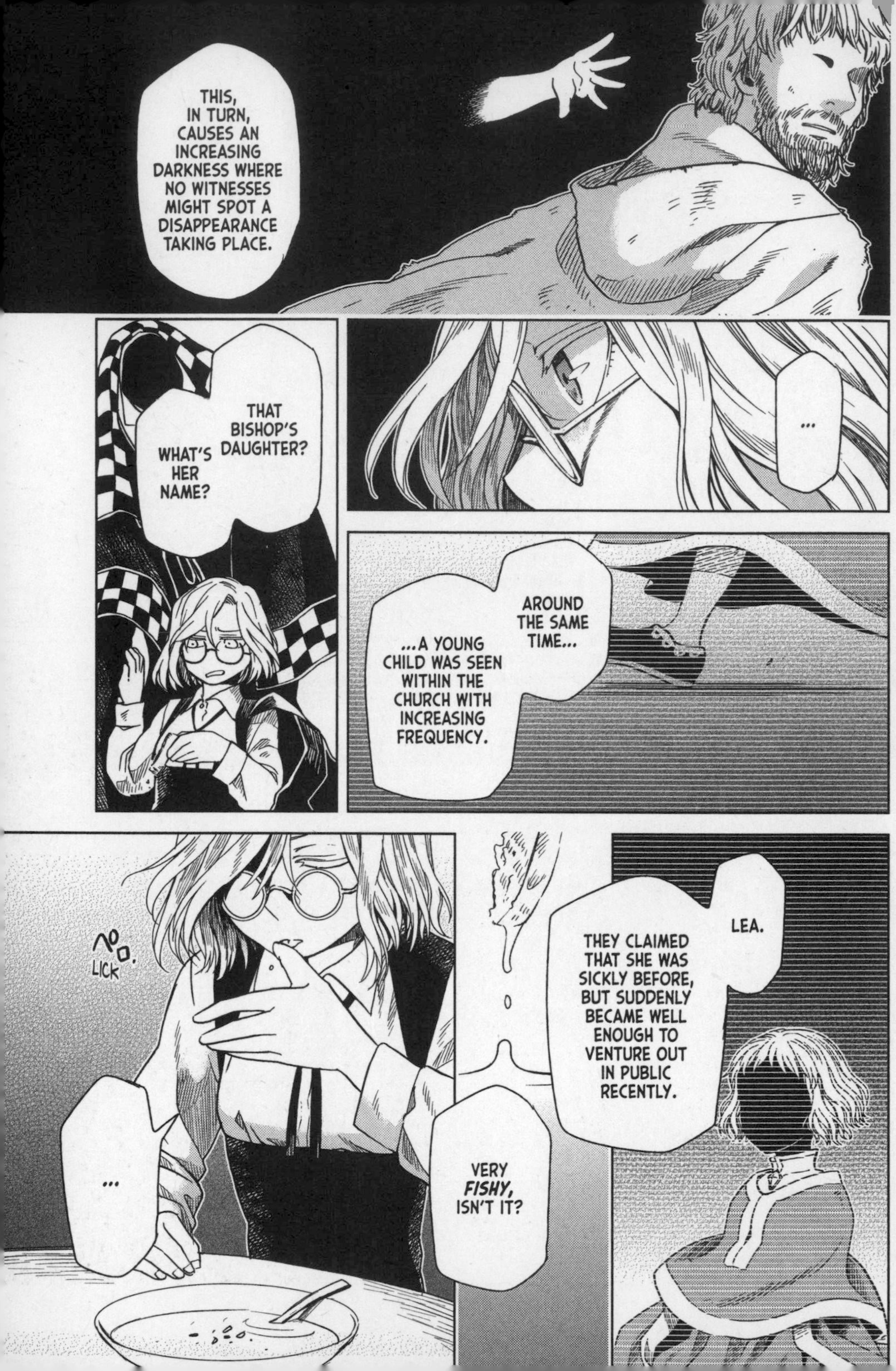
THIS, IN TURN, CAUSES AN INCREASING DARKNESS WHERE NO WITNESSES MIGHT SPOT A DISAPPEARANCE TAKING PLACE.
...
AROUND THE SAME TIME...
...A YOUNG CHILD WAS SEEN WITHIN THE CHURCH WITH INCREASING FREQUENCY.
THAT BISHOP'S DAUGHTER?
WHAT'S HER NAME?
LEA.
THEY CLAIMED THAT SHE WAS SICKLY BEFORE, BUT SUDDENLY BECAME WELL ENOUGH TO VENTURE OUT IN PUBLIC RECENTLY.
VERY *FISHY*, ISN'T IT?
ぺろ。
LICK
...

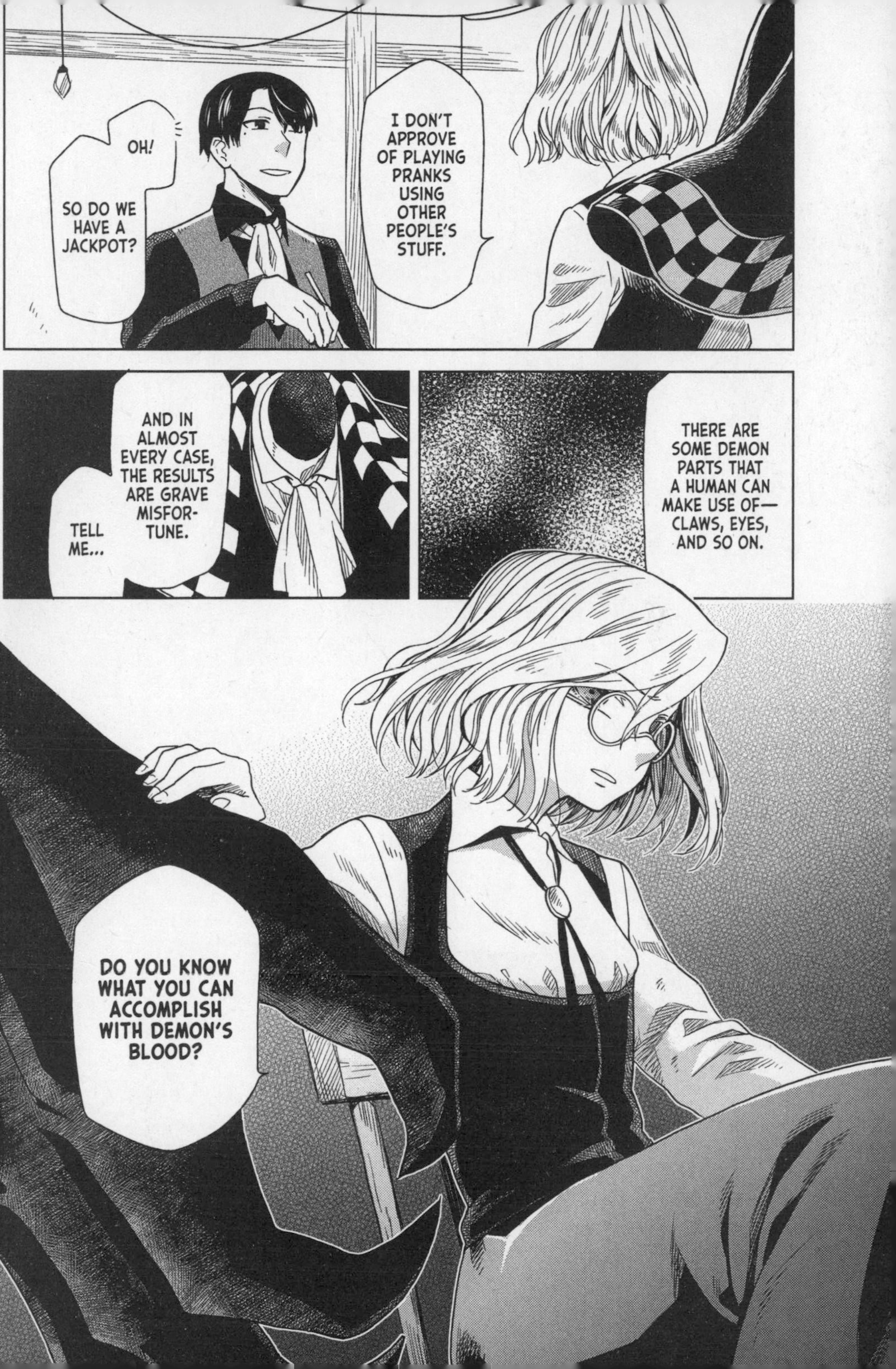
I DON'T APPROVE OF PLAYING PRANKS USING OTHER PEOPLE'S STUFF.
OH!
SO DO WE HAVE A JACKPOT?
THERE ARE SOME DEMON PARTS THAT A HUMAN CAN MAKE USE OF—CLAWS, EYES, AND SO ON.
AND IN ALMOST EVERY CASE, THE RESULTS ARE GRAVE MISFOR-TUNE.
TELL ME...
DO YOU KNOW WHAT YOU CAN ACCOMPLISH WITH DEMON'S BLOOD?

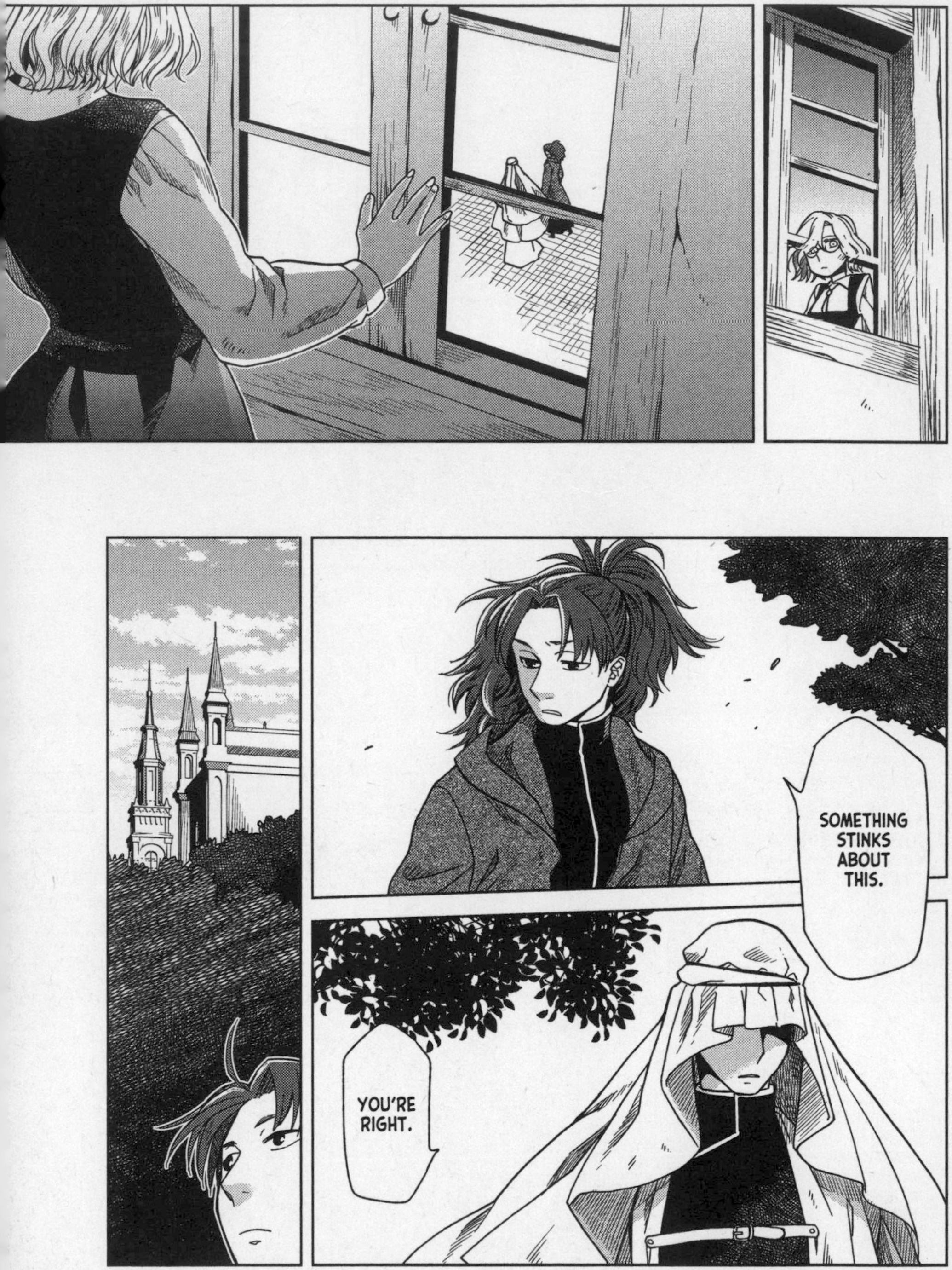
...
SOMETHING STINKS ABOUT THIS.
YOU'RE RIGHT.

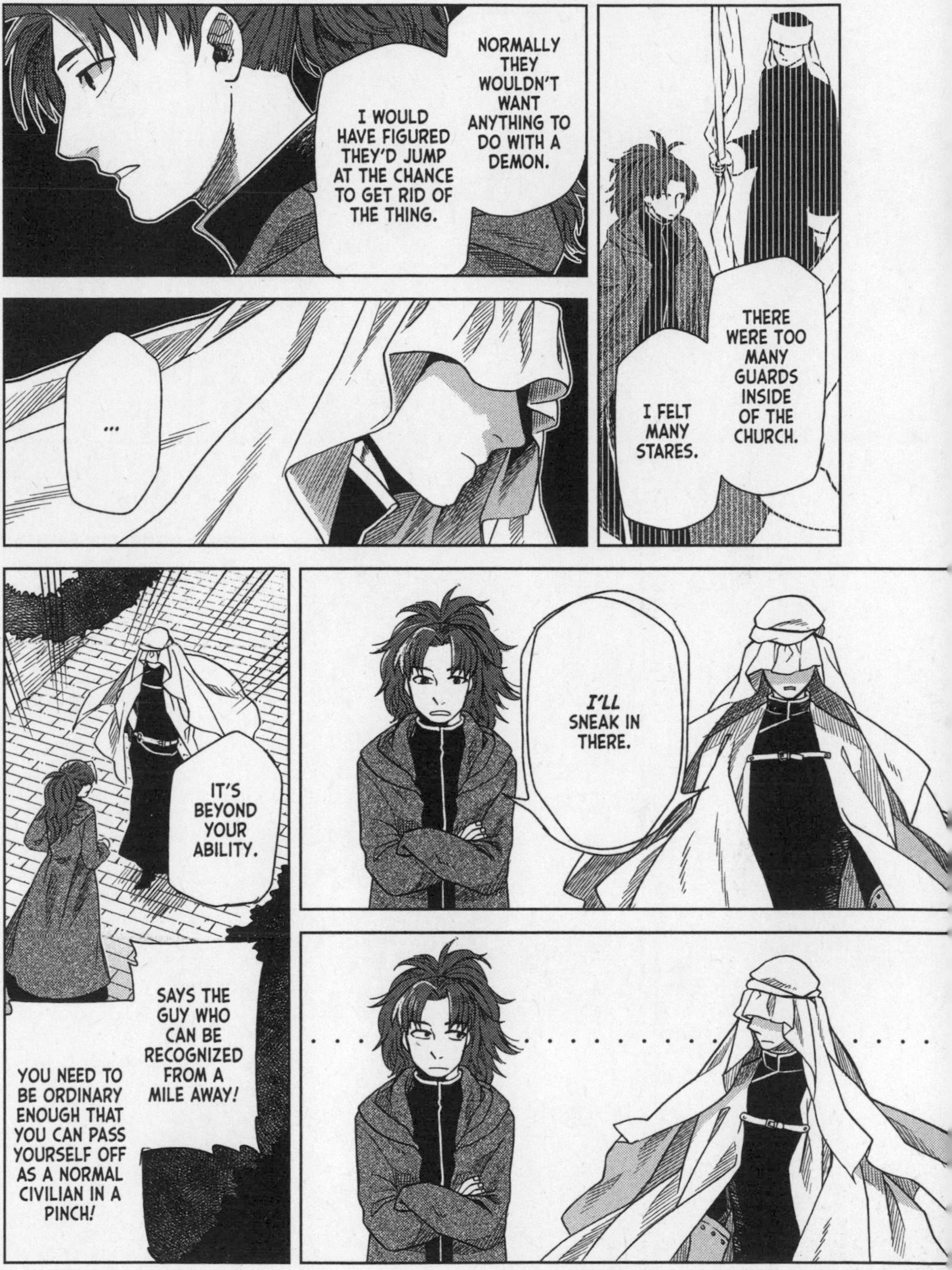
THERE WERE TOO MANY GUARDS INSIDE OF THE CHURCH.
I FELT MANY STARES.
NORMALLY THEY WOULDN'T WANT ANYTHING TO DO WITH A DEMON.
I WOULD HAVE FIGURED THEY'D JUMP AT THE CHANCE TO GET RID OF THE THING.
...
I'LL SNEAK IN THERE.
IT'S BEYOND YOUR ABILITY.
SAYS THE GUY WHO CAN BE RECOGNIZED FROM A MILE AWAY!
YOU NEED TO BE ORDINARY ENOUGH THAT YOU CAN PASS YOURSELF OFF AS A NORMAL CIVILIAN IN A PINCH!

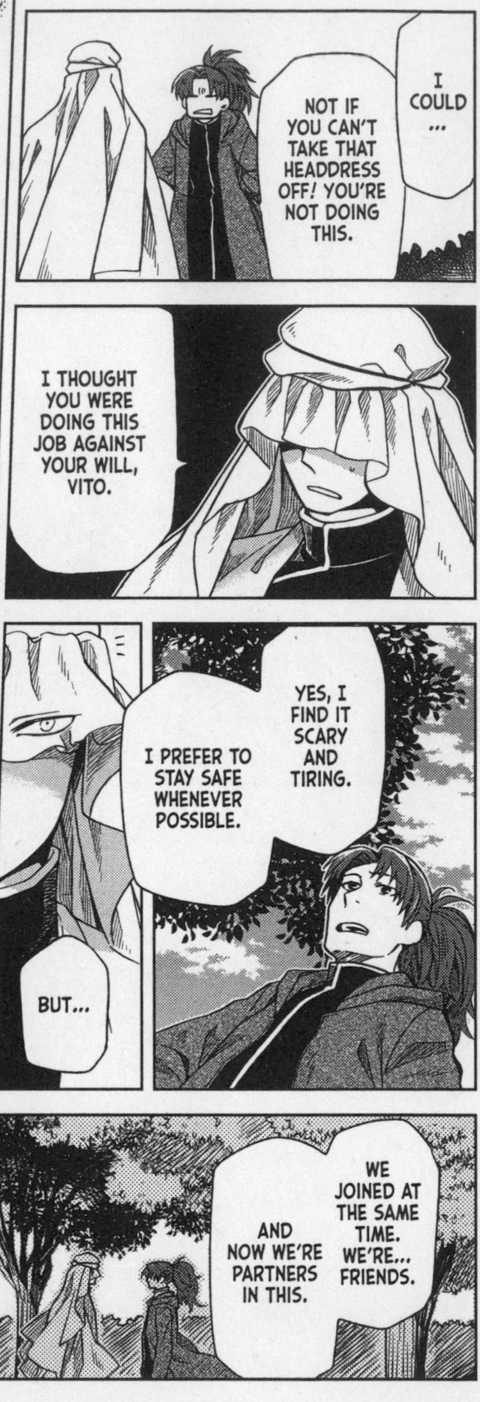
I COULD...
NOT IF YOU CAN'T TAKE THAT HEADDRESS OFF! YOU'RE NOT DOING THIS.
I THOUGHT YOU WERE DOING THIS JOB AGAINST YOUR WILL, VITO.
YES, I FIND IT SCARY AND TIRING.
I PREFER TO STAY SAFE WHENEVER POSSIBLE.
BUT...
WE JOINED AT THE SAME TIME. WE'RE... FRIENDS.
AND NOW WE'RE PARTNERS IN THIS.
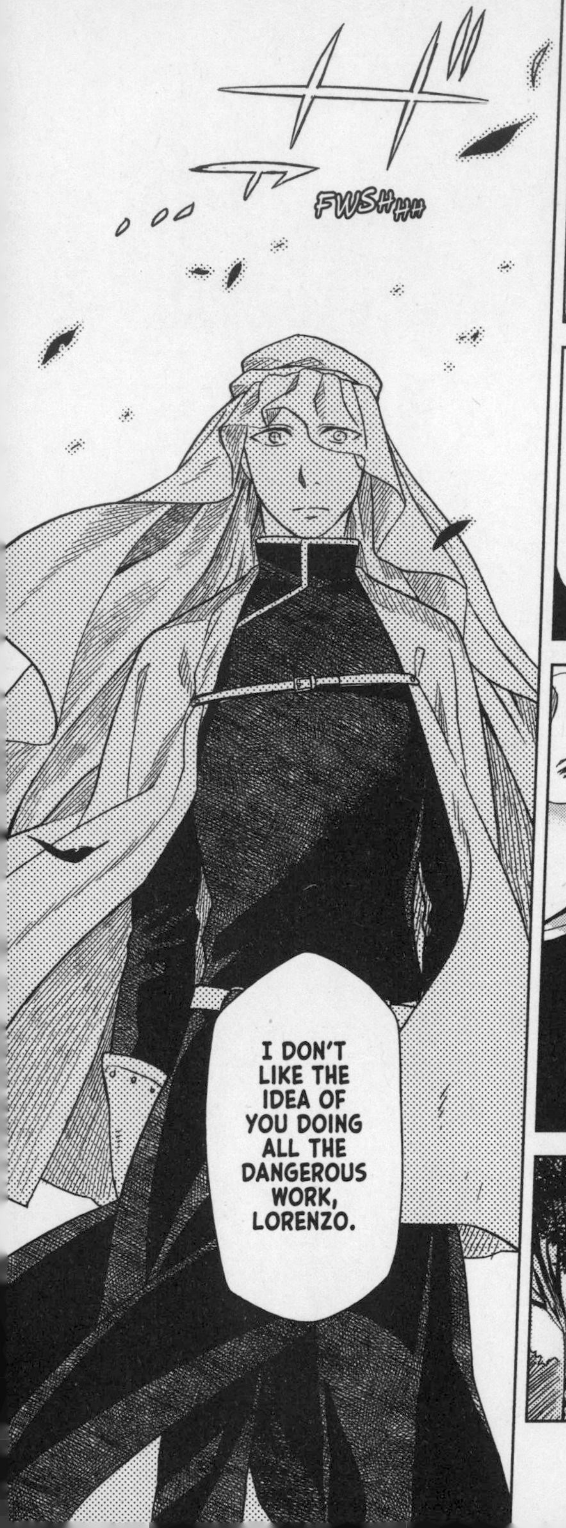
FWSHHH
I DON'T LIKE THE IDEA OF YOU DOING ALL THE DANGEROUS WORK, LORENZO.

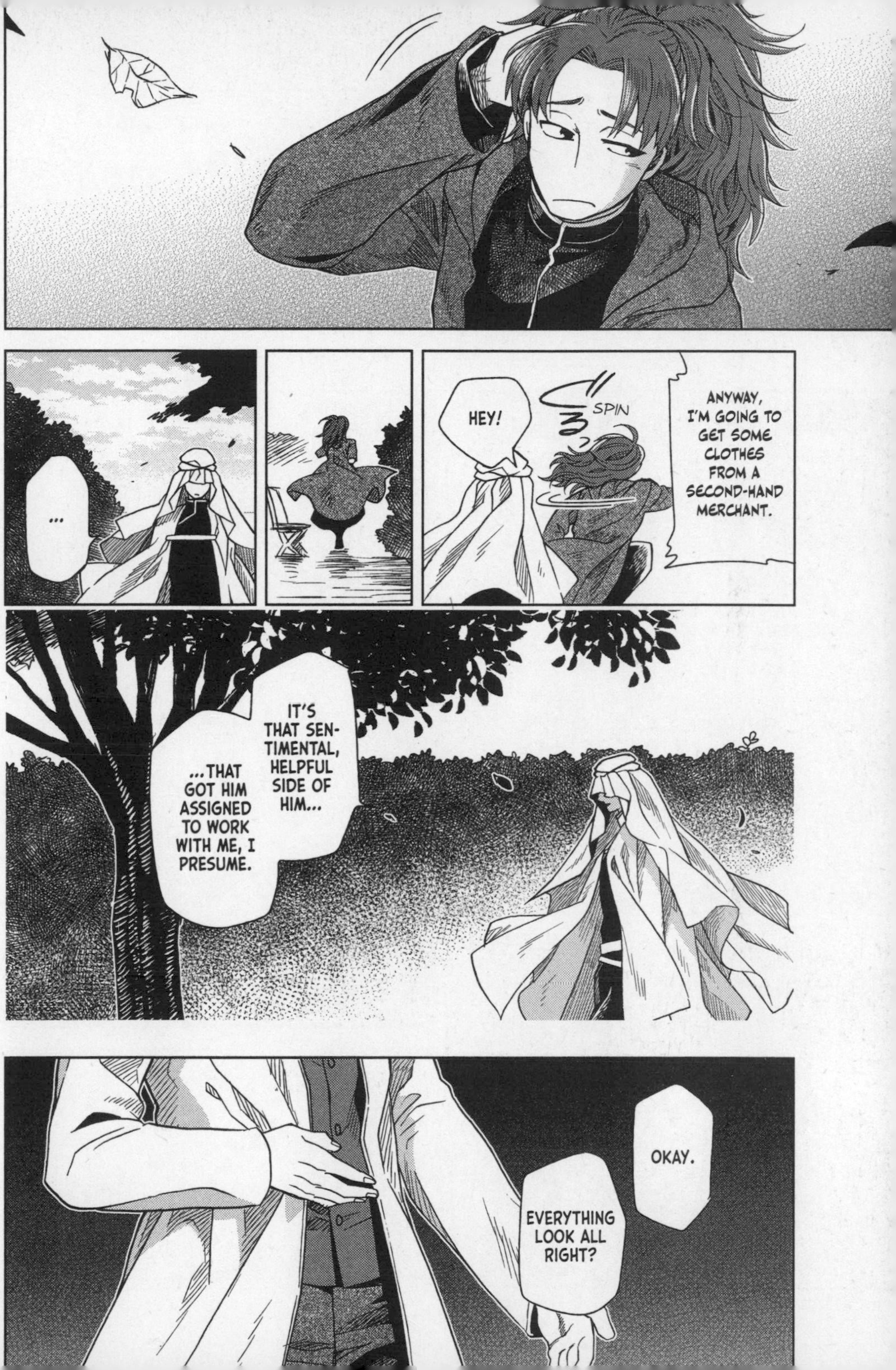
ANYWAY, I'M GOING TO GET SOME CLOTHES FROM A SECOND-HAND MERCHANT.
HEY!
SPIN
...
IT'S THAT SEN-TIMENTAL, HELPFUL SIDE OF HIM...
...THAT GOT HIM ASSIGNED TO WORK WITH ME, I PRESUME.
OKAY.
EVERYTHING LOOK ALL RIGHT?

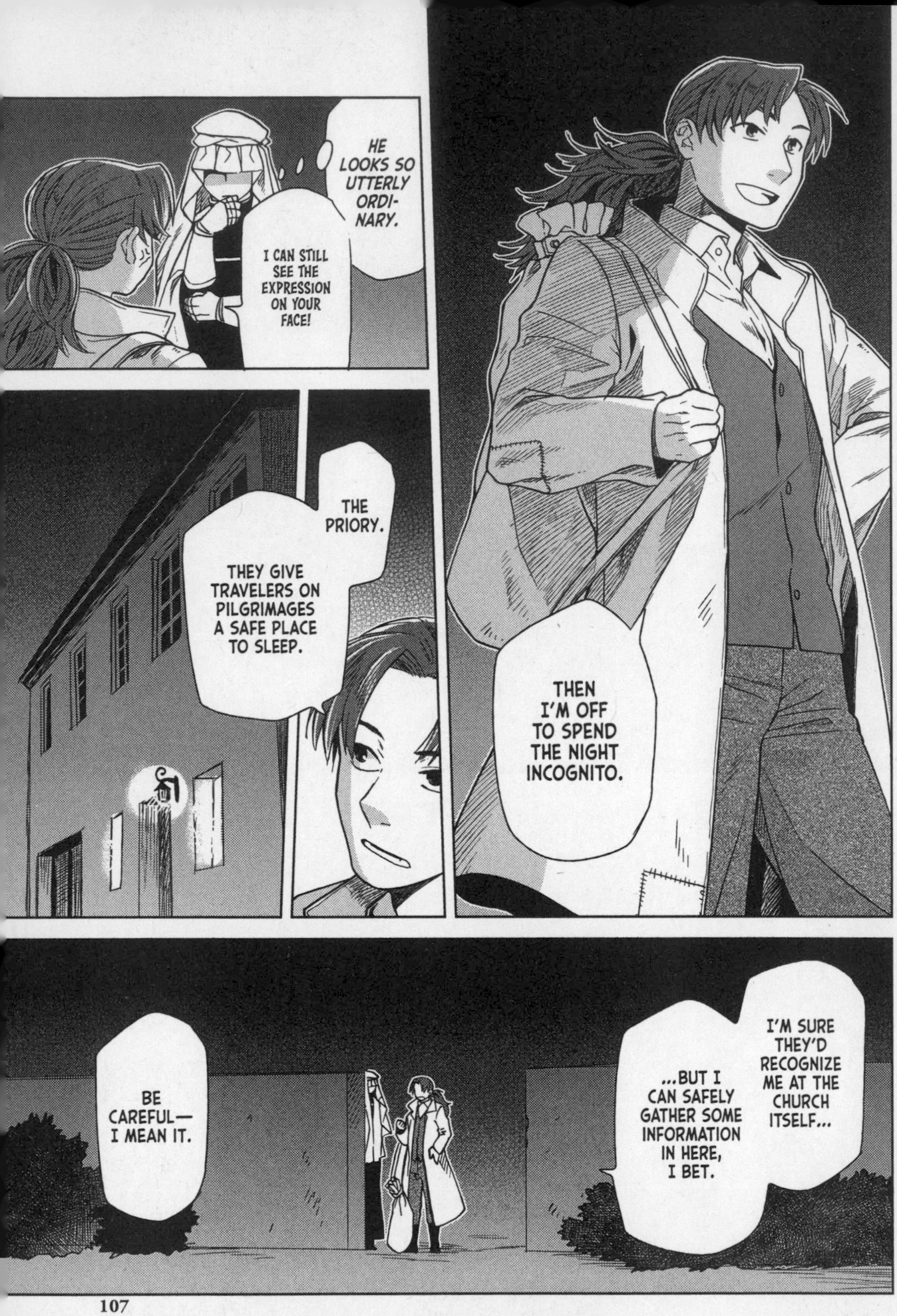
THEN I'M OFF TO SPEND THE NIGHT INCOGNITO.
HE LOOKS SO UTTERLY ORDINARY.
I CAN STILL SEE THE EXPRESSION ON YOUR FACE!
THE PRIORY.
THEY GIVE TRAVELERS ON PILGRIMAGES A SAFE PLACE TO SLEEP.
I'M SURE THEY'D RECOGNIZE ME AT THE CHURCH ITSELF...
...BUT I CAN SAFELY GATHER SOME INFORMATION IN HERE, I BET.
BE CAREFUL—I MEAN IT.

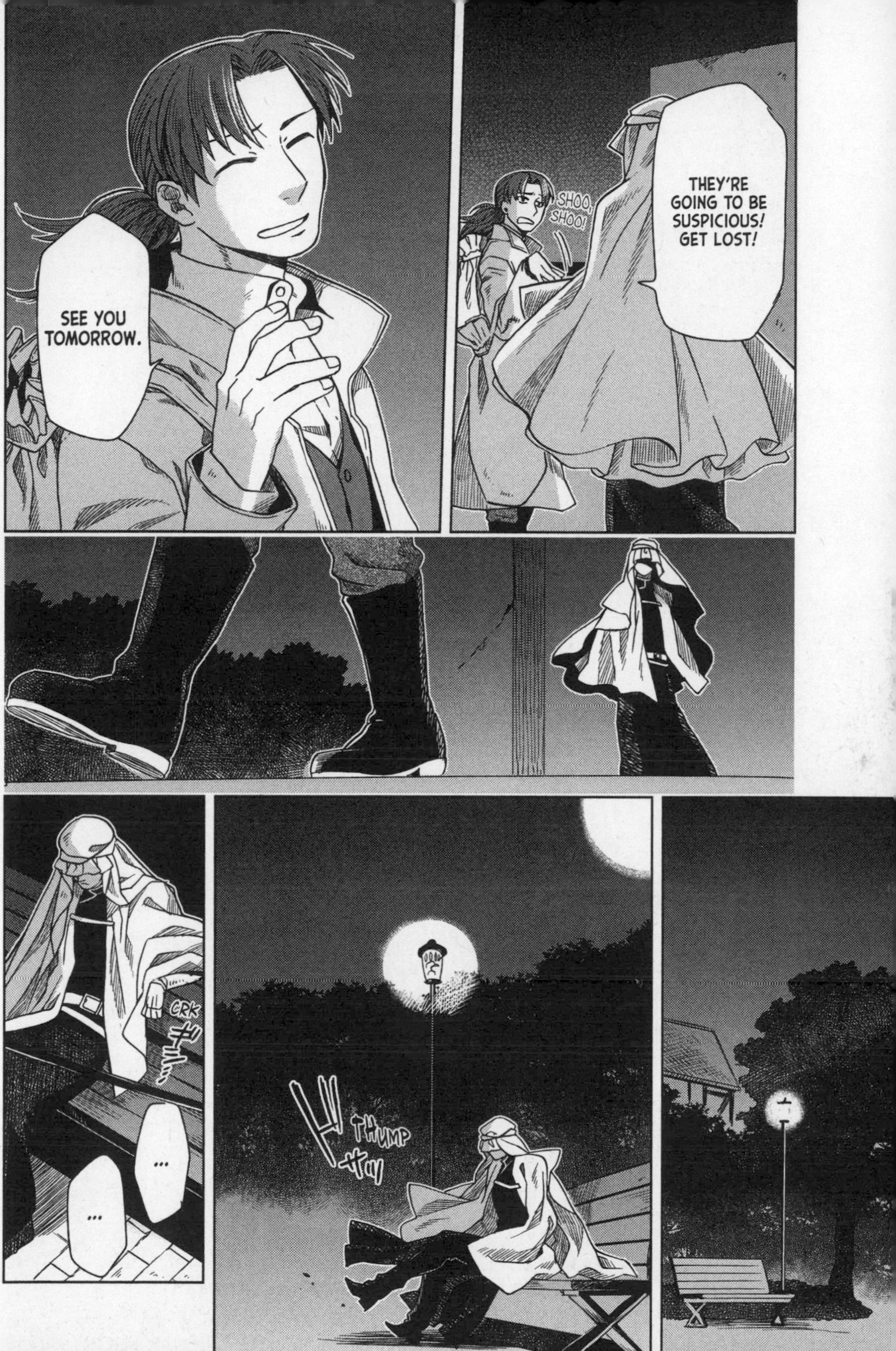
THEY'RE GOING TO BE SUSPICIOUS! GET LOST!
SHOO, SHOO!
SEE YOU TOMORROW.
THUMP
CRK
...
...

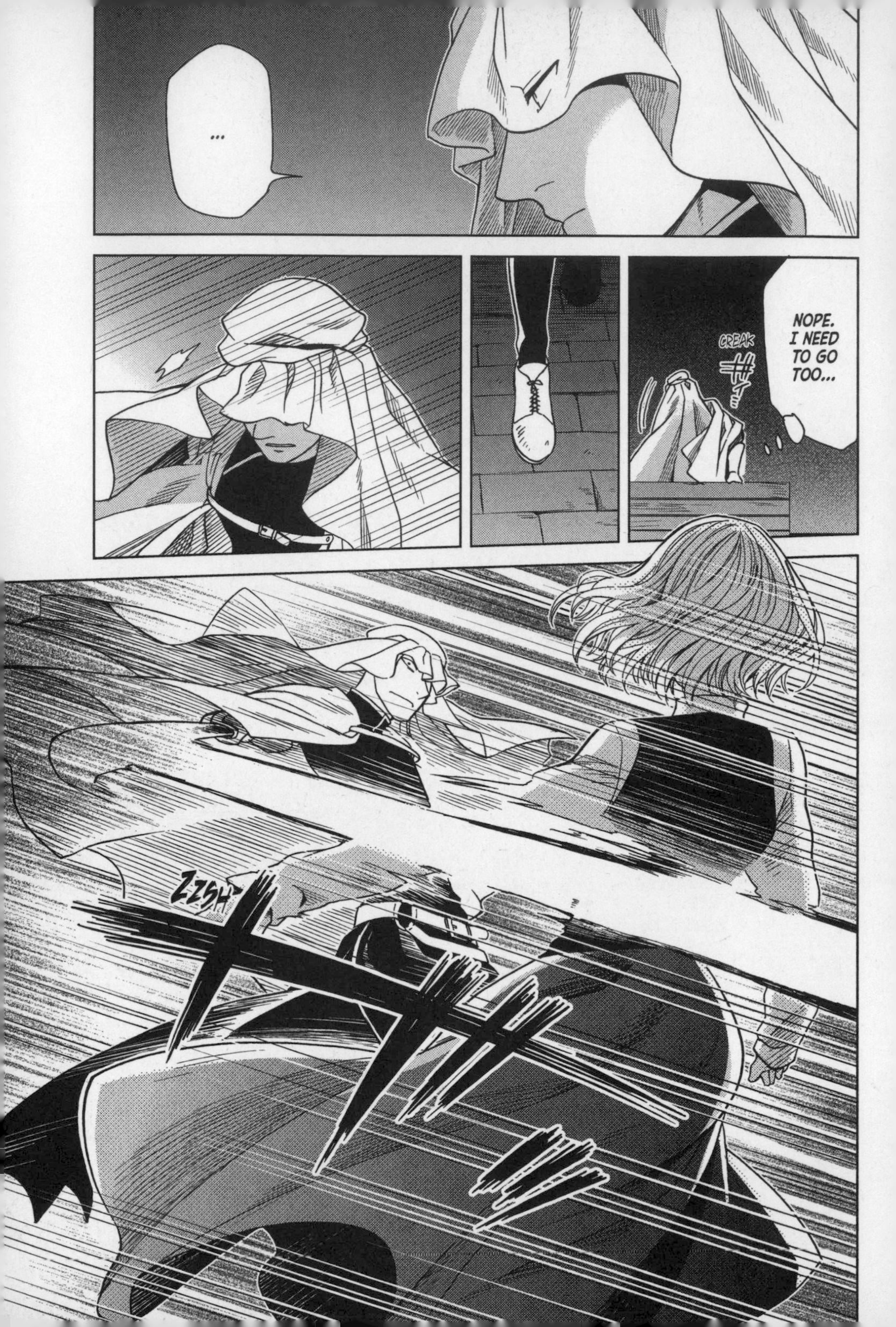
...
NOPE. I NEED TO GO TOO...
CREAK
ZZSH

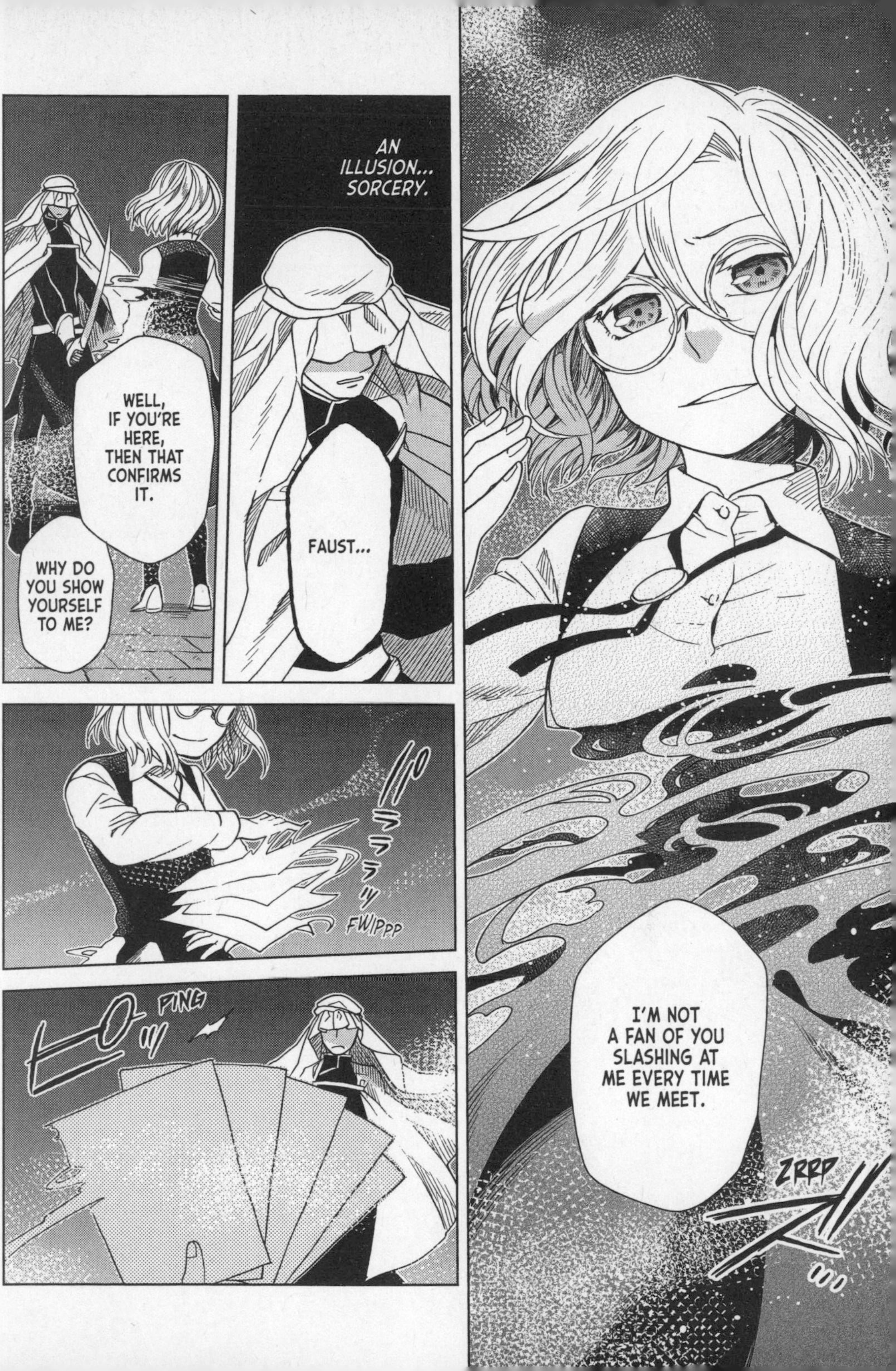
I'M NOT A FAN OF YOU SLASHING AT ME EVERY TIME WE MEET.
ZRRP
AN ILLUSION... SORCERY.
FAUST...
WELL, IF YOU'RE HERE, THEN THAT CONFIRMS IT.
WHY DO YOU SHOW YOURSELF TO ME?
FWIPPP
PING

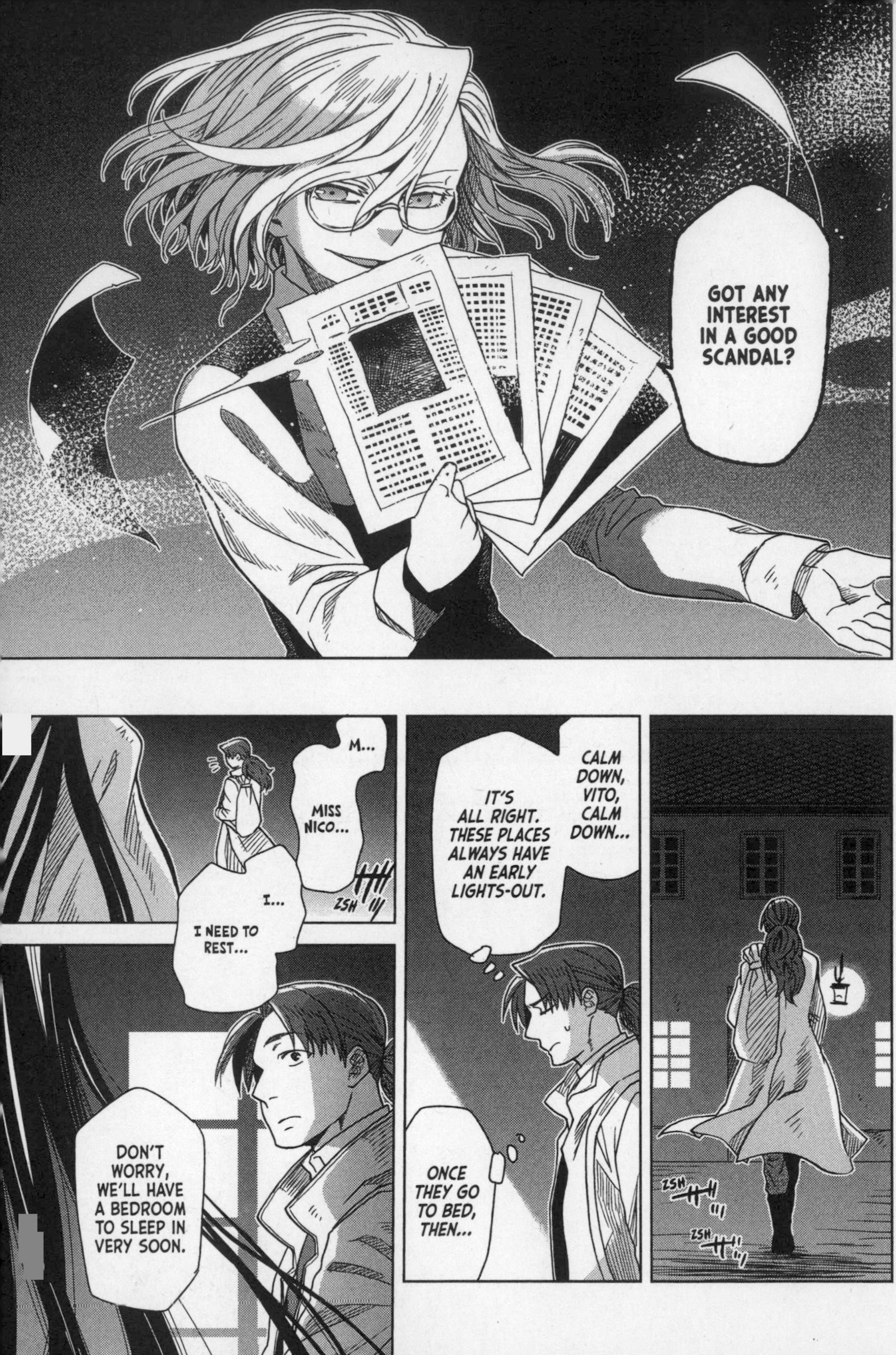
GOT ANY INTEREST IN A GOOD SCANDAL?
ZSH
ZSH
CALM DOWN, VITO, CALM DOWN...
IT'S ALL RIGHT. THESE PLACES ALWAYS HAVE AN EARLY LIGHTS-OUT.
ONCE THEY GO TO BED, THEN...
M...
MISS NICO...
ZSH
I...
I NEED TO REST...
DON'T WORRY, WE'LL HAVE A BEDROOM TO SLEEP IN VERY SOON.

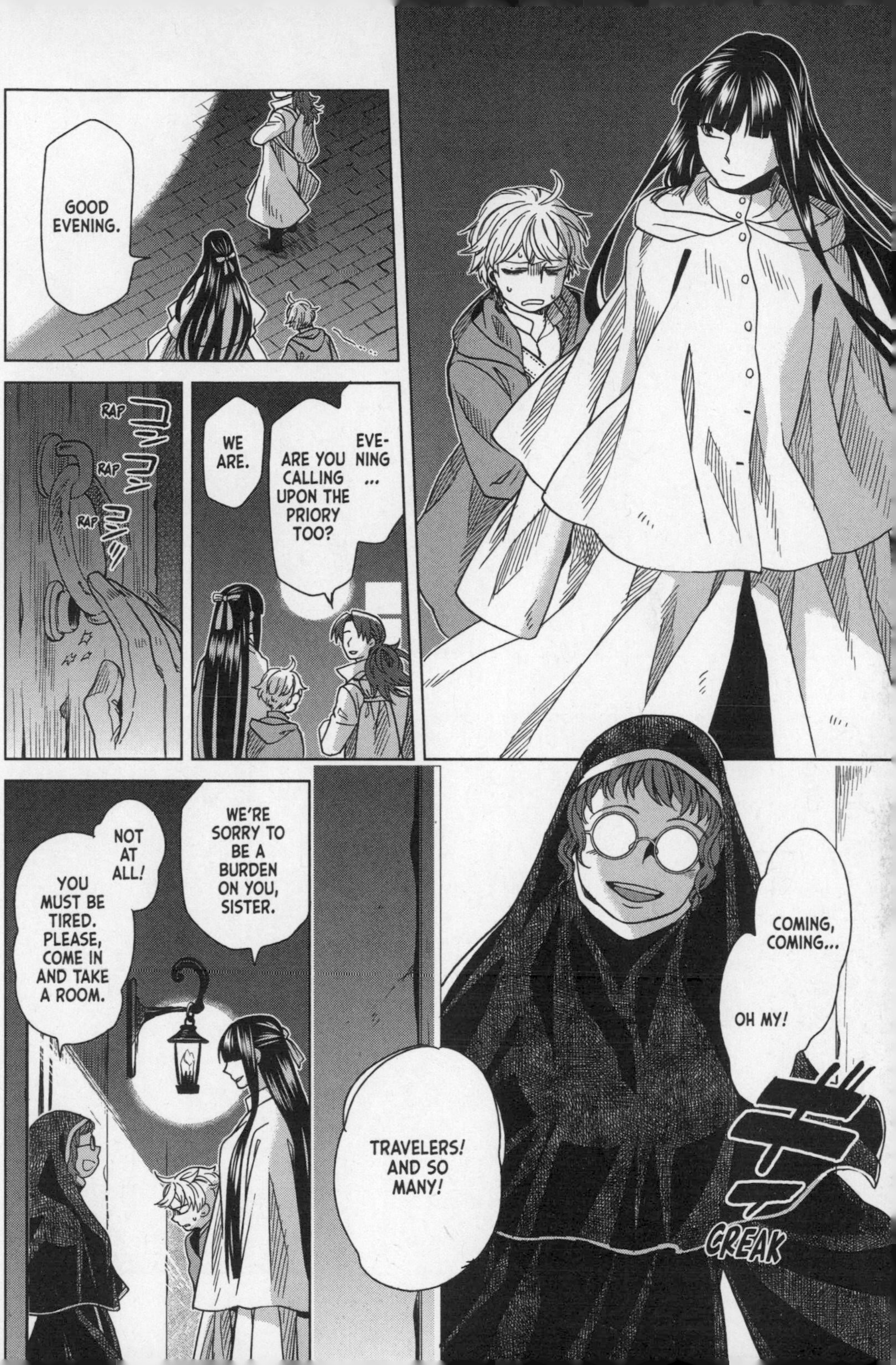
GOOD EVENING.
EVE-NING...
ARE YOU CALLING UPON THE PRIORY TOO?
WE ARE.
RAP
RAP
RAP
COMING, COMING...
OH MY!
TRAVELERS! AND SO MANY!
CREAK
WE'RE SORRY TO BE A BURDEN ON YOU, SISTER.
NOT AT ALL!
YOU MUST BE TIRED. PLEASE, COME IN AND TAKE A ROOM.

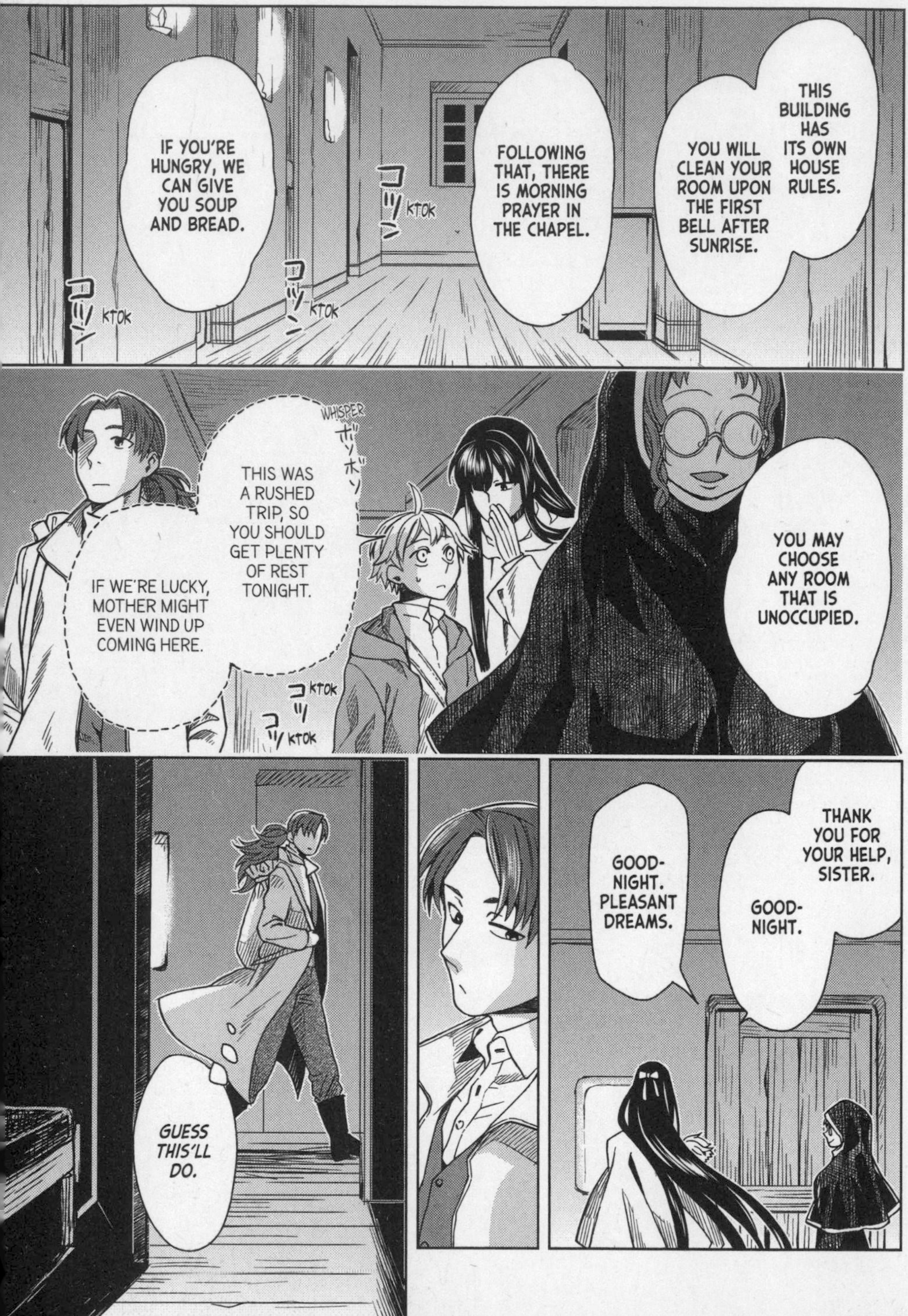
THIS BUILDING HAS ITS OWN HOUSE RULES.
YOU WILL CLEAN YOUR ROOM UPON THE FIRST BELL AFTER SUNRISE.
FOLLOWING THAT, THERE IS MORNING PRAYER IN THE CHAPEL.
KTOK
IF YOU'RE HUNGRY, WE CAN GIVE YOU SOUP AND BREAD.
KTOK
KTOK
YOU MAY CHOOSE ANY ROOM THAT IS UNOCCUPIED.
WHISPER
THIS WAS A RUSHED TRIP, SO YOU SHOULD GET PLENTY OF REST TONIGHT.
IF WE'RE LUCKY, MOTHER MIGHT EVEN WIND UP COMING HERE.
KTOK
KTOK
THANK YOU FOR YOUR HELP, SISTER.
GOOD-NIGHT.
GOOD-NIGHT. PLEASANT DREAMS.
GUESS THIS'LL DO.

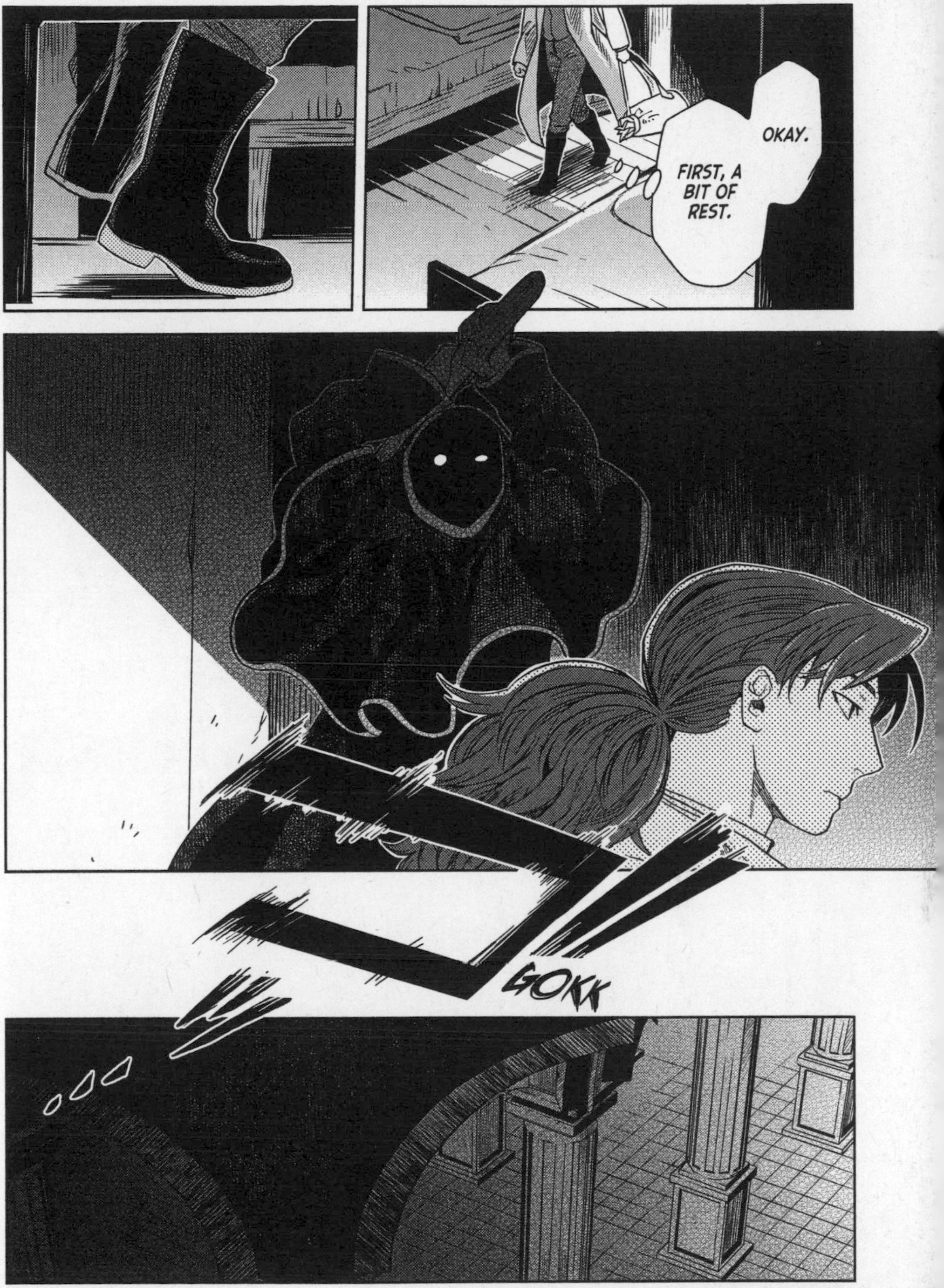
OKAY.
FIRST, A BIT OF REST.
GOKK

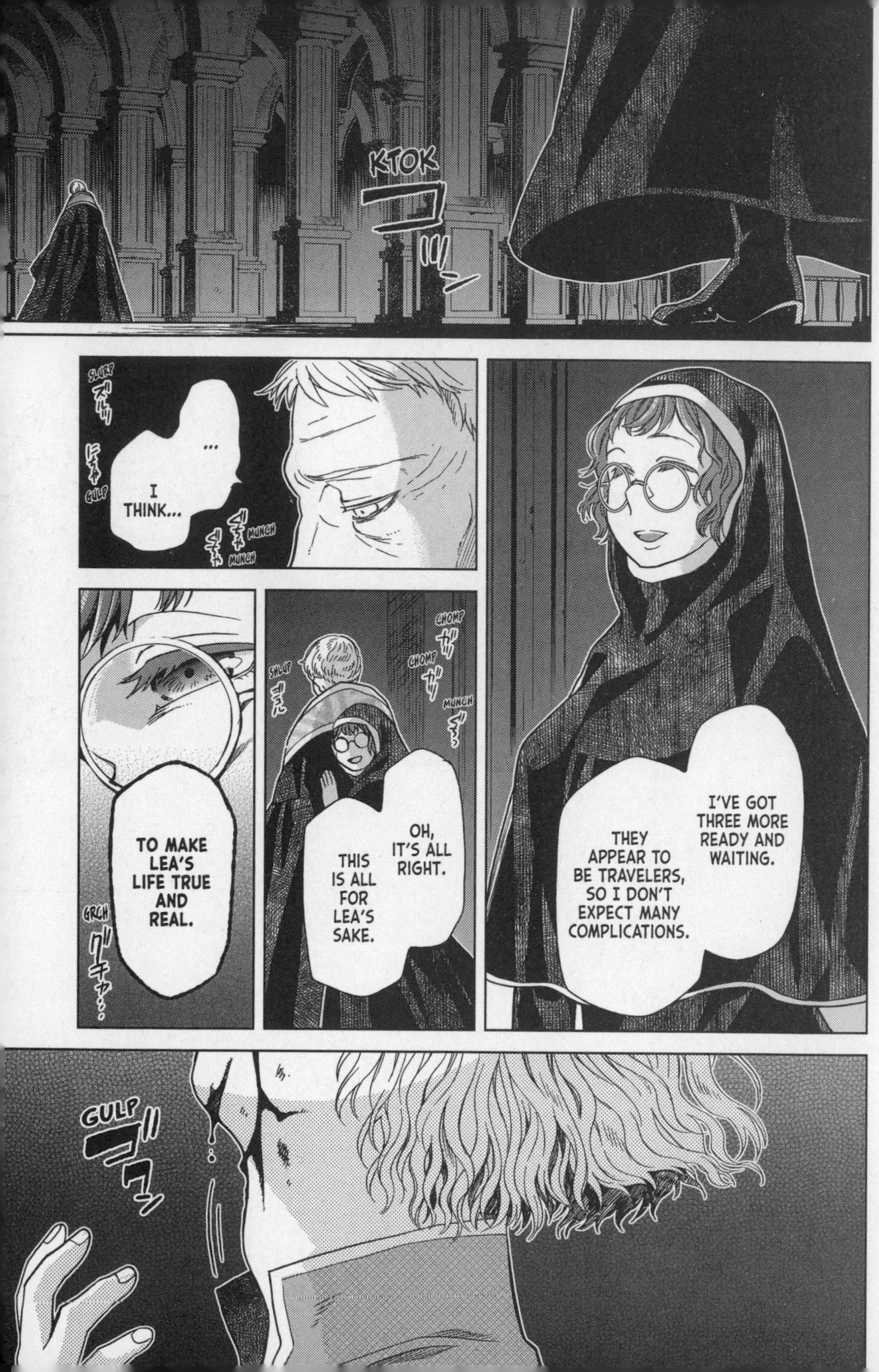
KTOK
I'VE GOT THREE MORE READY AND WAITING.
THEY APPEAR TO BE TRAVELERS, SO I DON'T EXPECT MANY COMPLICATIONS.
SLURP
GULP
...
I THINK...
MUNCH
MUNCH
CHOMP
CHOMP
SHLUP
MUNCH
OH, IT'S ALL RIGHT.
THIS IS ALL FOR LEA'S SAKE.
TO MAKE LEA'S LIFE TRUE AND REAL.
GRCH
GULP

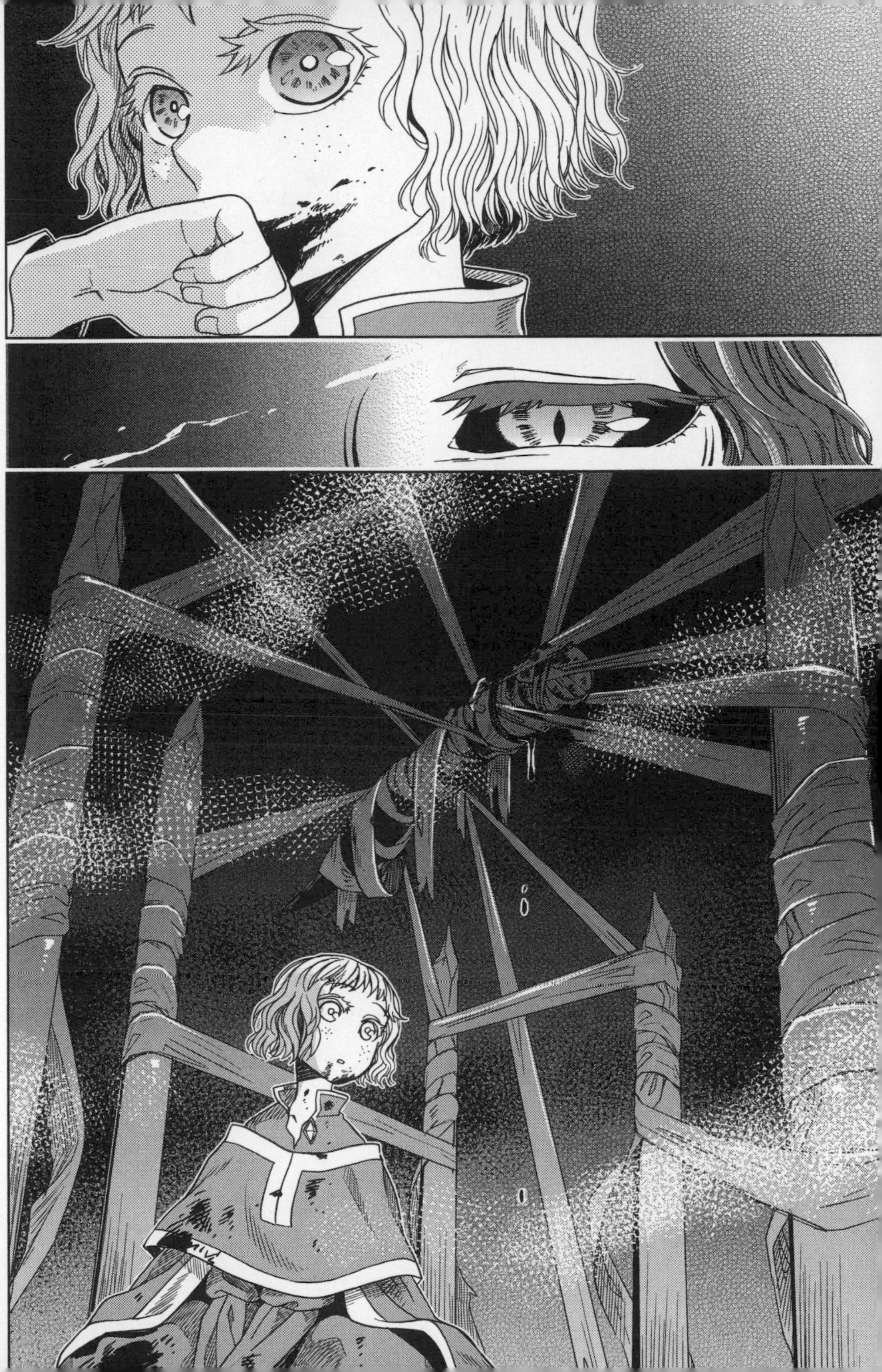

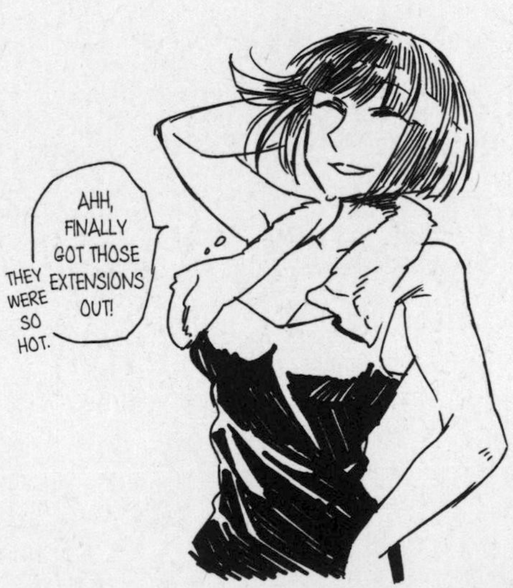
AHH, FINALLY GOT THOSE EXTENSIONS OUT!
THEY WERE SO HOT.

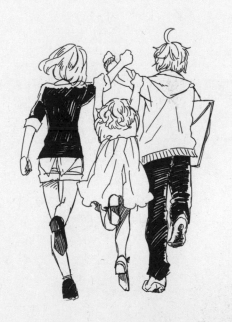

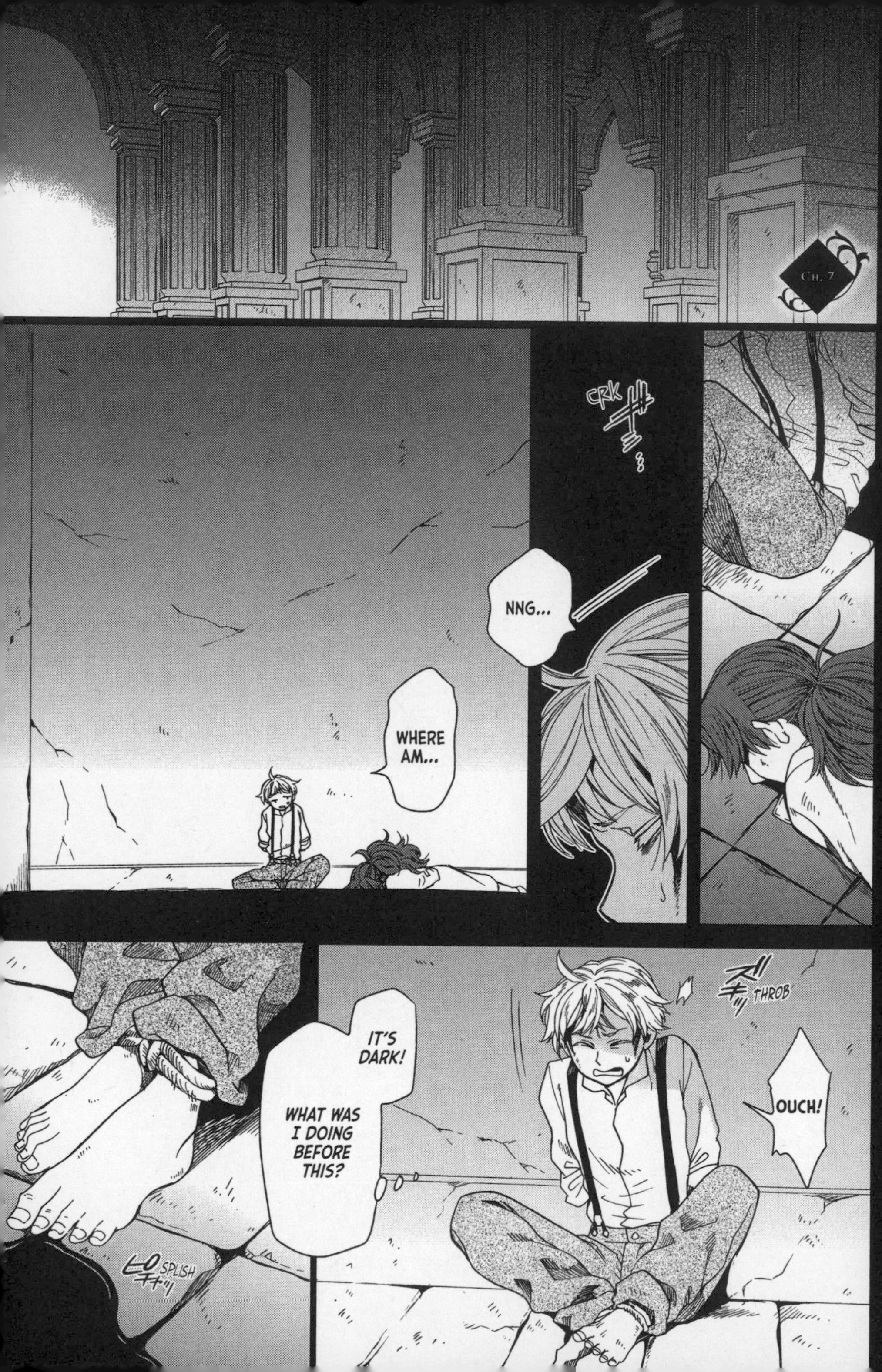
Ch. 7
CRK
NNG...
WHERE AM...
THROB
OUCH!
IT'S DARK!
WHAT WAS I DOING BEFORE THIS?
SPLISH

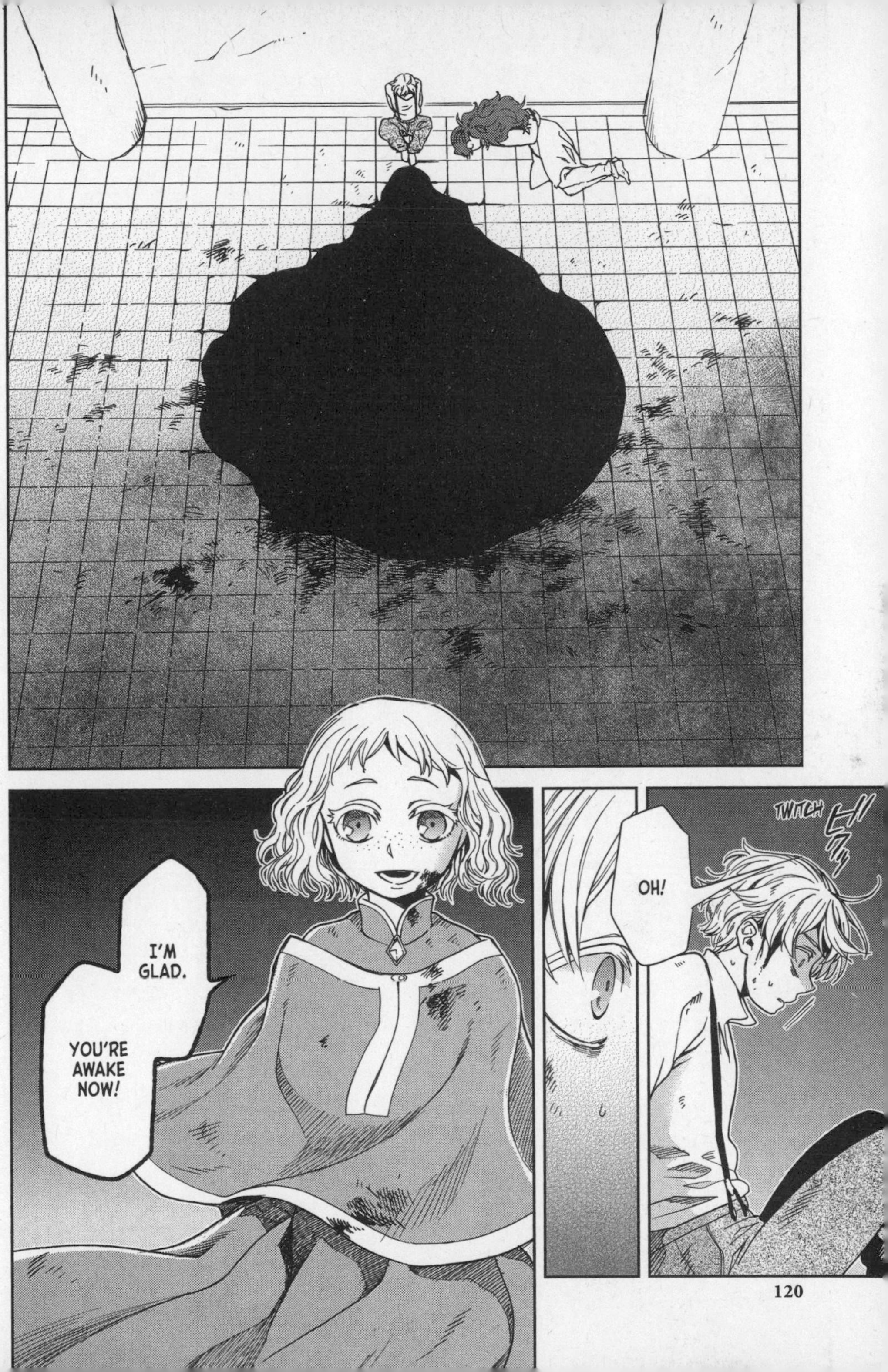
TWITCH
OH!
I'M GLAD.
YOU'RE AWAKE NOW!

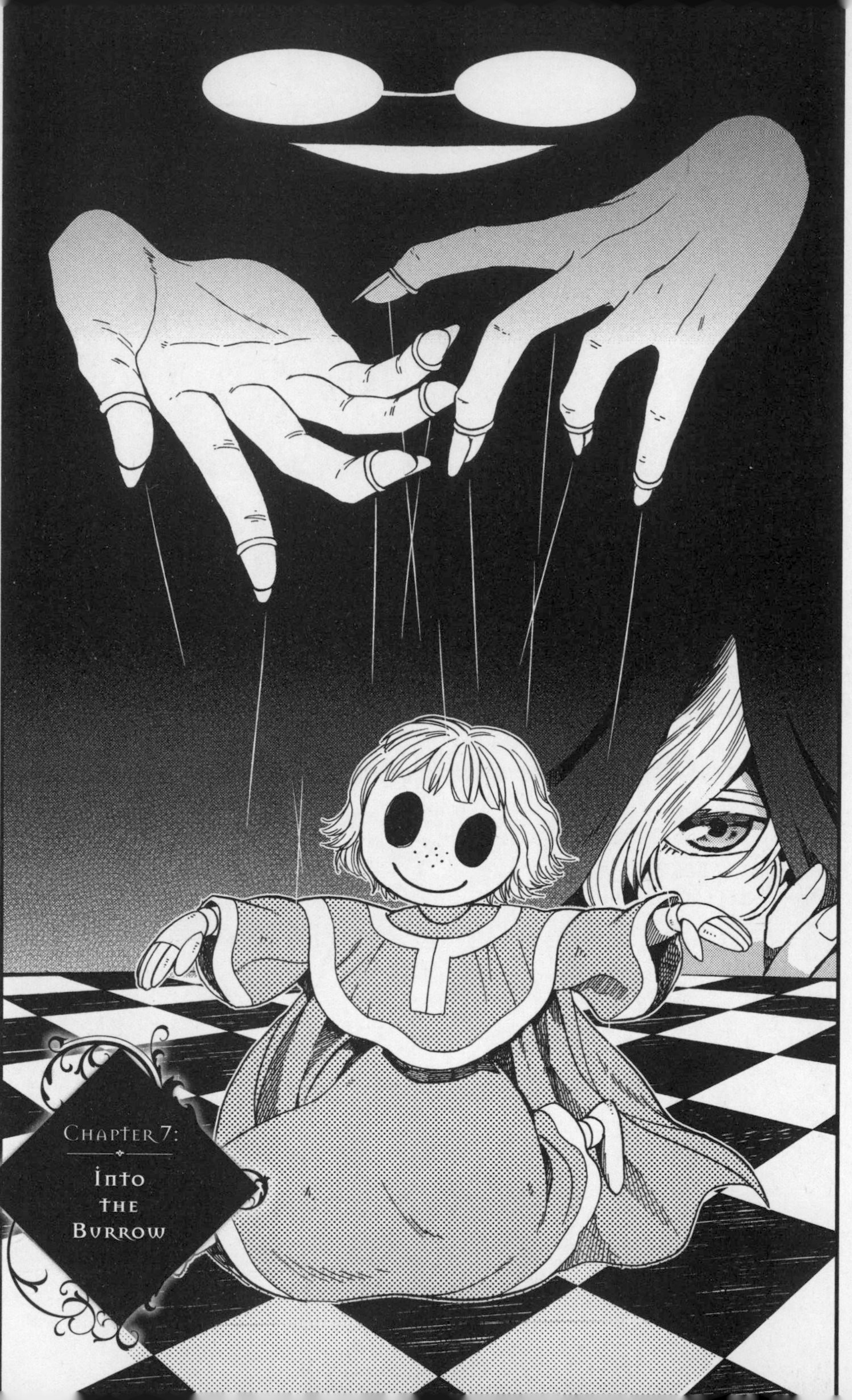
Chapter 7:
Into the Burrow

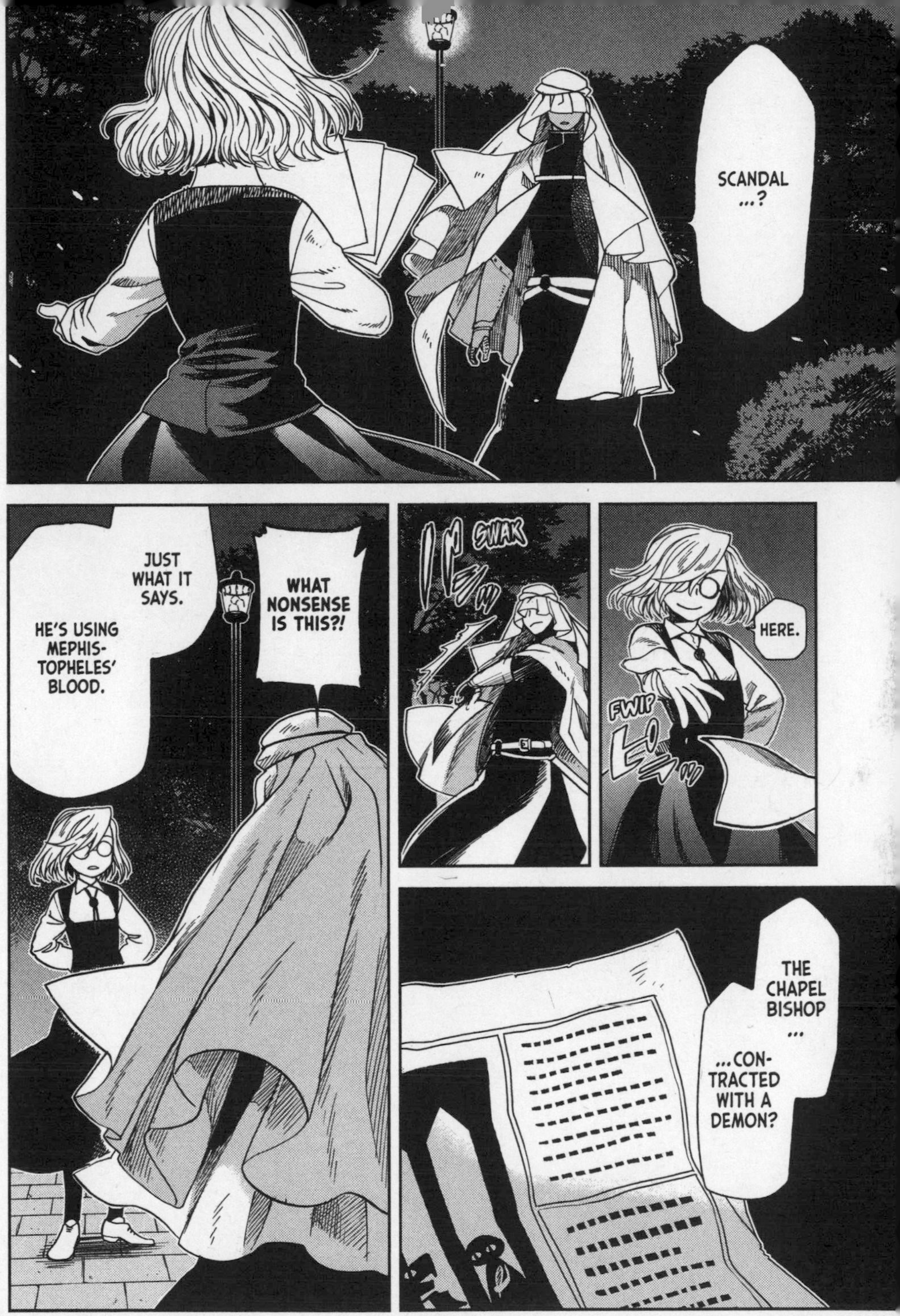
SCANDAL ...?
HERE.
FWIP
SWAK
THE CHAPEL BISHOP ...
...CONTRACTED WITH A DEMON?
WHAT NONSENSE IS THIS?!
JUST WHAT IT SAYS.
HE'S USING MEPHISTOPHELES' BLOOD.

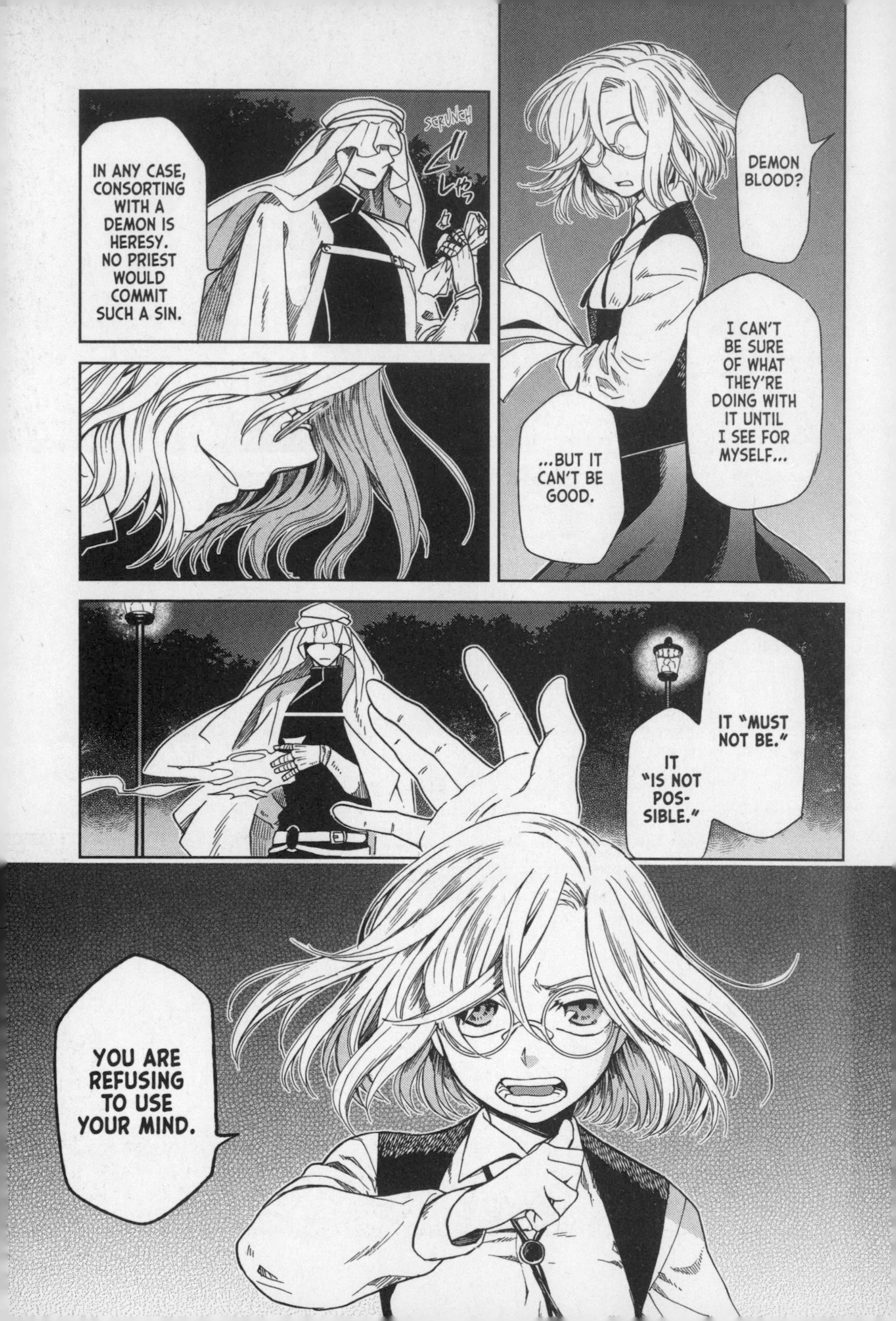
DEMON BLOOD?
I CAN'T BE SURE OF WHAT THEY'RE DOING WITH IT UNTIL I SEE FOR MYSELF...
...BUT IT CAN'T BE GOOD.
SCRUNCH
IN ANY CASE, CONSORTING WITH A DEMON IS HERESY. NO PRIEST WOULD COMMIT SUCH A SIN.
IT "MUST NOT BE."
IT "IS NOT POS-SIBLE."
YOU ARE REFUSING TO USE YOUR MIND.

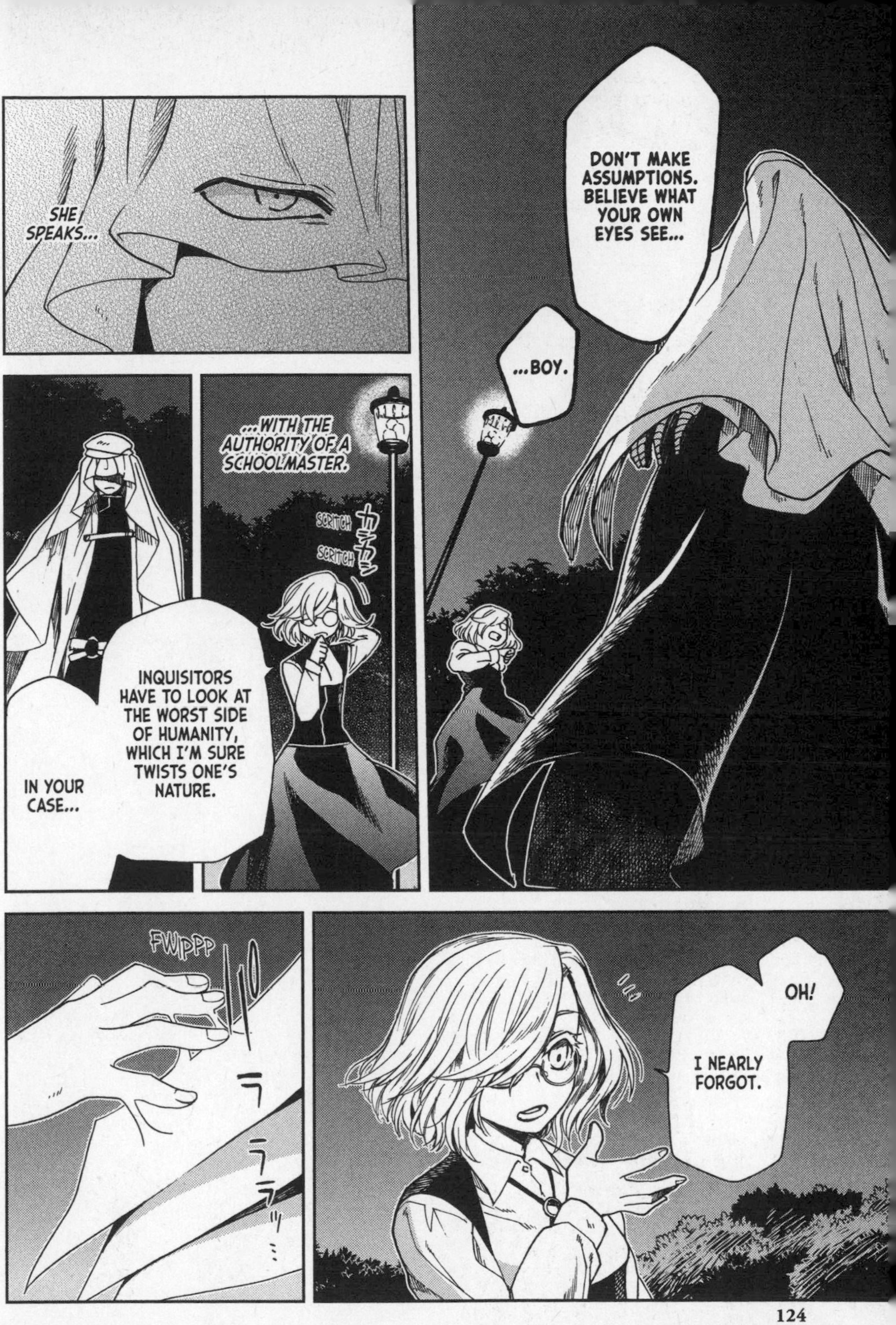
DON'T MAKE ASSUMPTIONS. BELIEVE WHAT YOUR OWN EYES SEE...
...BOY.
SHE SPEAKS...
...WITH THE AUTHORITY OF A SCHOOLMASTER.
SCRITCH
SCRITCH
INQUISITORS HAVE TO LOOK AT THE WORST SIDE OF HUMANITY, WHICH I'M SURE TWISTS ONE'S NATURE.
IN YOUR CASE...
OH!
I NEARLY FORGOT.
FWIPPP

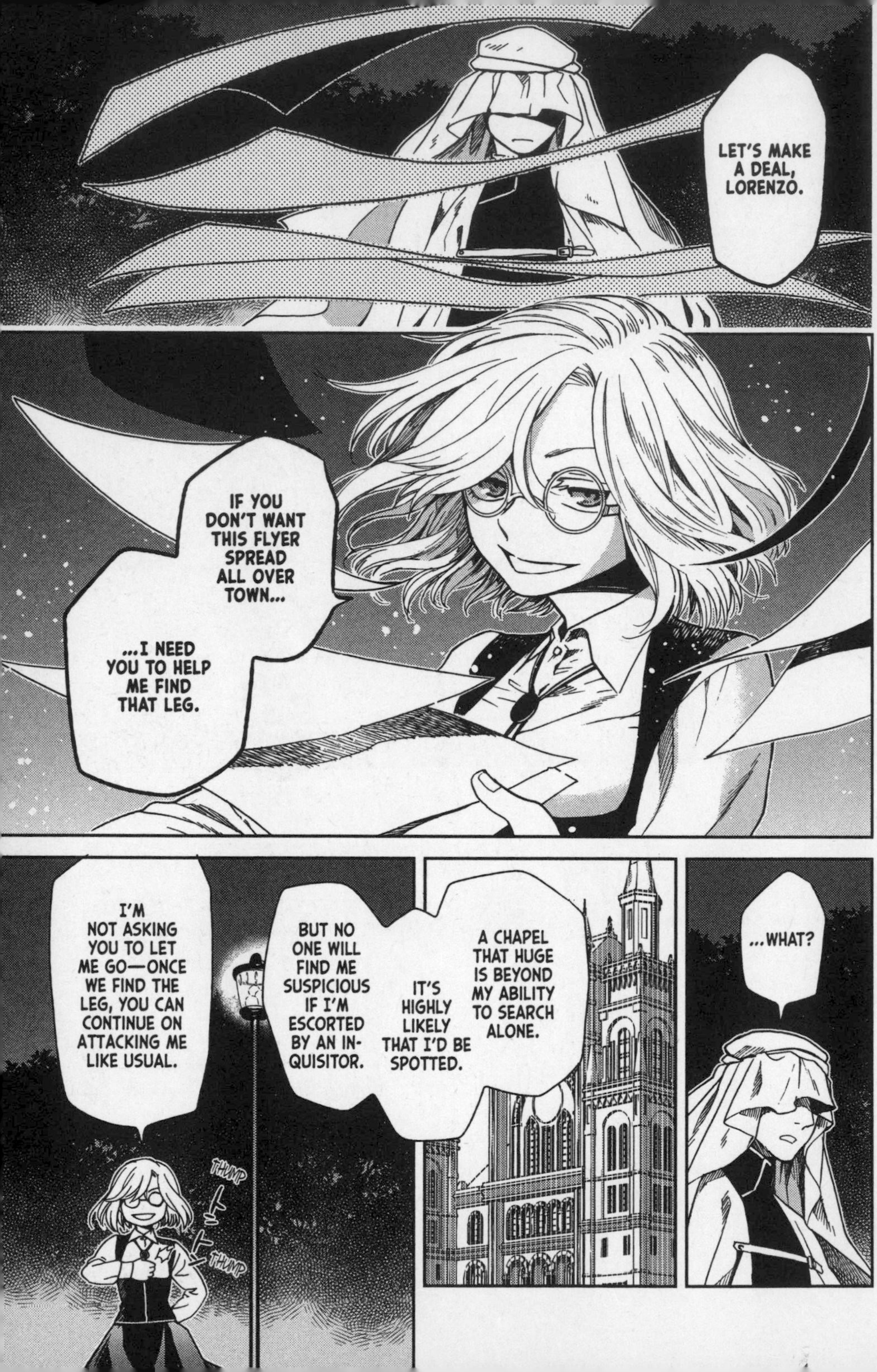
LET'S MAKE A DEAL, LORENZO.
IF YOU DON'T WANT THIS FLYER SPREAD ALL OVER TOWN...
...I NEED YOU TO HELP ME FIND THAT LEG.
...WHAT?
A CHAPEL THAT HUGE IS BEYOND MY ABILITY TO SEARCH ALONE.
IT'S HIGHLY LIKELY THAT I'D BE SPOTTED.
BUT NO ONE WILL FIND ME SUSPICIOUS IF I'M ESCORTED BY AN INQUISITOR.
I'M NOT ASKING YOU TO LET ME GO—ONCE WE FIND THE LEG, YOU CAN CONTINUE ON ATTACKING ME LIKE USUAL.
THUMP
THUMP

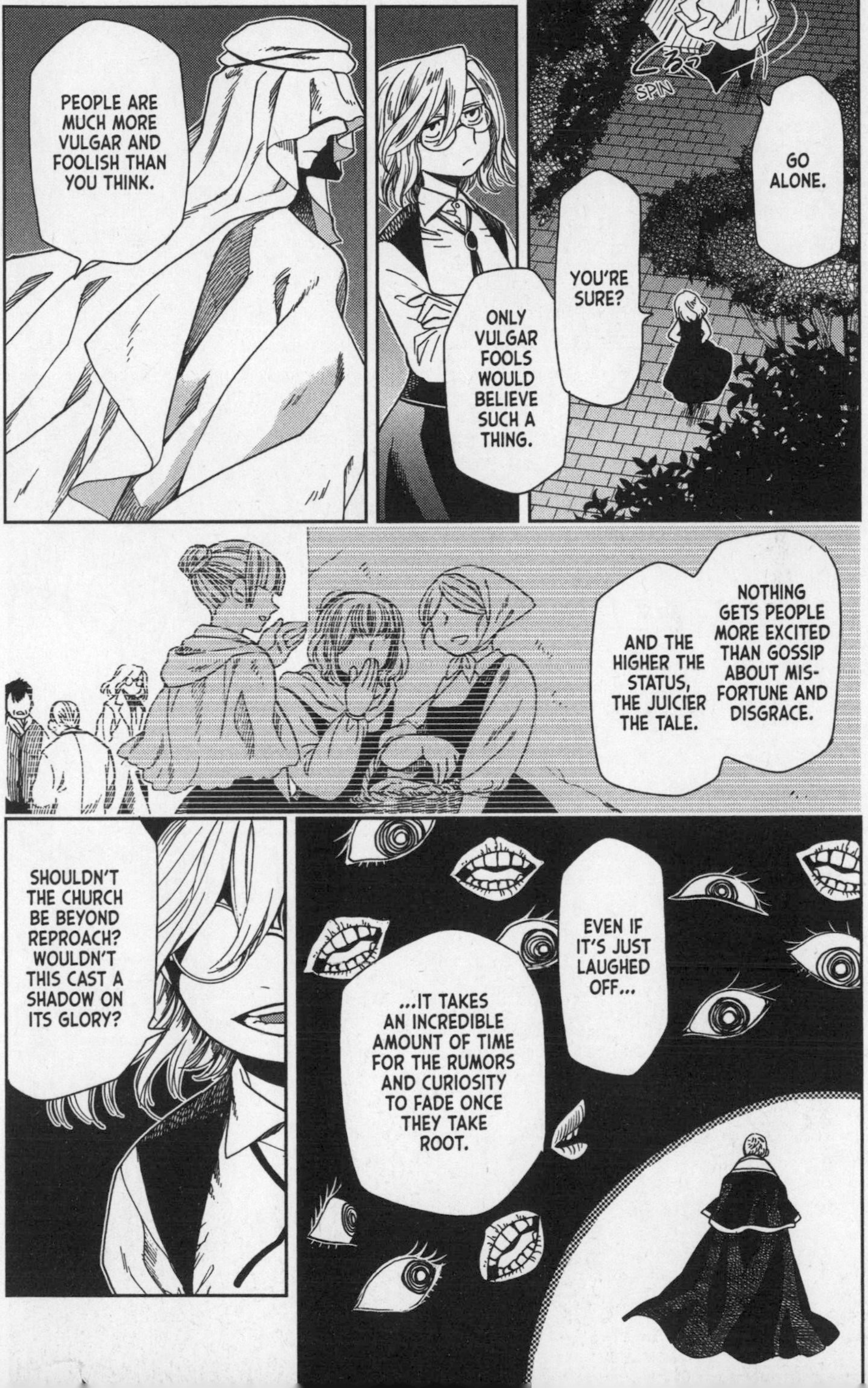
SPIN
GO ALONE.
YOU'RE SURE?
ONLY VULGAR FOOLS WOULD BELIEVE SUCH A THING.
PEOPLE ARE MUCH MORE VULGAR AND FOOLISH THAN YOU THINK.
NOTHING GETS PEOPLE MORE EXCITED THAN GOSSIP ABOUT MIS-FORTUNE AND DISGRACE.
AND THE HIGHER THE STATUS, THE JUICIER THE TALE.
EVEN IF IT'S JUST LAUGHED OFF...
...IT TAKES AN INCREDIBLE AMOUNT OF TIME FOR THE RUMORS AND CURIOSITY TO FADE ONCE THEY TAKE ROOT.
SHOULDN'T THE CHURCH BE BEYOND REPROACH? WOULDN'T THIS CAST A SHADOW ON ITS GLORY?

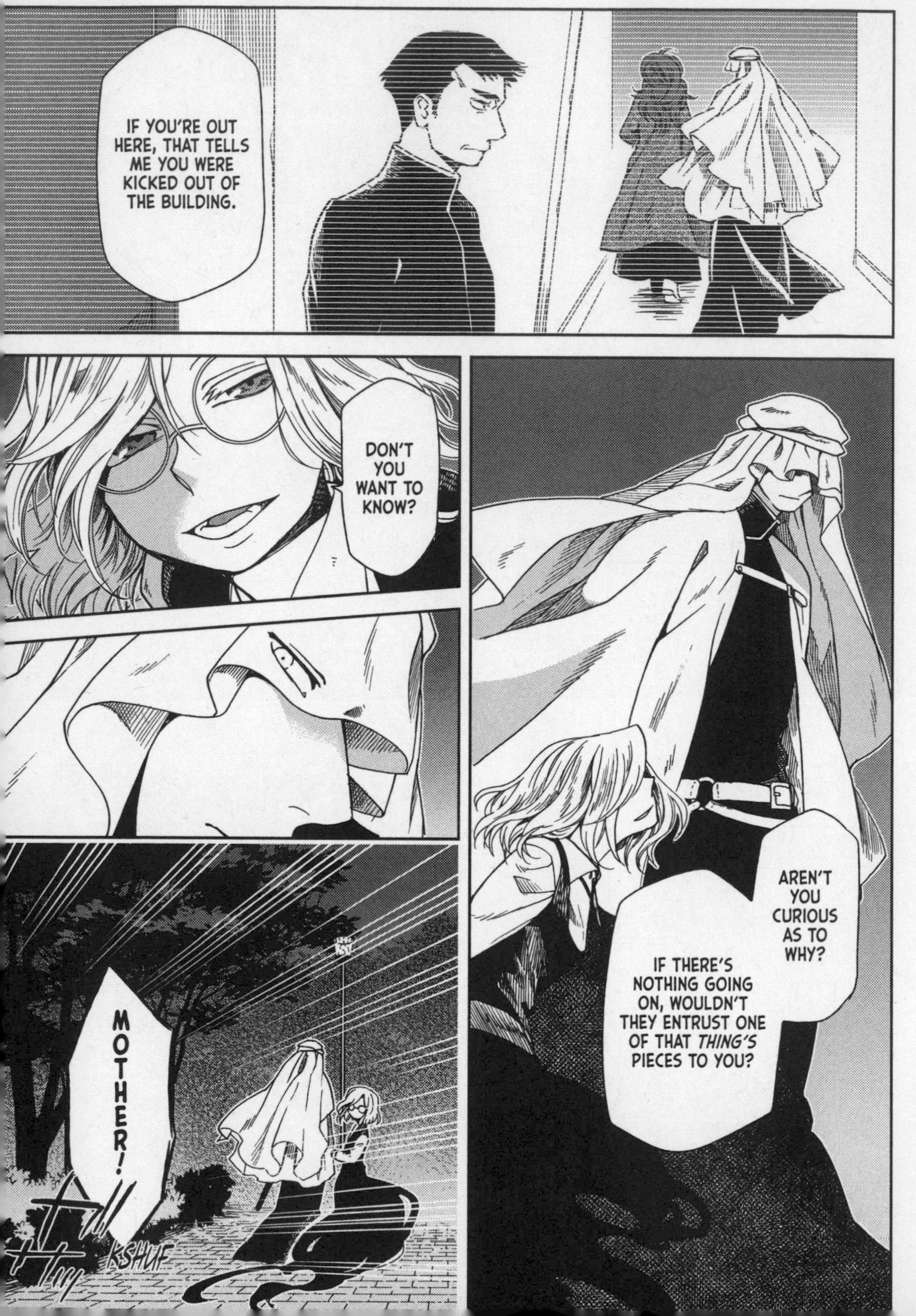
IF YOU'RE OUT HERE, THAT TELLS ME YOU WERE KICKED OUT OF THE BUILDING.
AREN'T YOU CURIOUS AS TO WHY?
IF THERE'S NOTHING GOING ON, WOULDN'T THEY ENTRUST ONE OF THAT *THING'S* PIECES TO YOU?
DON'T YOU WANT TO KNOW?
MOTHER!
KSHUF

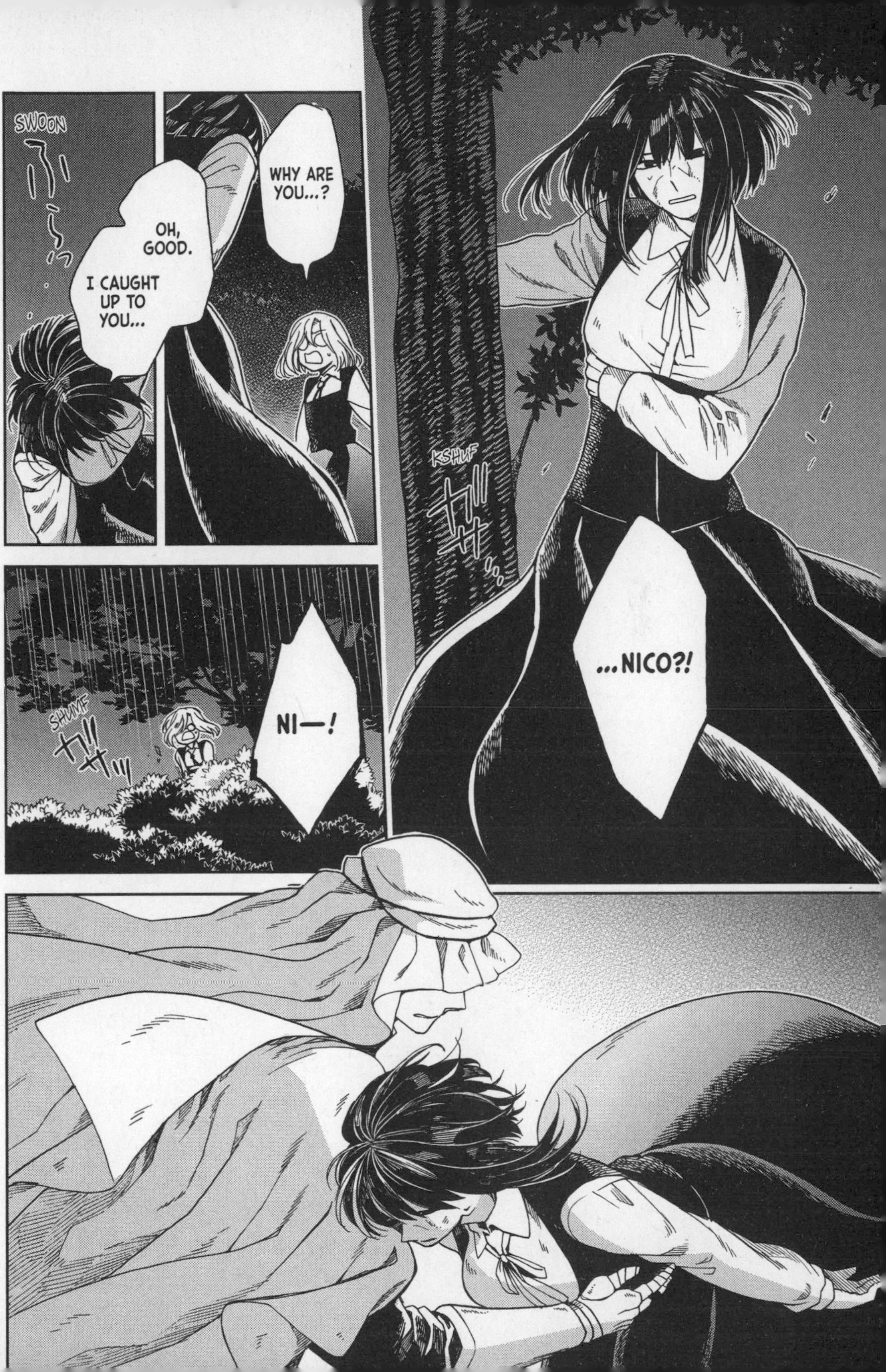
KSHUF
...NICO?!
WHY ARE YOU...?
SWOON
OH, GOOD.
I CAUGHT UP TO YOU...
SHUMF
NI—!

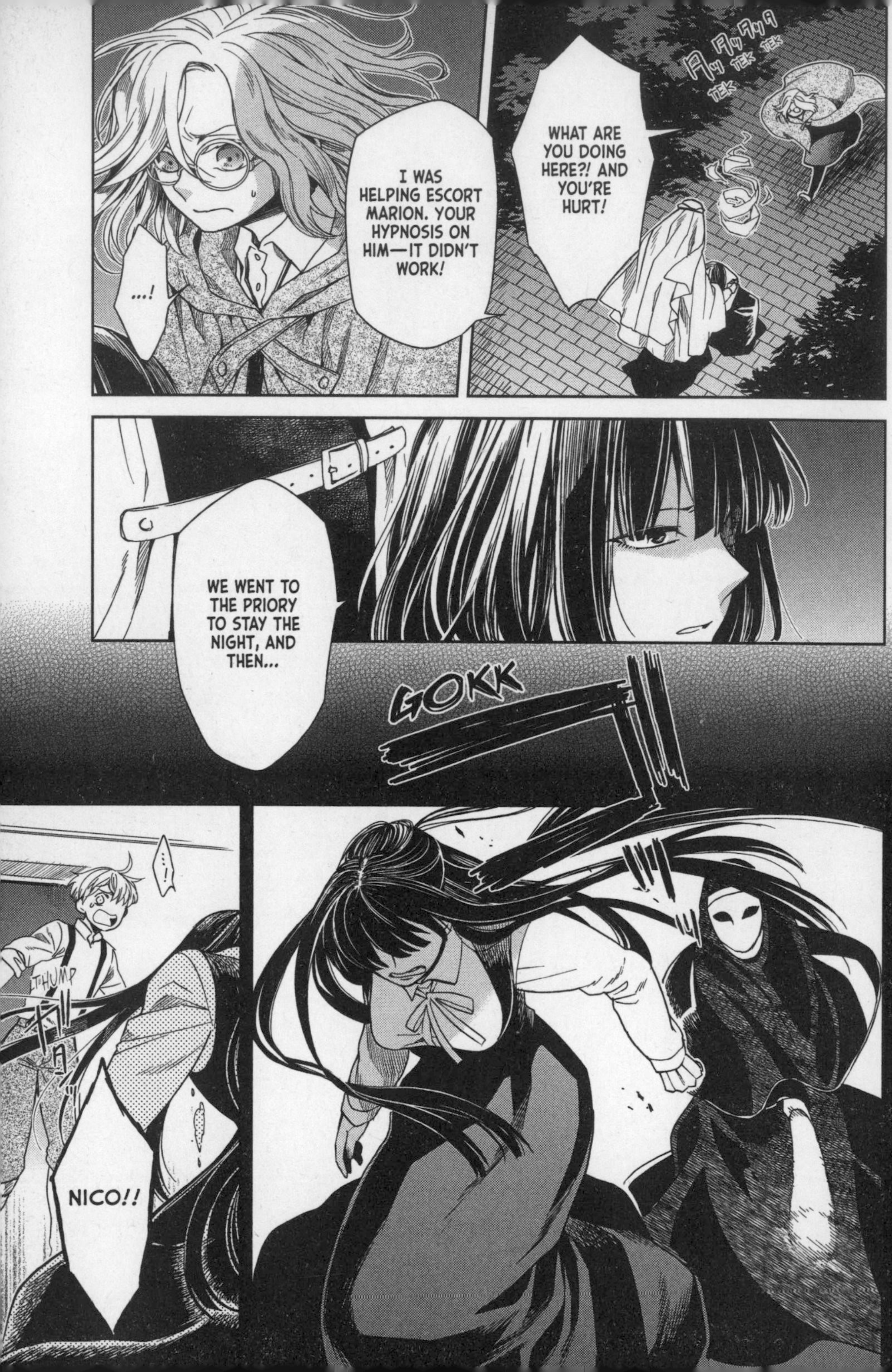
TEK TEK TEK
WHAT ARE YOU DOING HERE?! AND YOU'RE HURT!
I WAS HELPING ESCORT MARION. YOUR HYPNOSIS ON HIM—IT DIDN'T WORK!
...!
WE WENT TO THE PRIORY TO STAY THE NIGHT, AND THEN...
GOKK
...!
THUMP
NICO!!

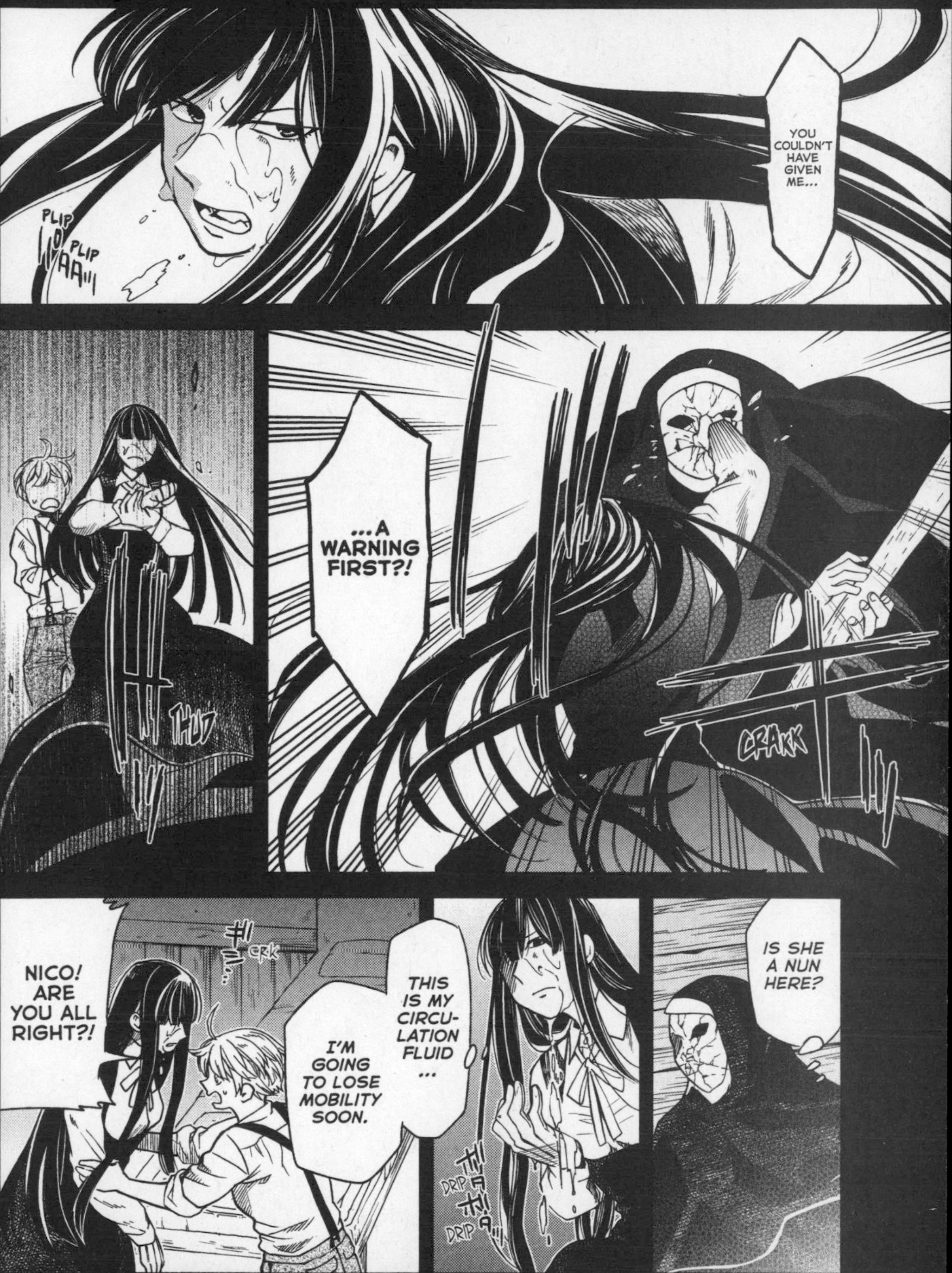
YOU COULDN'T HAVE GIVEN ME...
PLIP PLIP
...A WARNING FIRST?!
CRAKK
THUD
IS SHE A NUN HERE?
THIS IS MY CIRCULATION FLUID ...
I'M GOING TO LOSE MOBILITY SOON.
DRIP DRIP
NICO! ARE YOU ALL RIGHT?!
CRK

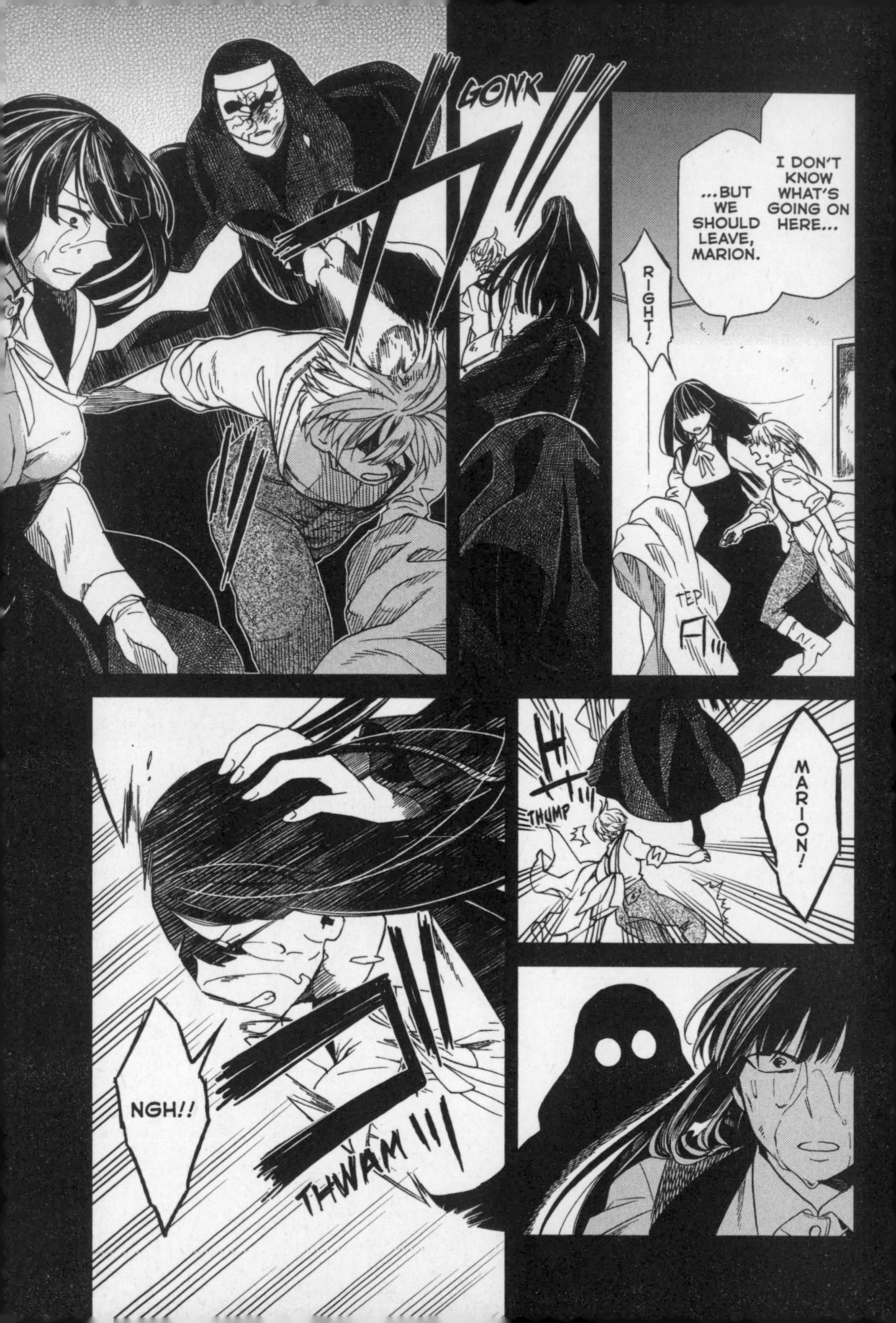

I DON'T KNOW WHAT'S GOING ON HERE...
...BUT WE SHOULD LEAVE, MARION.
RIGHT!
TEP
GONK
MARION!
THUMP
NGH!!
THWAM

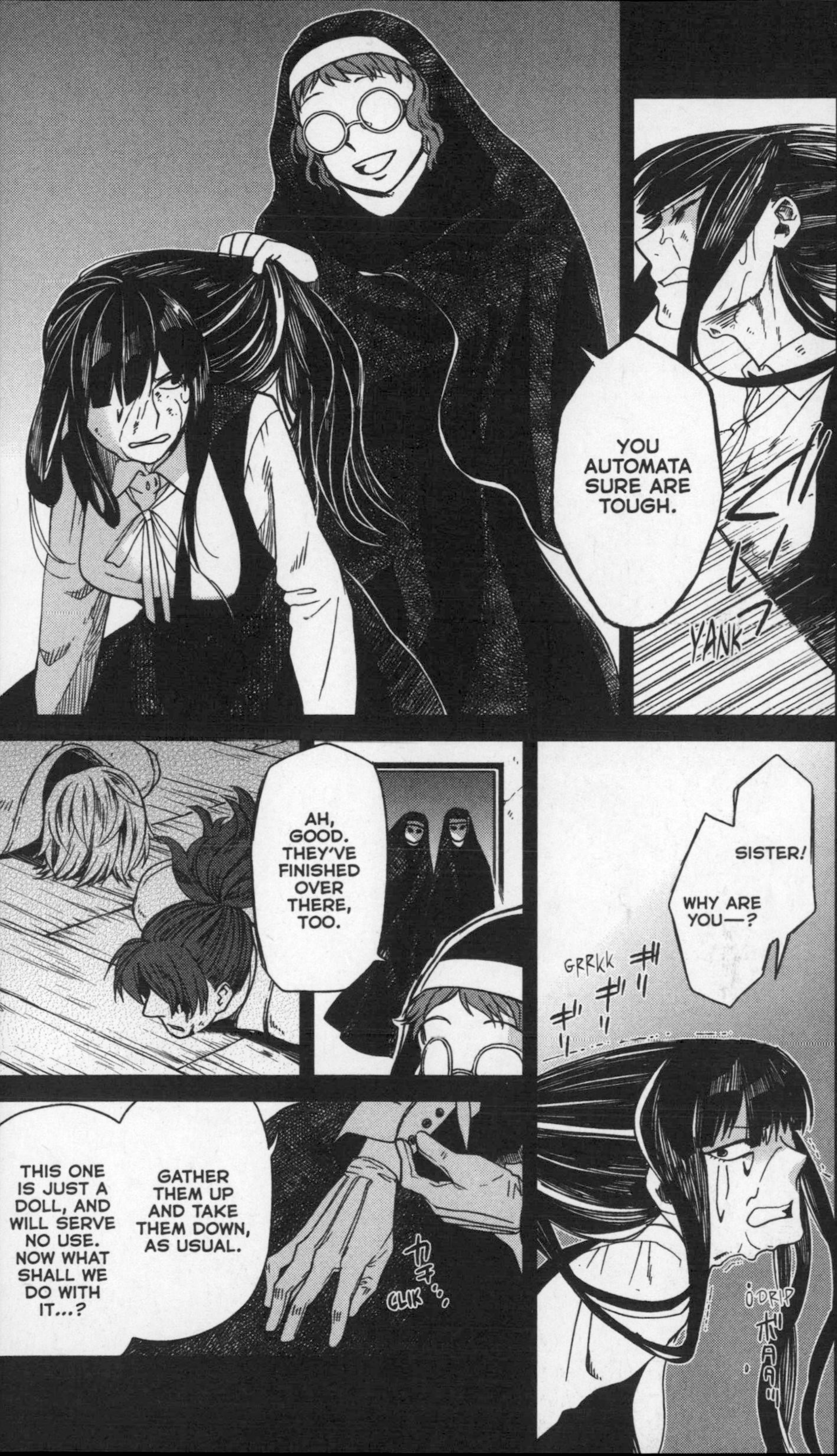
YOU AUTOMATA SURE ARE TOUGH.
YANK
SISTER!
WHY ARE YOU—?
GRRKK
DRIP
AH, GOOD. THEY'VE FINISHED OVER THERE, TOO.
GATHER THEM UP AND TAKE THEM DOWN, AS USUAL.
CLIK
THIS ONE IS JUST A DOLL, AND WILL SERVE NO USE. NOW WHAT SHALL WE DO WITH IT...?

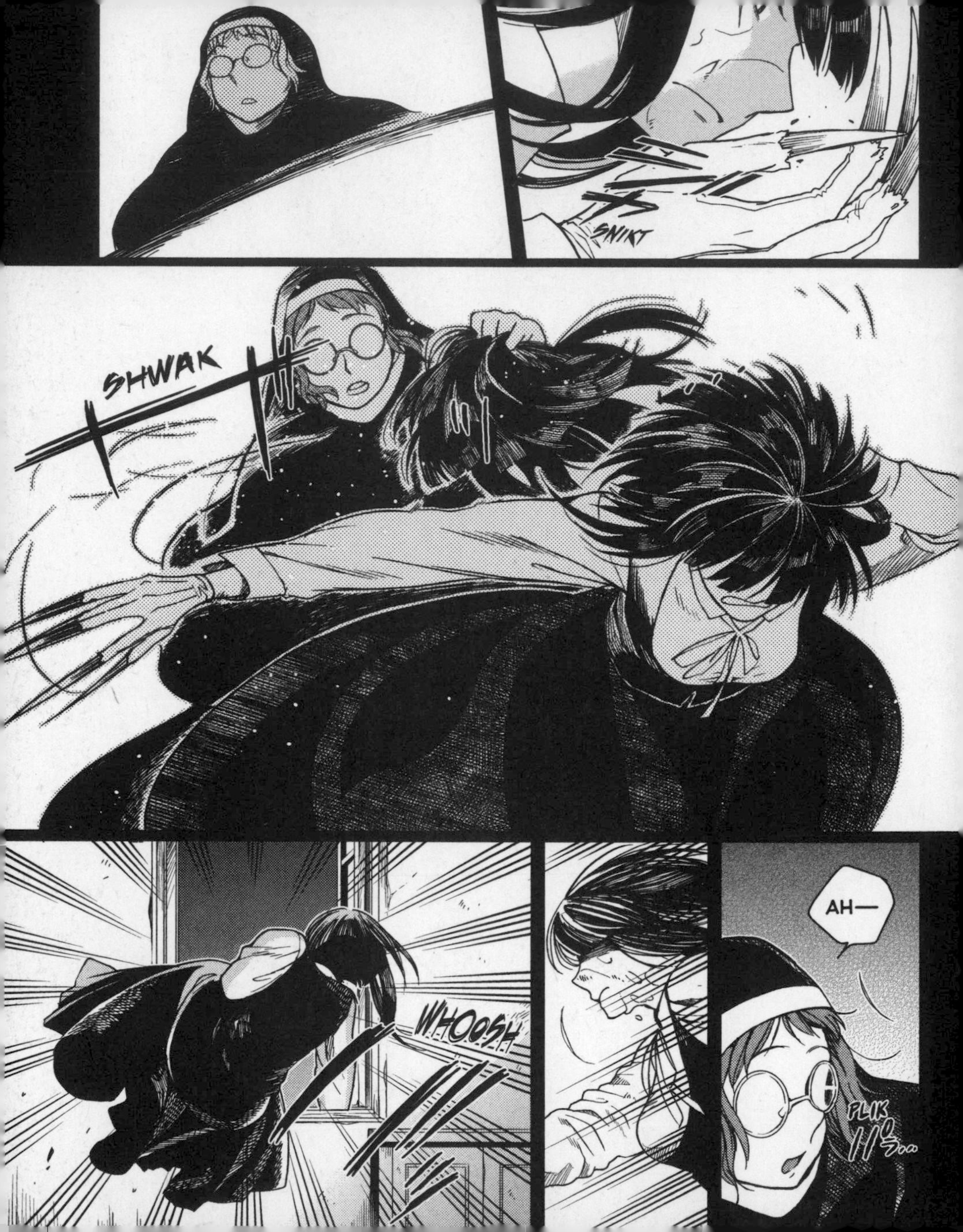
SNIKT
SHWAK
AH—
FLIK
WHOOSH

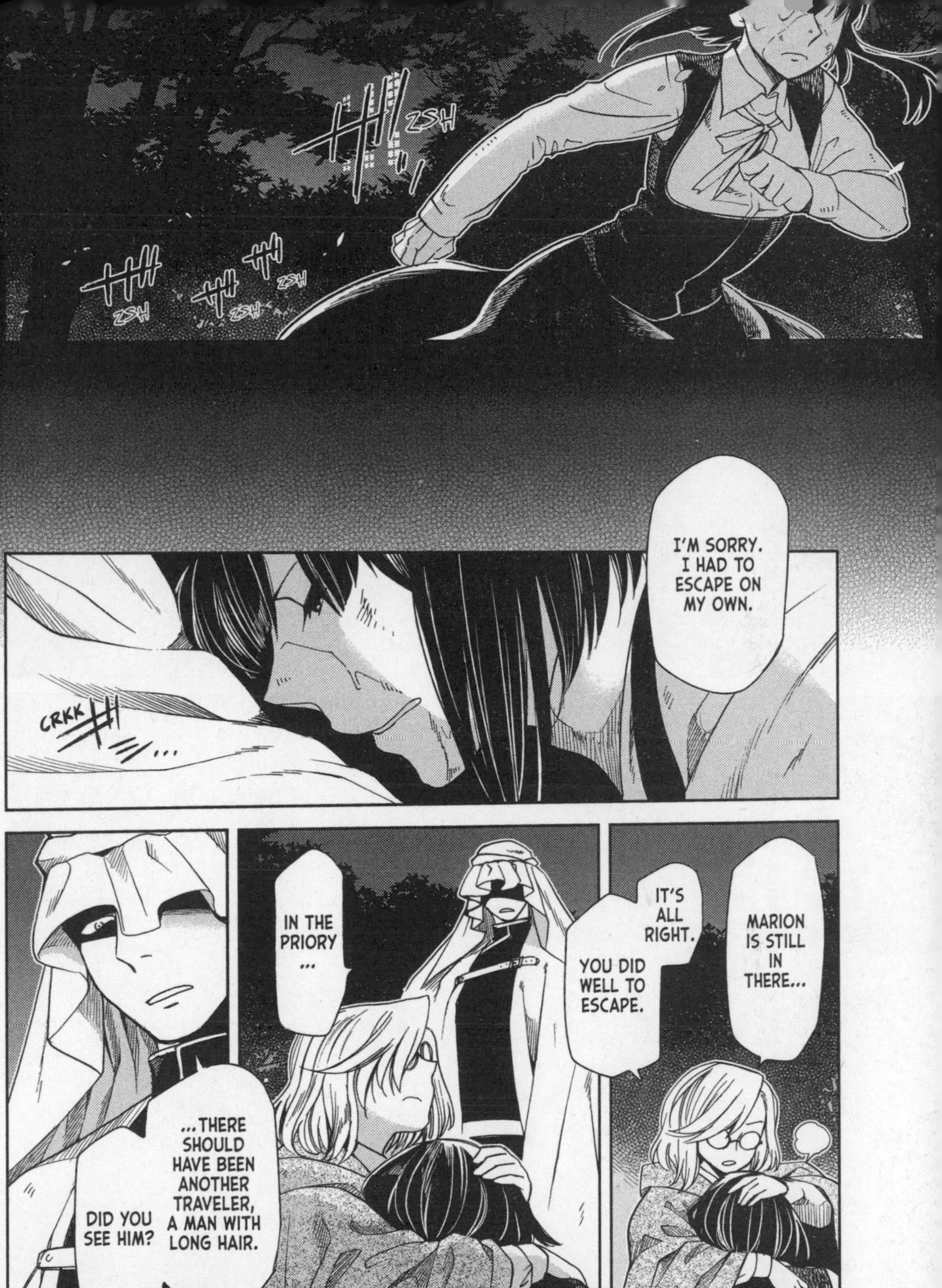
ZSH
ZSH
ZSH
ZSH
I'M SORRY. I HAD TO ESCAPE ON MY OWN.
CRKK
MARION IS STILL IN THERE...
IT'S ALL RIGHT.
YOU DID WELL TO ESCAPE.
IN THE PRIORY ...
...THERE SHOULD HAVE BEEN ANOTHER TRAVELER, A MAN WITH LONG HAIR.
DID YOU SEE HIM?

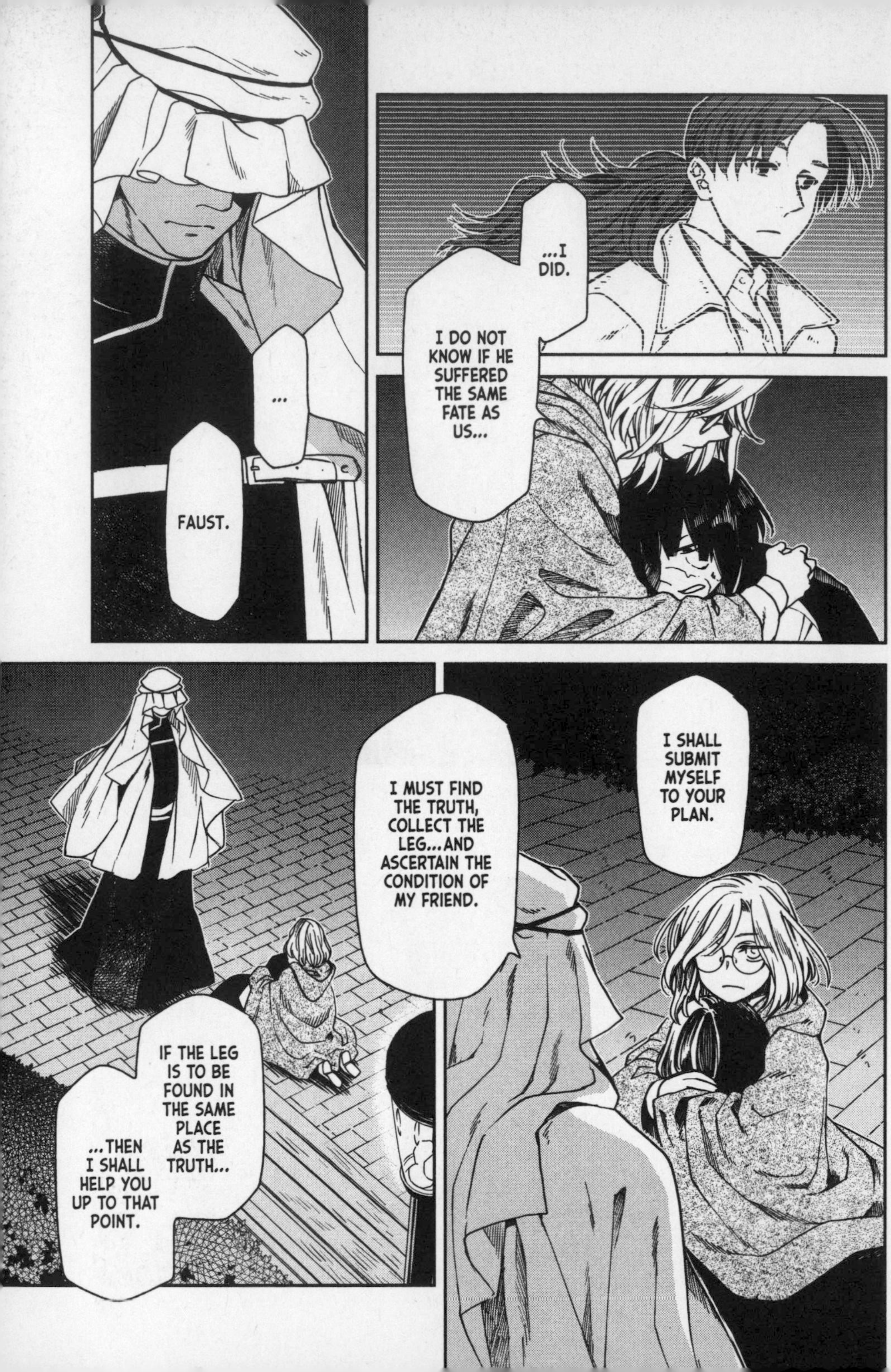
...I DID.
I DO NOT KNOW IF HE SUFFERED THE SAME FATE AS US...
...
FAUST.
I SHALL SUBMIT MYSELF TO YOUR PLAN.
I MUST FIND THE TRUTH, COLLECT THE LEG...AND ASCERTAIN THE CONDITION OF MY FRIEND.
IF THE LEG IS TO BE FOUND IN THE SAME PLACE AS THE TRUTH...
...THEN I SHALL HELP YOU UP TO THAT POINT.

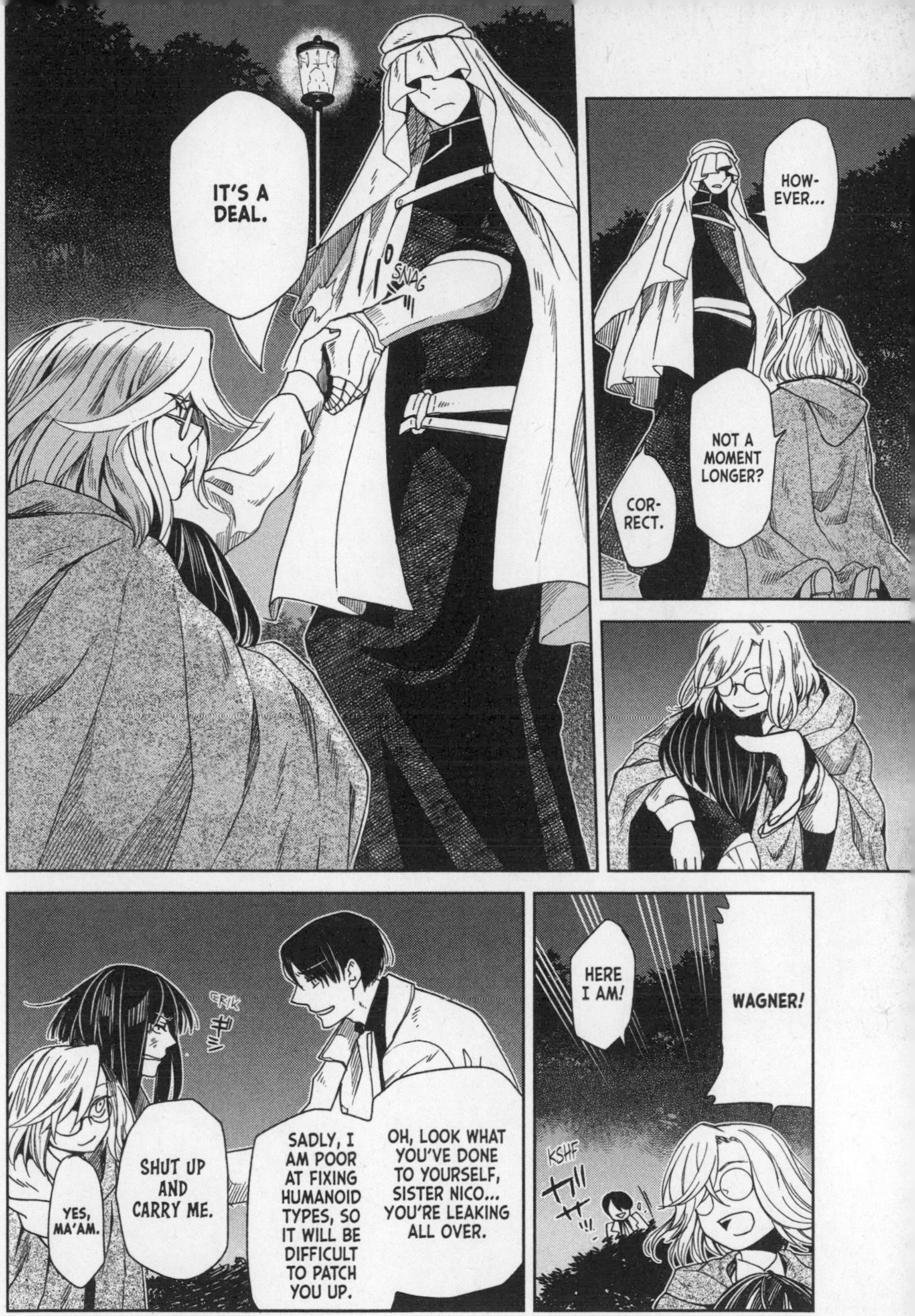
HOW-EVER...
NOT A MOMENT LONGER?
CORRECT.
IT'S A DEAL.
SNAG
WAGNER!
HERE I AM!
KSHF
OH, LOOK WHAT YOU'VE DONE TO YOURSELF, SISTER NICO... YOU'RE LEAKING ALL OVER.
SADLY, I AM POOR AT FIXING HUMANOID TYPES, SO IT WILL BE DIFFICULT TO PATCH YOU UP.
SHUT UP AND CARRY ME.
YES, MA'AM.
CRIK

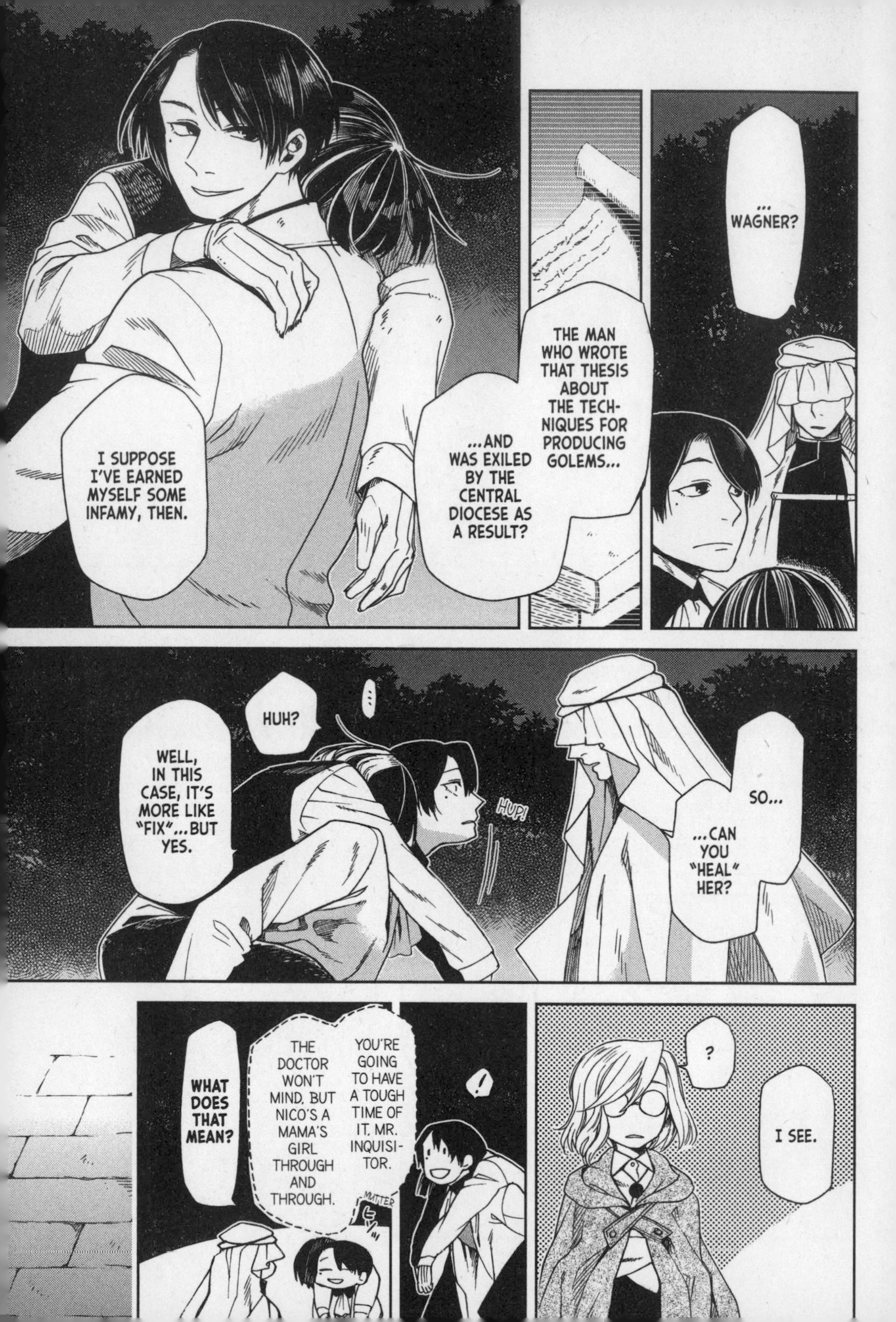
...WAGNER?
THE MAN WHO WROTE THAT THESIS ABOUT THE TECHNIQUES FOR PRODUCING GOLEMS...
...AND WAS EXILED BY THE CENTRAL DIOCESE AS A RESULT?
I SUPPOSE I'VE EARNED MYSELF SOME INFAMY, THEN.
SO...
...CAN YOU "HEAL" HER?
HUP!
...
HUH?
WELL, IN THIS CASE, IT'S MORE LIKE "FIX"...BUT YES.
?
I SEE.
!
YOU'RE GOING TO HAVE A TOUGH TIME OF IT, MR. INQUISITOR.
THE DOCTOR WON'T MIND, BUT NICO'S A MAMA'S GIRL THROUGH AND THROUGH.
MUTTER
WHAT DOES THAT MEAN?

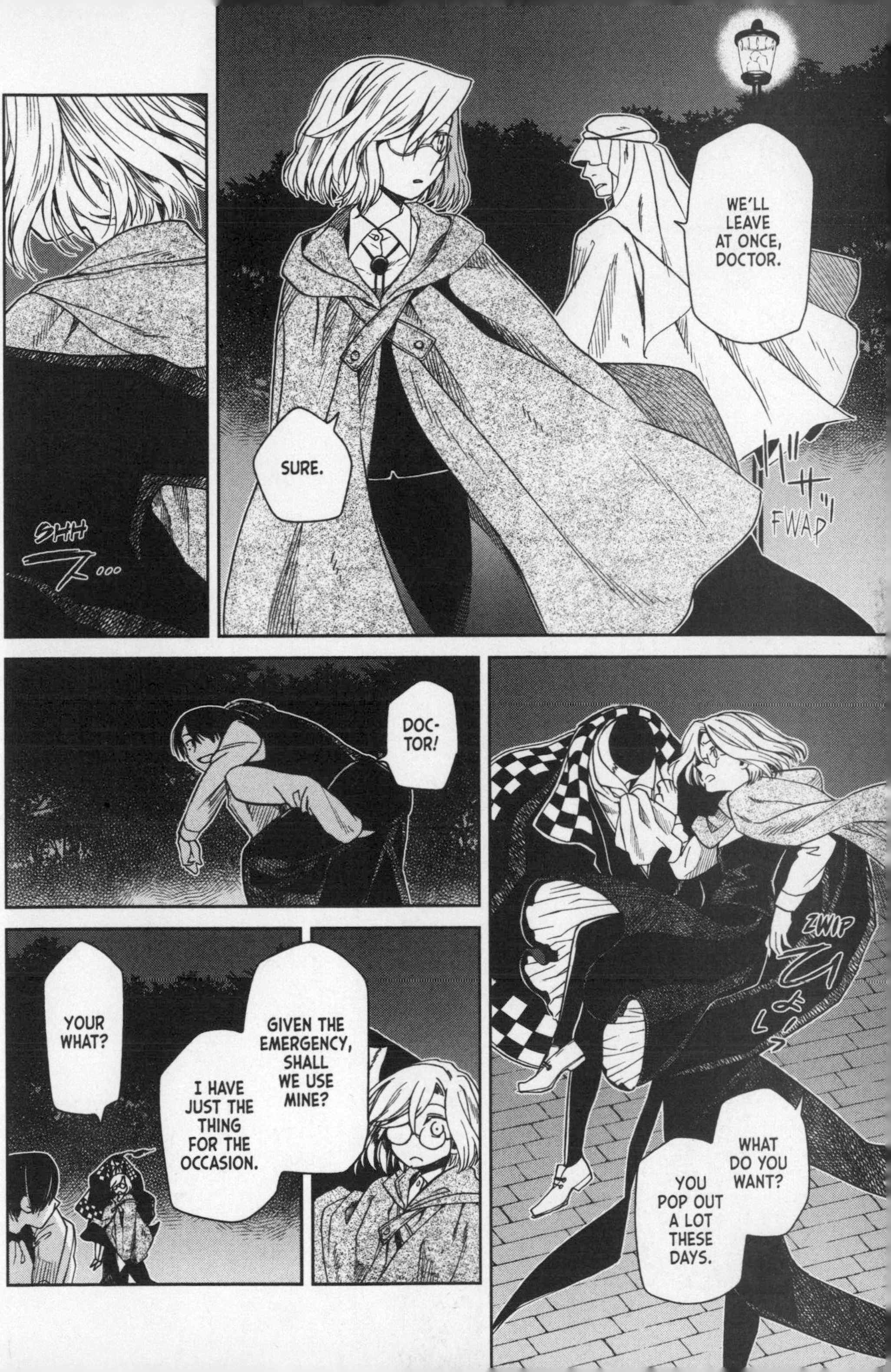
WE'LL LEAVE AT ONCE, DOCTOR.
FWAP
SURE.
SHH
ZWIP
WHAT DO YOU WANT?
YOU POP OUT A LOT THESE DAYS.
DOC-TOR!
GIVEN THE EMERGENCY, SHALL WE USE MINE?
YOUR WHAT?
I HAVE JUST THE THING FOR THE OCCASION.

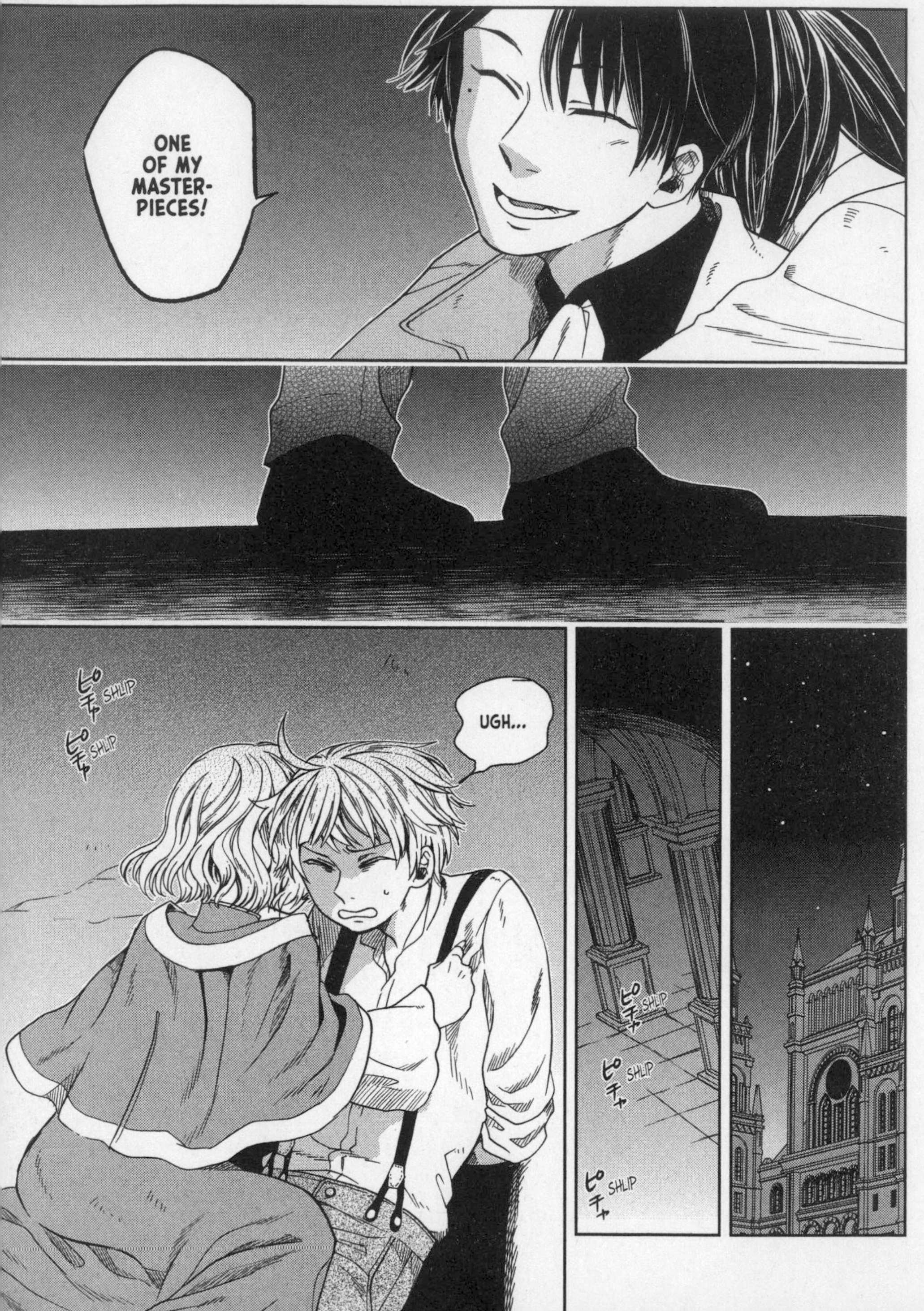
ONE OF MY MASTER-PIECES!
ピチャ SHLIP
ピチャ SHLIP
ピチャ SHLIP
UGH...
ピチャ SHLIP
ピチャ SHLIP

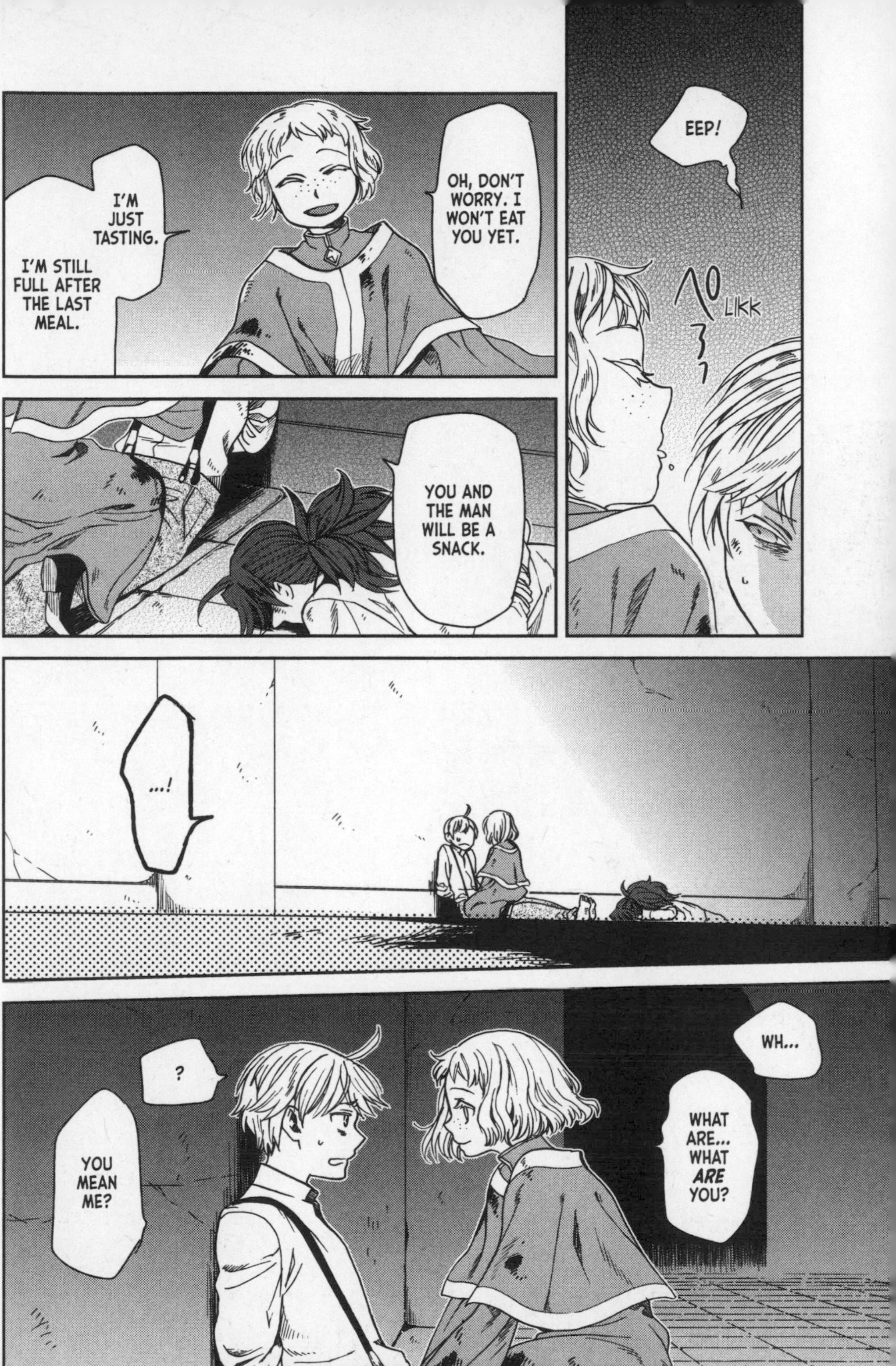
EEP!
LIKK
OH, DON'T WORRY. I WON'T EAT YOU YET.
I'M JUST TASTING.
I'M STILL FULL AFTER THE LAST MEAL.
YOU AND THE MAN WILL BE A SNACK.
...!
WH...
WHAT ARE... WHAT *ARE* YOU?
?
YOU MEAN ME?

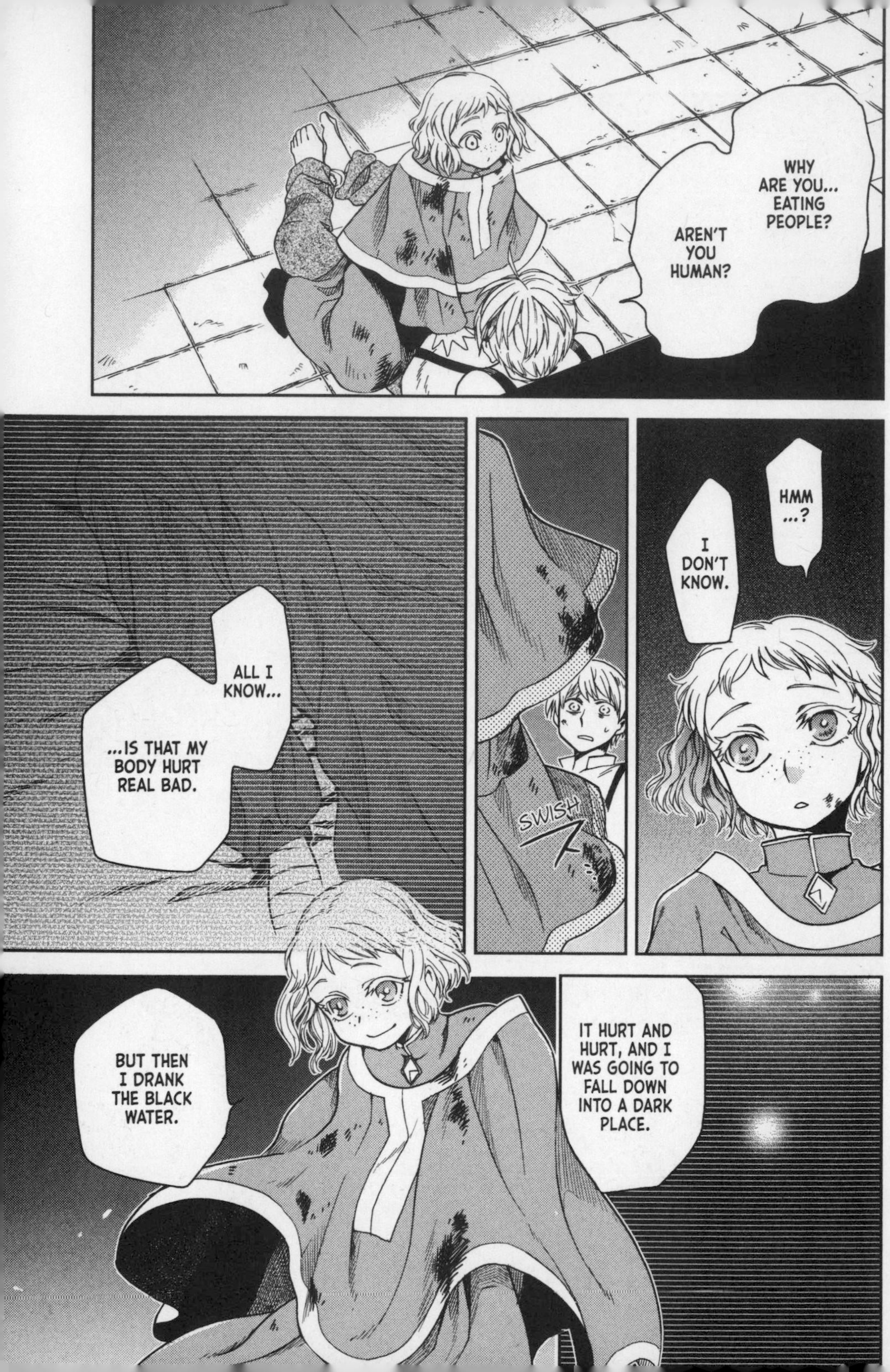
WHY ARE YOU... EATING PEOPLE?
AREN'T YOU HUMAN?
HMM ...?
I DON'T KNOW.
SWISH
ALL I KNOW...
...IS THAT MY BODY HURT REAL BAD.
IT HURT AND HURT, AND I WAS GOING TO FALL DOWN INTO A DARK PLACE.
BUT THEN I DRANK THE BLACK WATER.

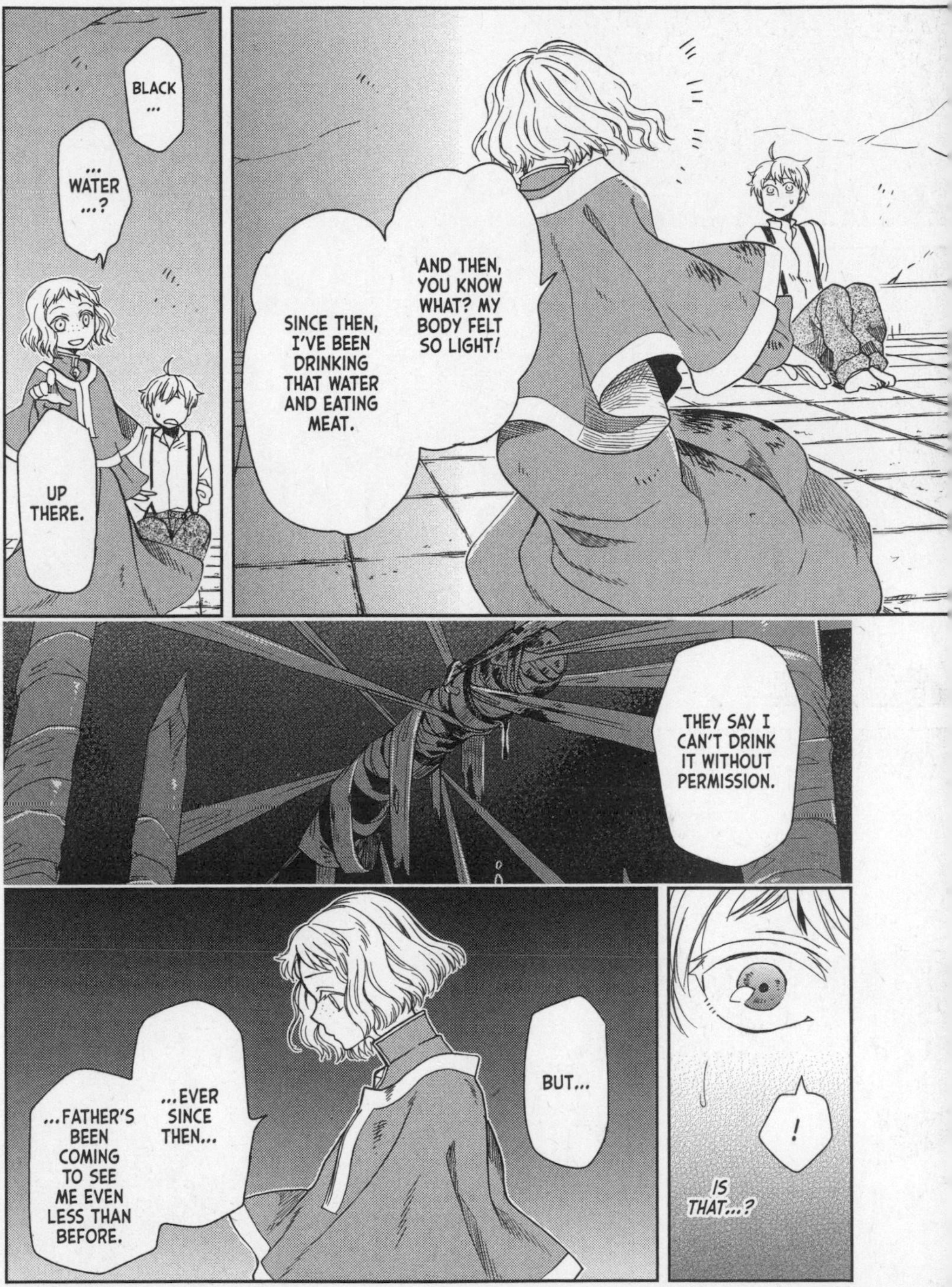
AND THEN, YOU KNOW WHAT? MY BODY FELT SO LIGHT!
SINCE THEN, I'VE BEEN DRINKING THAT WATER AND EATING MEAT.
BLACK...
...WATER...?
UP THERE.
THEY SAY I CAN'T DRINK IT WITHOUT PERMISSION.
!
IS THAT...?
BUT...
...EVER SINCE THEN...
...FATHER'S BEEN COMING TO SEE ME EVEN LESS THAN BEFORE.

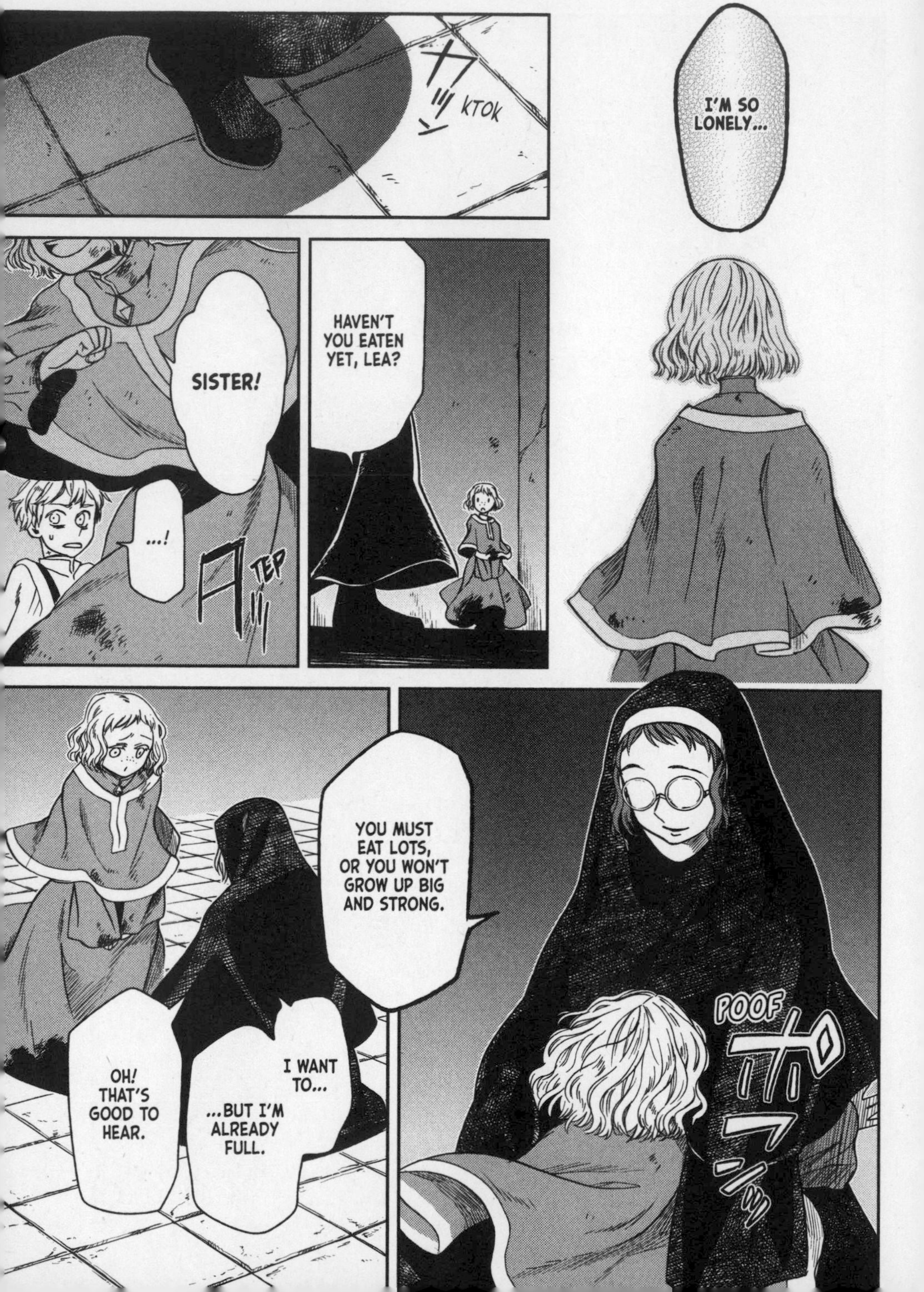
I'M SO LONELY...
KTOK
HAVEN'T YOU EATEN YET, LEA?
SISTER!
...!
TEP
YOU MUST EAT LOTS, OR YOU WON'T GROW UP BIG AND STRONG.
POOF
I WANT TO...
...BUT I'M ALREADY FULL.
OH! THAT'S GOOD TO HEAR.

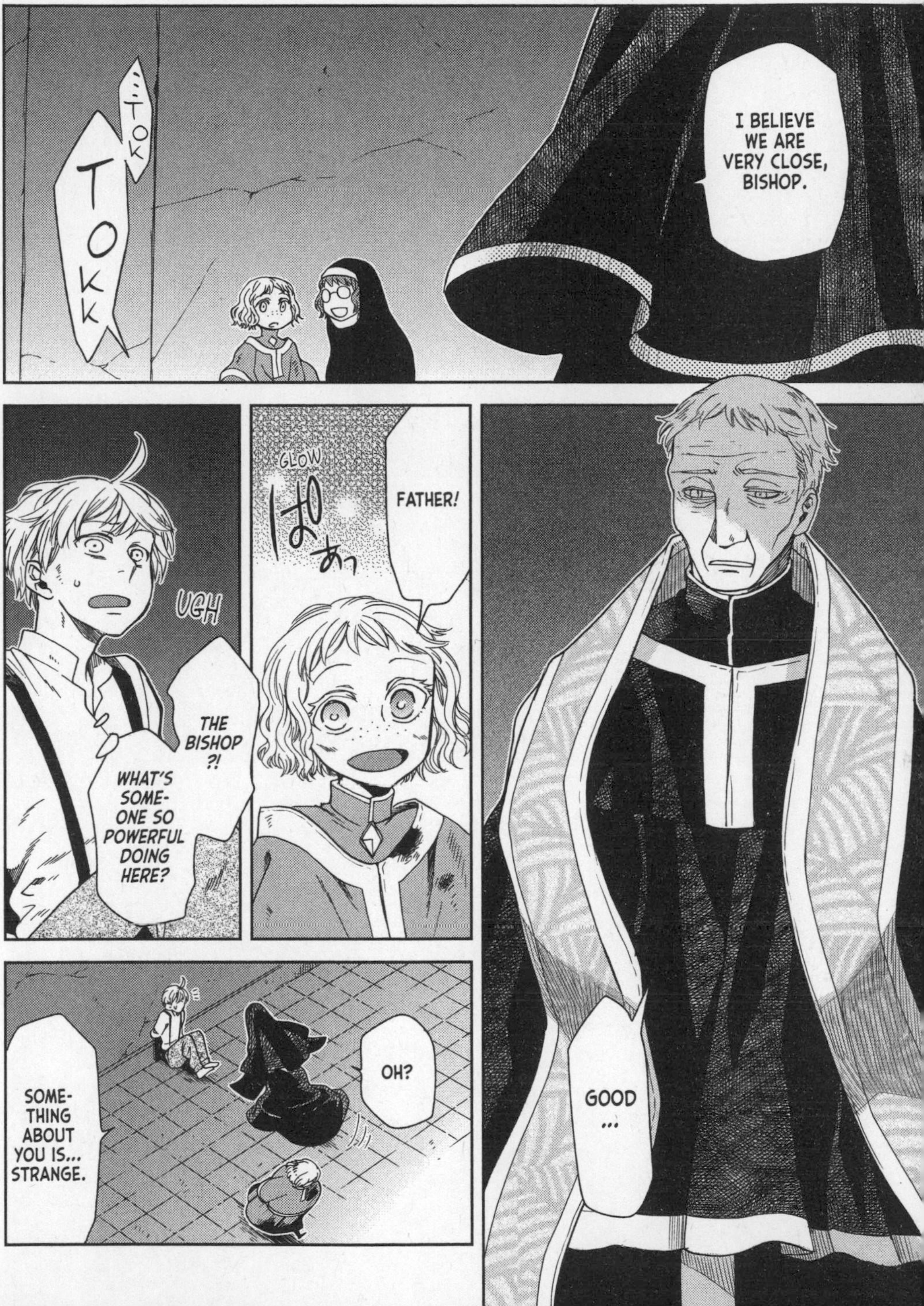
I BELIEVE WE ARE VERY CLOSE, BISHOP.
TOK
TOKK
GOOD ...
GLOW
ぱあっ
FATHER!
UGH
THE BISHOP ?!
WHAT'S SOME-ONE SO POWERFUL DOING HERE?
OH?
SOME-THING ABOUT YOU IS... STRANGE.

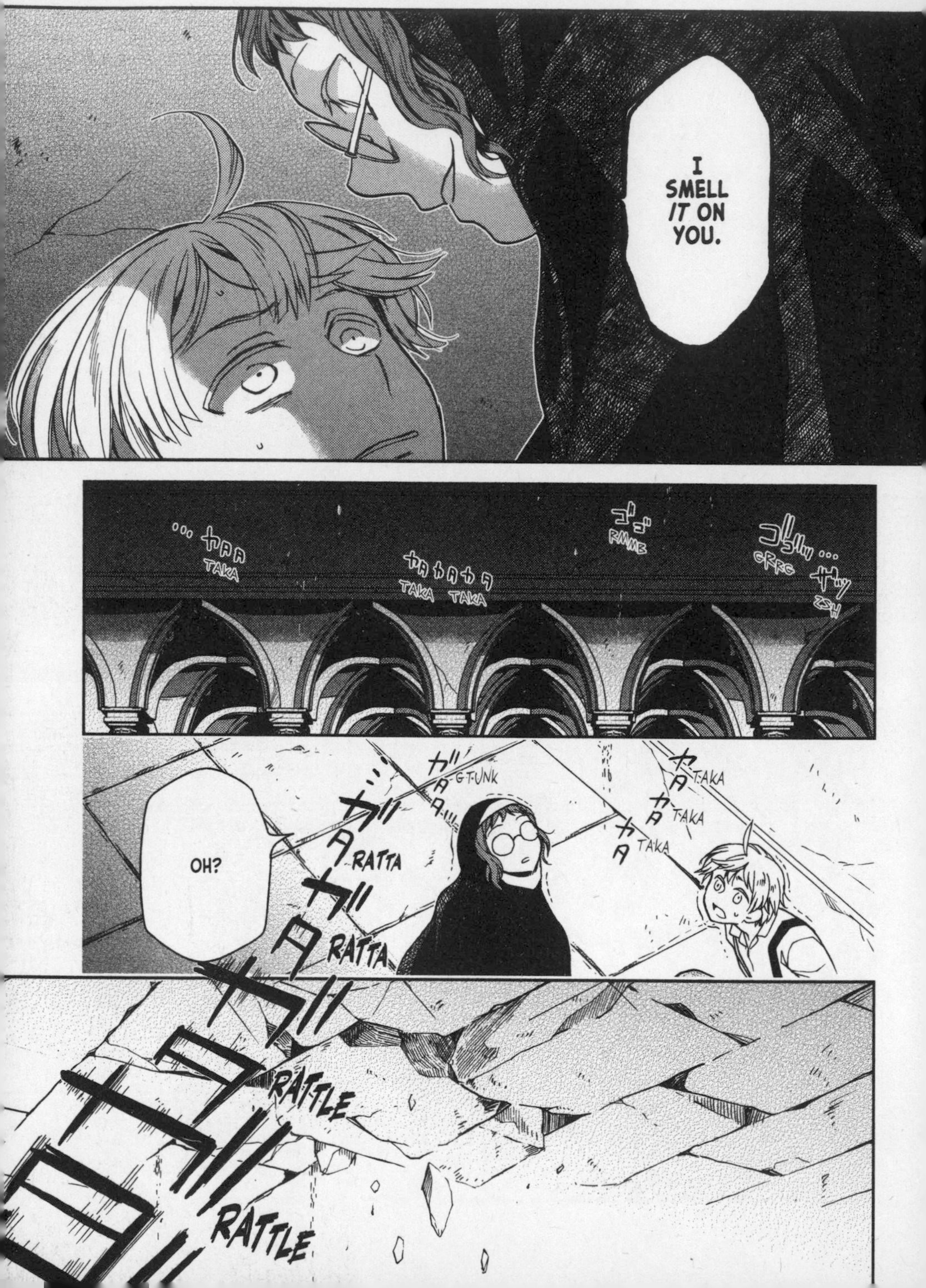
I SMELL IT ON YOU.
GRRG
ZSH
RMMB
TAKA TAKA
TAKA
TAKA
TAKA
TAKA
G-TUNK
RATTA
RATTA
OH?
RATTLE
RATTLE

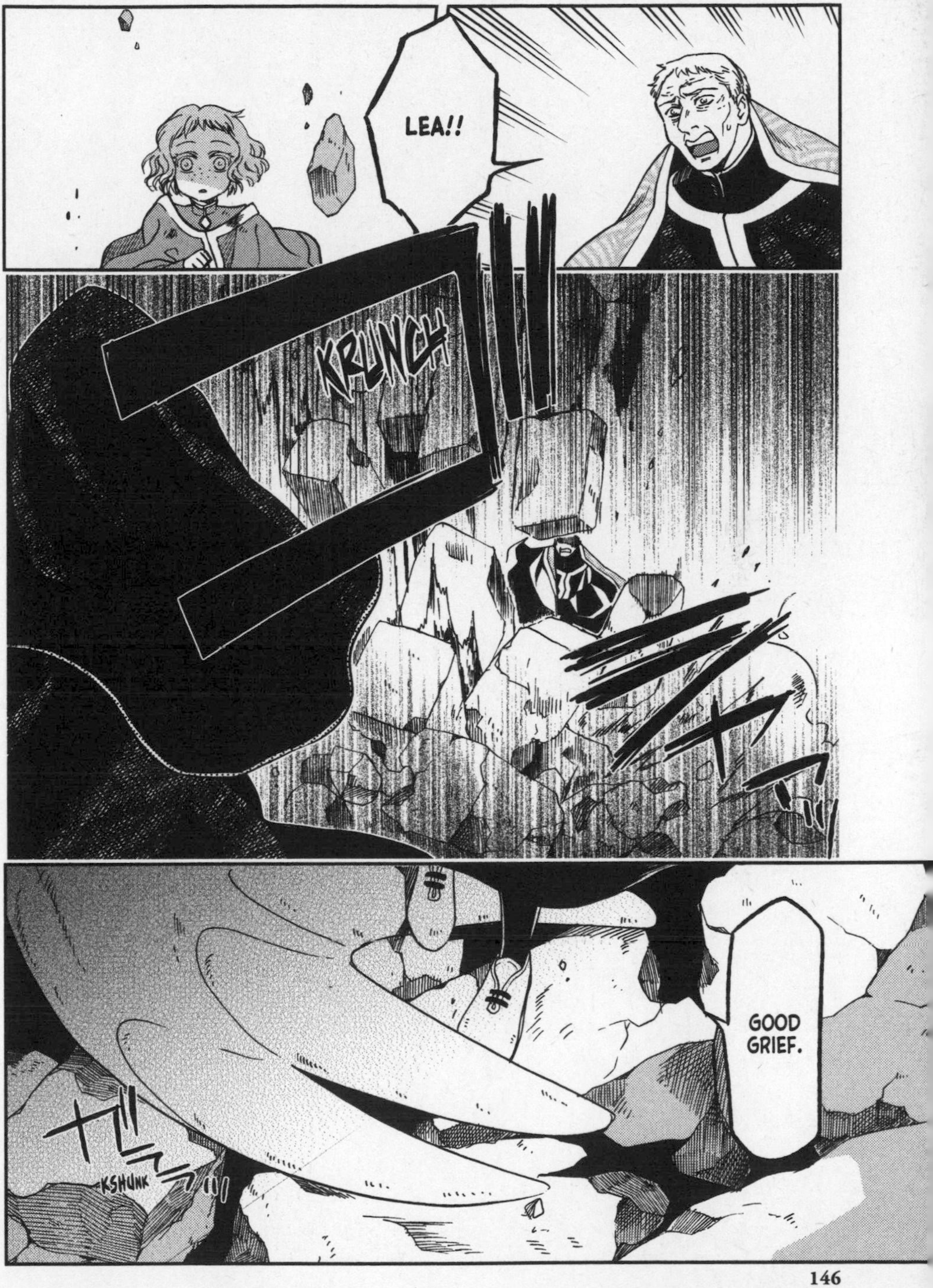
LEA!!
KRUNCH
GOOD GRIEF.
KSHUNK

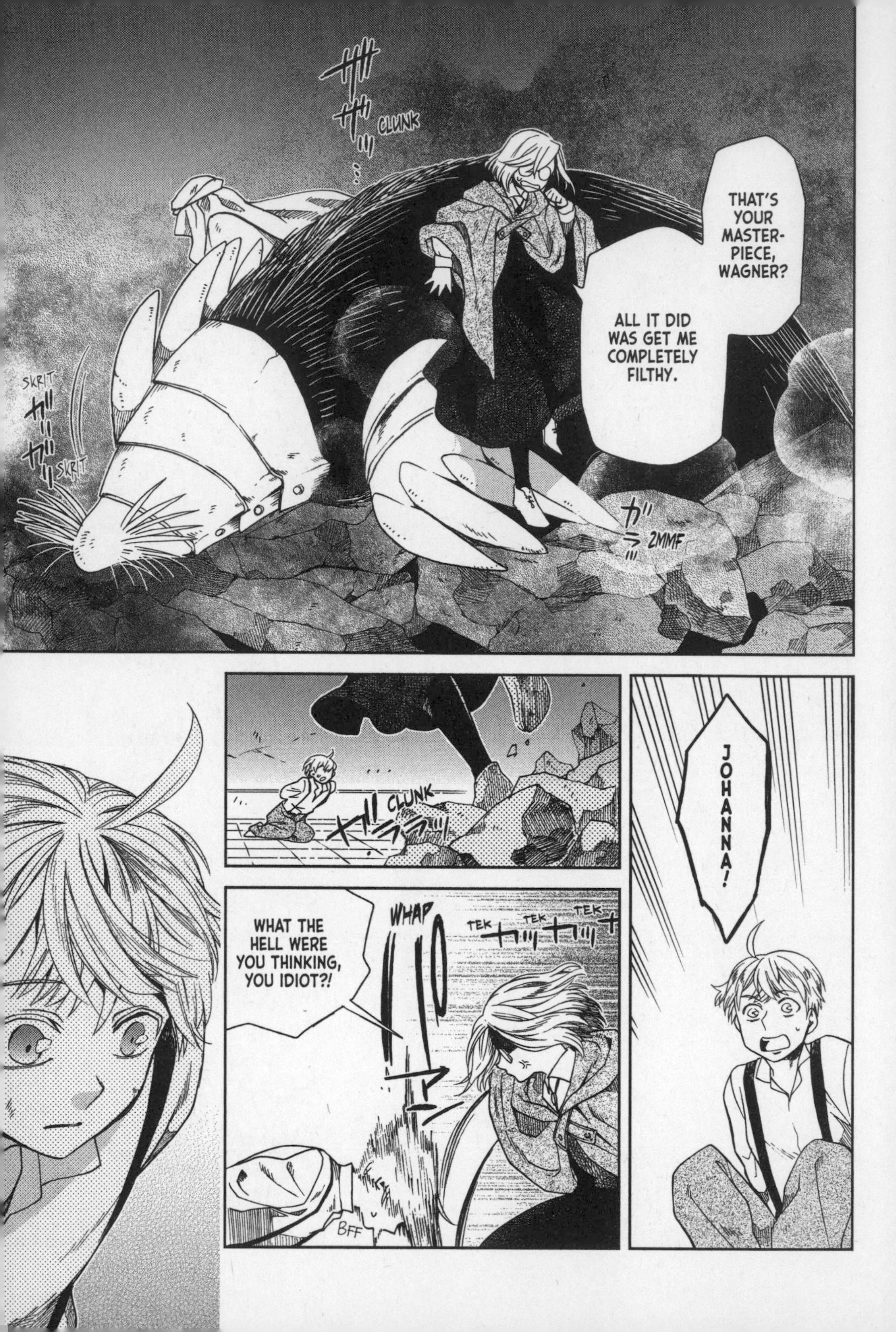
THAT'S YOUR MASTER-PIECE, WAGNER?
ALL IT DID WAS GET ME COMPLETELY FILTHY.
CLUNK
SKRIT
SKRIT
ZMMF
JOHANNA!
CLUNK
TEK TEK TEK
WHAP
WHAT THE HELL WERE YOU THINKING, YOU IDIOT?!
BFF

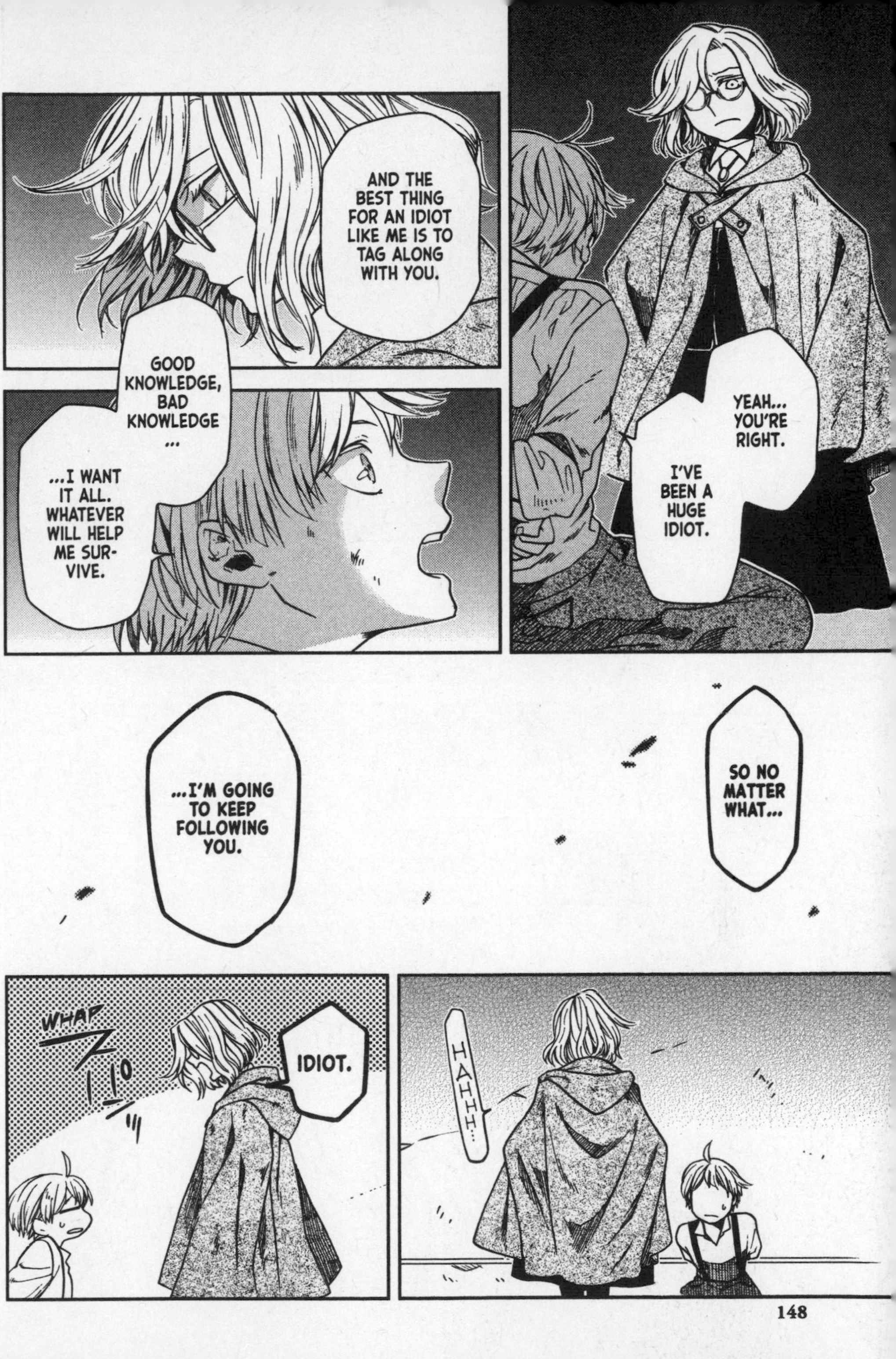
YEAH... YOU'RE RIGHT.
I'VE BEEN A HUGE IDIOT.
AND THE BEST THING FOR AN IDIOT LIKE ME IS TO TAG ALONG WITH YOU.
GOOD KNOWLEDGE, BAD KNOWLEDGE...
...I WANT IT ALL. WHATEVER WILL HELP ME SUR-VIVE.
SO NO MATTER WHAT...
...I'M GOING TO KEEP FOLLOWING YOU.
HAHHH...
WHAP
IDIOT.

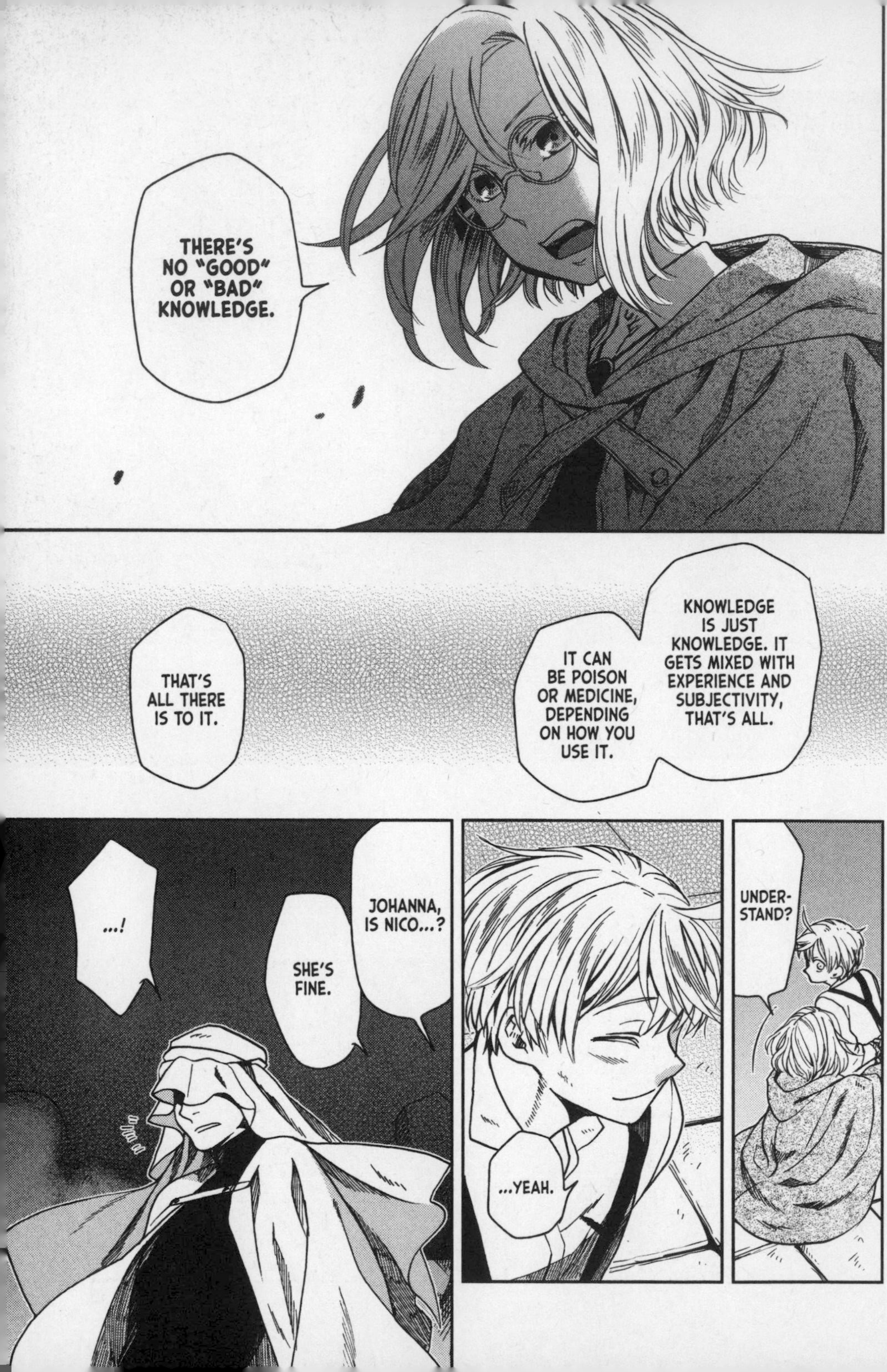
THERE'S NO "GOOD" OR "BAD" KNOWLEDGE.
KNOWLEDGE IS JUST KNOWLEDGE. IT GETS MIXED WITH EXPERIENCE AND SUBJECTIVITY, THAT'S ALL.
IT CAN BE POISON OR MEDICINE, DEPENDING ON HOW YOU USE IT.
THAT'S ALL THERE IS TO IT.
UNDER-STAND?
...YEAH.
JOHANNA, IS NICO...?
SHE'S FINE.
...!

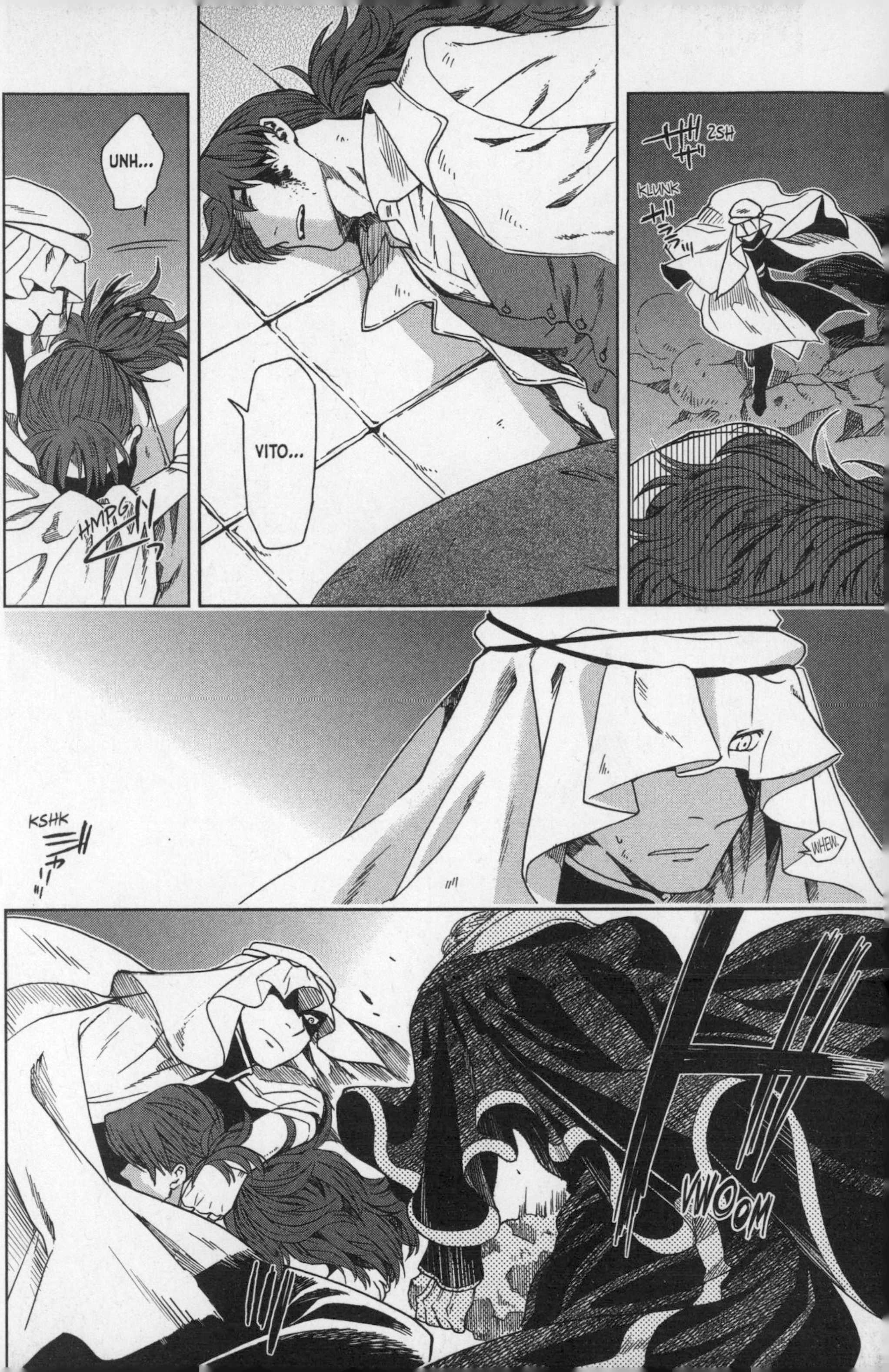
ZSH
KLUNK
VITO...
UNH...
HMPG
WHEW.
KSHK
VWOOM

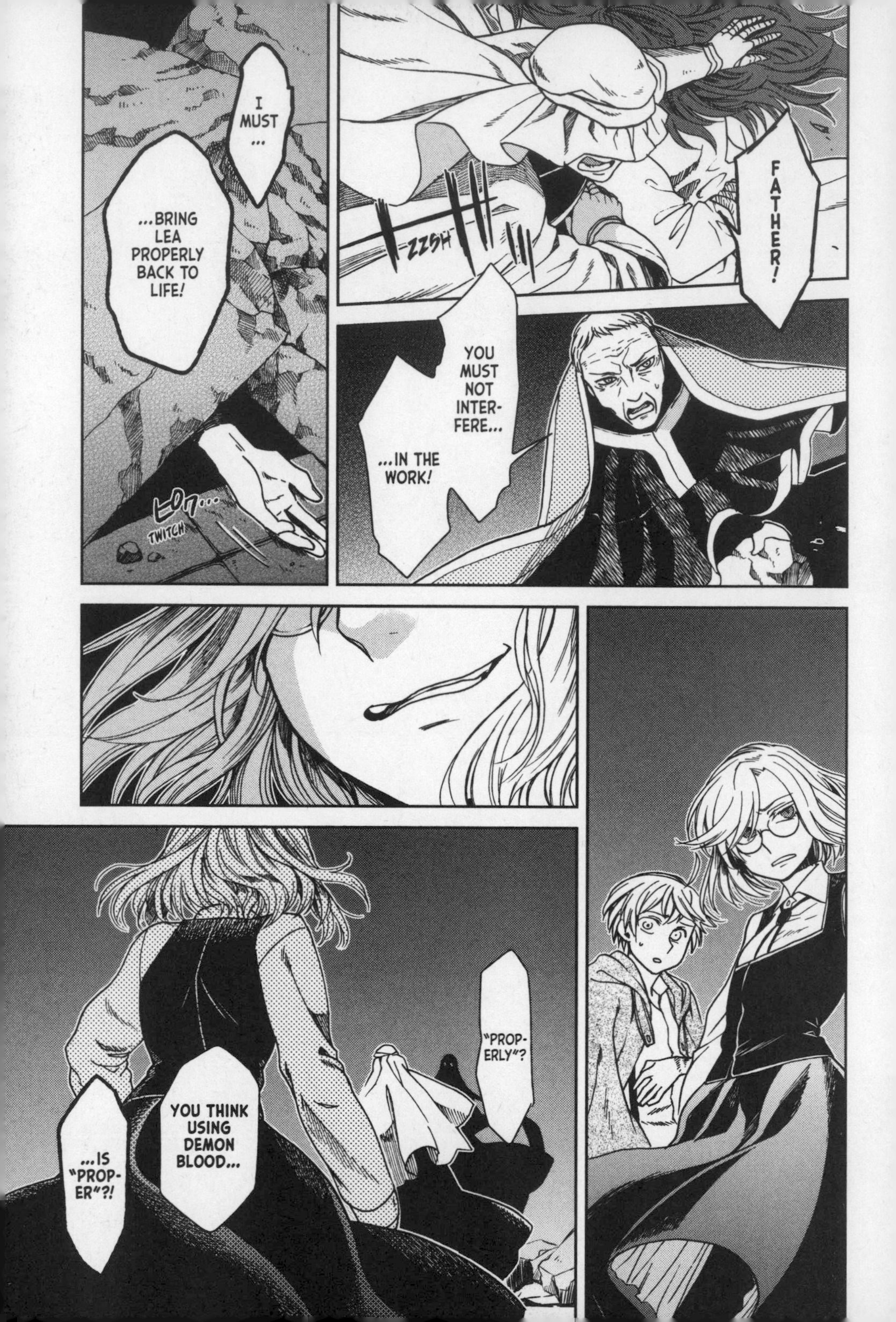
FATHER!
ZZSH
YOU MUST NOT INTERFERE...
...IN THE WORK!
I MUST...
...BRING LEA PROPERLY BACK TO LIFE!
ヒクッ...
TWITCH
"PROPERLY"?
YOU THINK USING DEMON BLOOD...
...IS "PROPER"?!

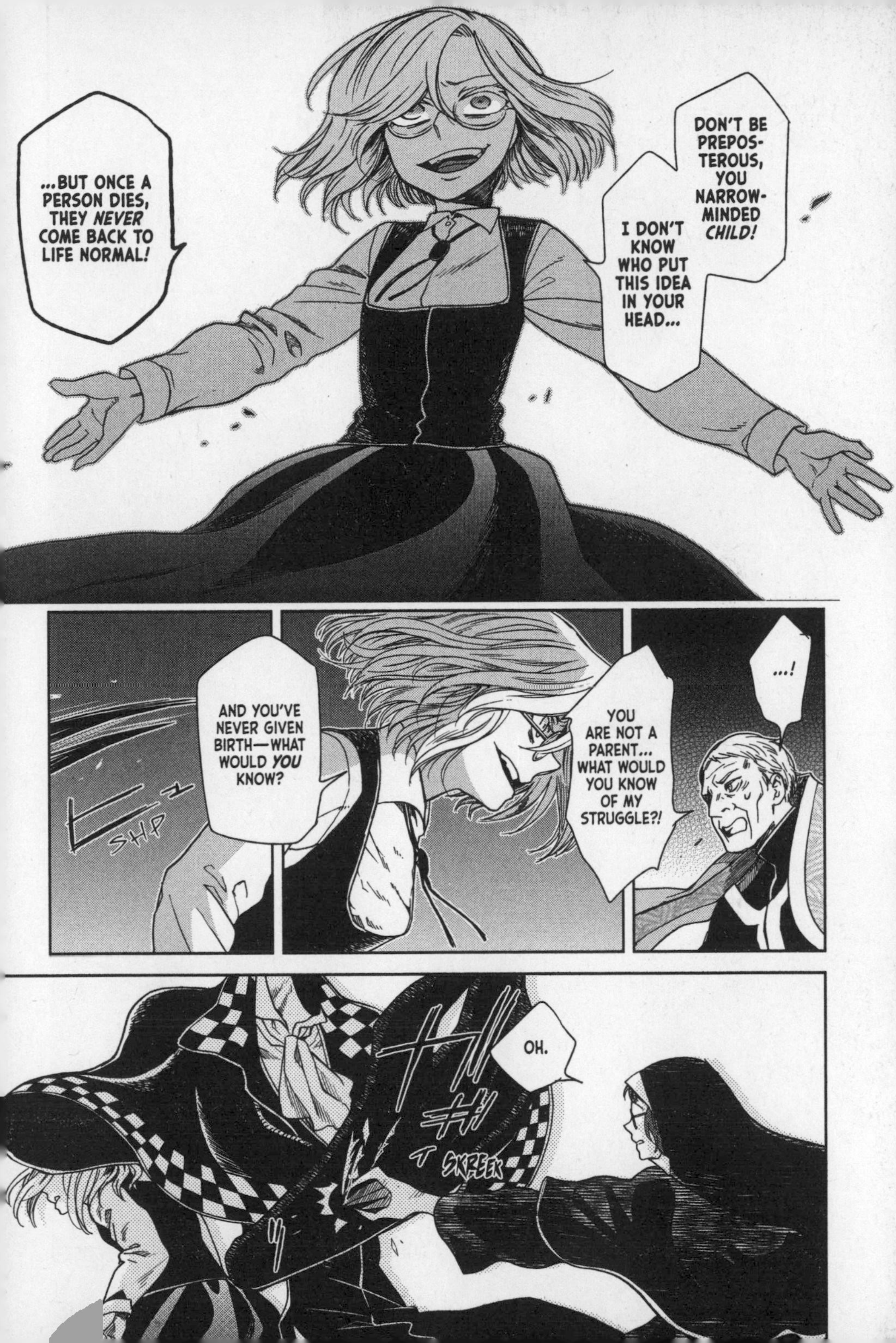
DON'T BE PREPOSTEROUS, YOU NARROW-MINDED *CHILD!*
I DON'T KNOW WHO PUT THIS IDEA IN YOUR HEAD...
...BUT ONCE A PERSON DIES, THEY *NEVER* COME BACK TO LIFE NORMAL!
...!
YOU ARE NOT A PARENT... WHAT WOULD YOU KNOW OF MY STRUGGLE?!
AND YOU'VE NEVER GIVEN BIRTH—WHAT WOULD *YOU* KNOW?
SHP
OH.
SKREEK

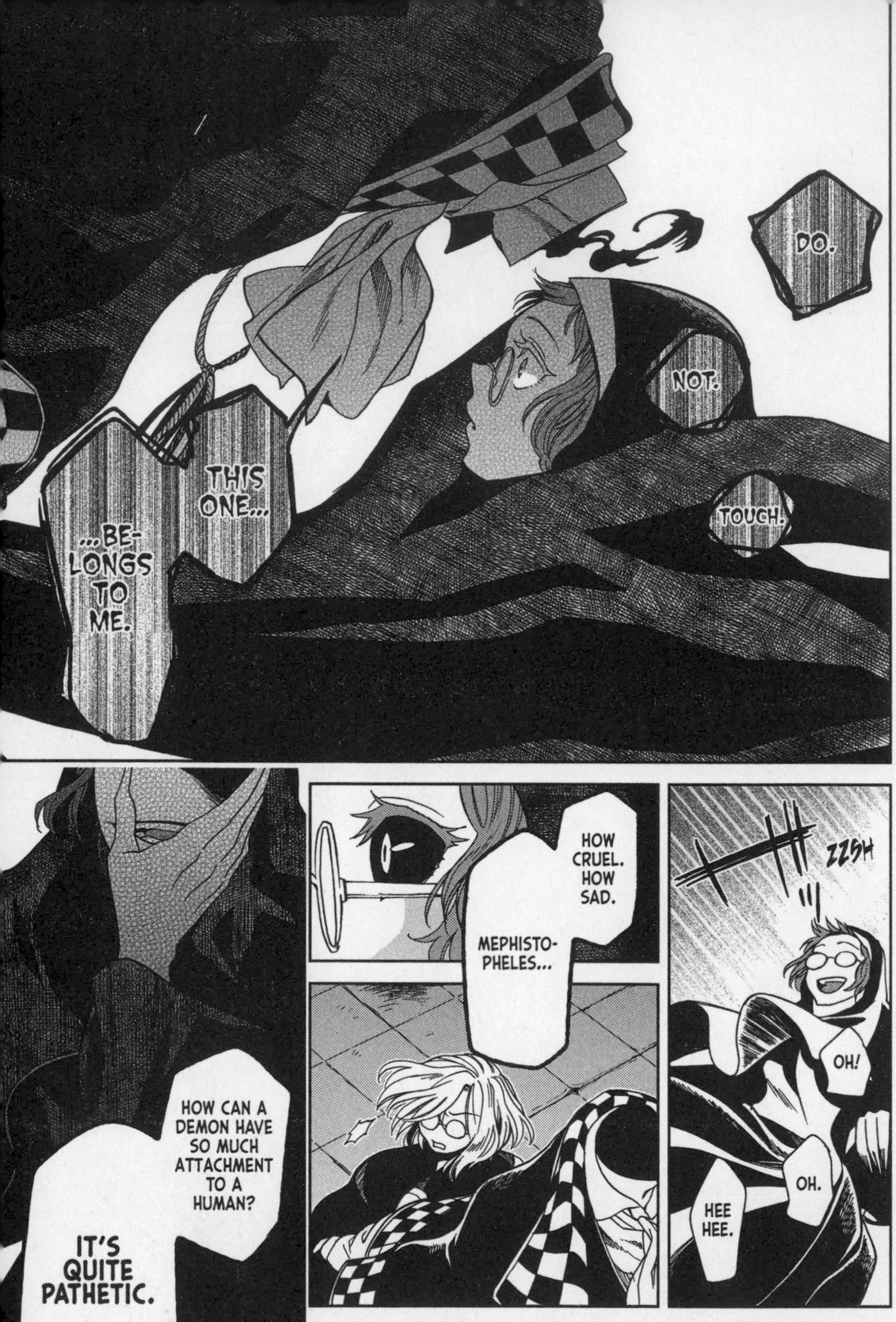
DO.
NOT.
TOUCH.
THIS ONE...
...BE-LONGS TO ME.
ZZSH
OH!
OH.
HEE HEE.
HOW CRUEL. HOW SAD.
MEPHISTO-PHELES...
HOW CAN A DEMON HAVE SO MUCH ATTACHMENT TO A HUMAN?
IT'S QUITE PATHETIC.

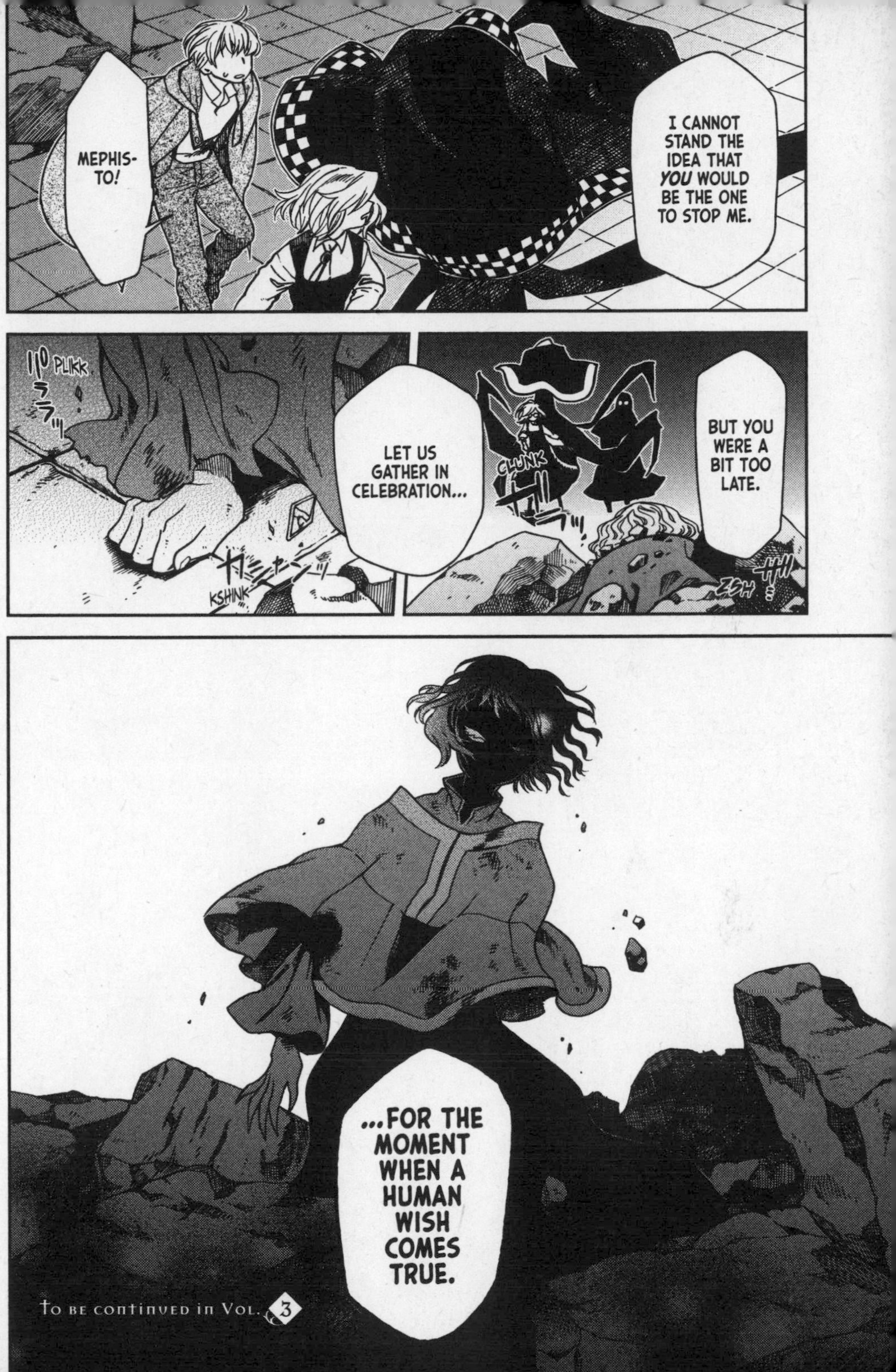
I CANNOT STAND THE IDEA THAT *YOU* WOULD BE THE ONE TO STOP ME.
MEPHIS-TO!
BUT YOU WERE A BIT TOO LATE.
ZSH
CLUNK
LET US GATHER IN CELEBRATION...
PLIKK
KSHINK
...FOR THE MOMENT WHEN A HUMAN WISH COMES TRUE.
To be continued in Vol. 3

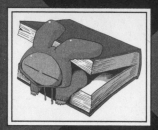

KORE YAMAZAKI

It is with both joy and shame that I present Volume 2 of *Frau Faust*. I know the story's rather slow, but my hope is that you'll enjoy the leisurely pace. My family's really going to let me hear it for this one.

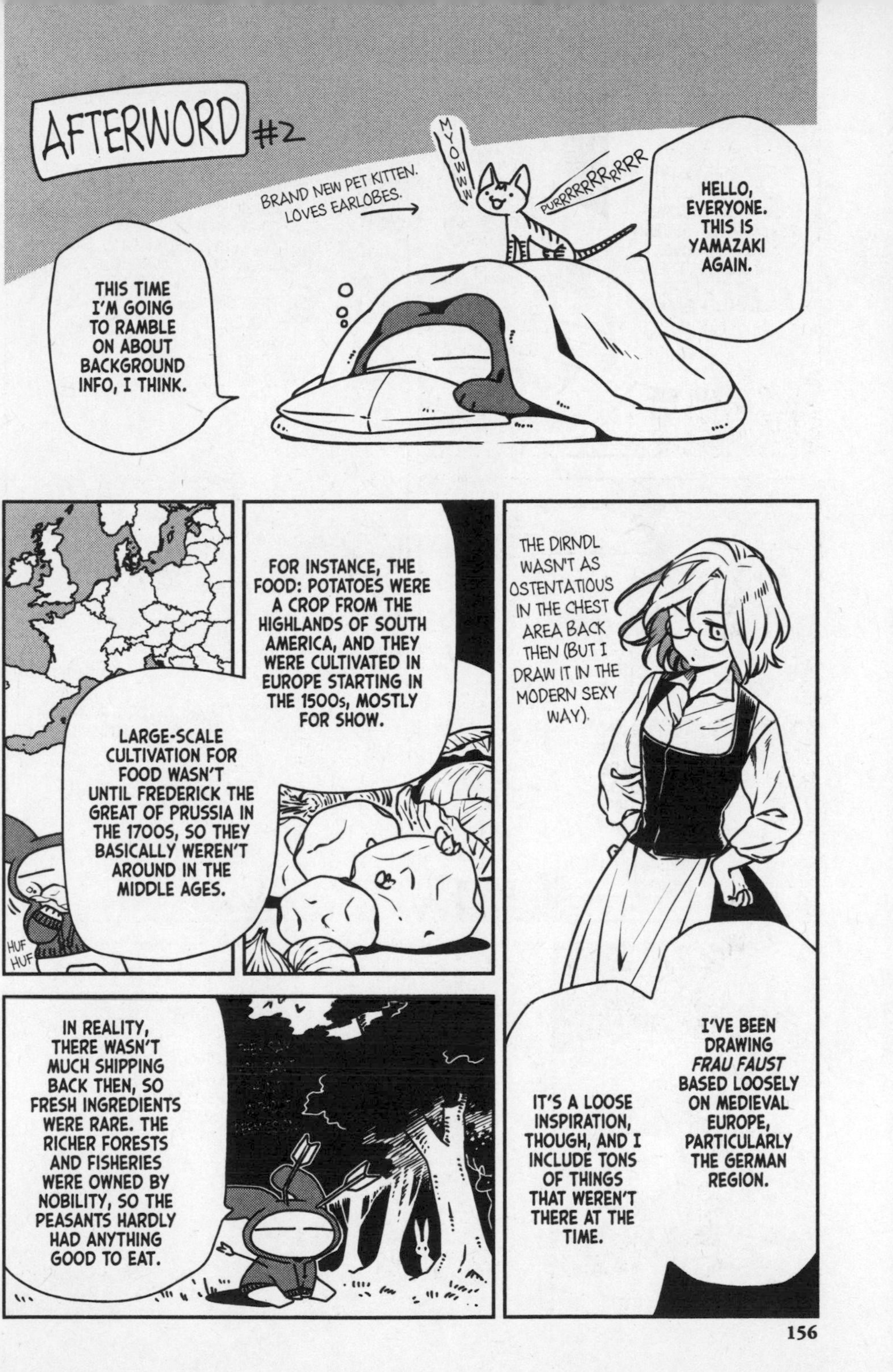
AFTERWORD #2
HELLO, EVERYONE. THIS IS YAMAZAKI AGAIN.
MYOWWW
PURRRRRRRRRRR
BRAND NEW PET KITTEN. LOVES EARLOBES.
THIS TIME I'M GOING TO RAMBLE ON ABOUT BACKGROUND INFO, I THINK.
I'VE BEEN DRAWING *FRAU FAUST* BASED LOOSELY ON MEDIEVAL EUROPE, PARTICULARLY THE GERMAN REGION.
IT'S A LOOSE INSPIRATION, THOUGH, AND I INCLUDE TONS OF THINGS THAT WEREN'T THERE AT THE TIME.
THE DIRNDL WASN'T AS OSTENTATIOUS IN THE CHEST AREA BACK THEN (BUT I DRAW IT IN THE MODERN SEXY WAY).
FOR INSTANCE, THE FOOD: POTATOES WERE A CROP FROM THE HIGHLANDS OF SOUTH AMERICA, AND THEY WERE CULTIVATED IN EUROPE STARTING IN THE 1500s, MOSTLY FOR SHOW.
LARGE-SCALE CULTIVATION FOR FOOD WASN'T UNTIL FREDERICK THE GREAT OF PRUSSIA IN THE 1700S, SO THEY BASICALLY WEREN'T AROUND IN THE MIDDLE AGES.
HUF HUF
IN REALITY, THERE WASN'T MUCH SHIPPING BACK THEN, SO FRESH INGREDIENTS WERE RARE. THE RICHER FORESTS AND FISHERIES WERE OWNED BY NOBILITY, SO THE PEASANTS HARDLY HAD ANYTHING GOOD TO EAT.

TO SAY NOTHING OF WHAT WAS POSSIBLE WITH THEIR TECHNOLOGY

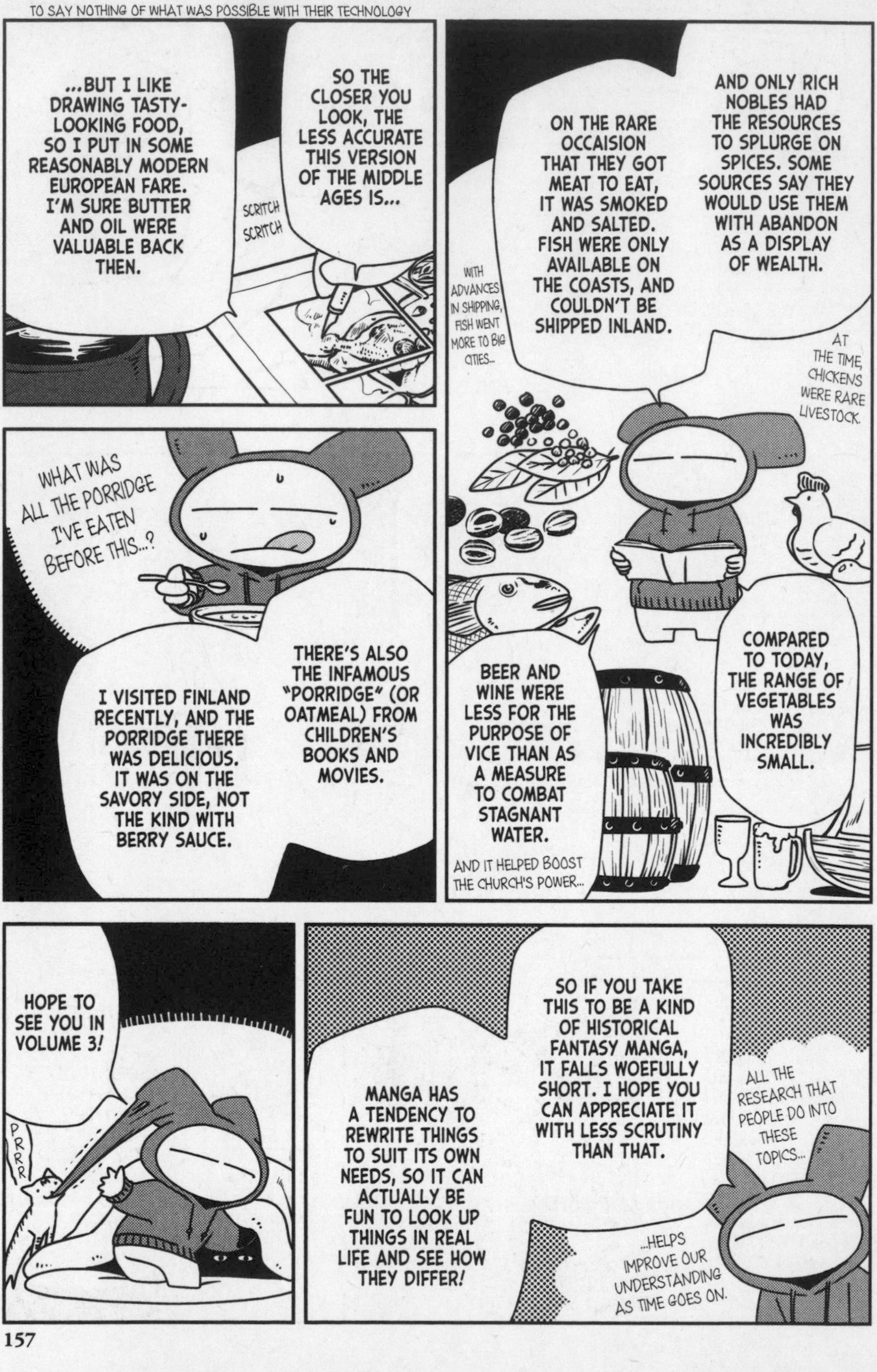
AND ONLY RICH NOBLES HAD THE RESOURCES TO SPLURGE ON SPICES. SOME SOURCES SAY THEY WOULD USE THEM WITH ABANDON AS A DISPLAY OF WEALTH.
ON THE RARE OCCAISION THAT THEY GOT MEAT TO EAT, IT WAS SMOKED AND SALTED. FISH WERE ONLY AVAILABLE ON THE COASTS, AND COULDN'T BE SHIPPED INLAND.
WITH ADVANCES IN SHIPPING, FISH WENT MORE TO BIG CITIES...
AT THE TIME, CHICKENS WERE RARE LIVESTOCK.
COMPARED TO TODAY, THE RANGE OF VEGETABLES WAS INCREDIBLY SMALL.
BEER AND WINE WERE LESS FOR THE PURPOSE OF VICE THAN AS A MEASURE TO COMBAT STAGNANT WATER.
AND IT HELPED BOOST THE CHURCH'S POWER...
SO THE CLOSER YOU LOOK, THE LESS ACCURATE THIS VERSION OF THE MIDDLE AGES IS...
...BUT I LIKE DRAWING TASTY-LOOKING FOOD, SO I PUT IN SOME REASONABLY MODERN EUROPEAN FARE. I'M SURE BUTTER AND OIL WERE VALUABLE BACK THEN.
SCRITCH SCRITCH
WHAT WAS ALL THE PORRIDGE I'VE EATEN BEFORE THIS...?
THERE'S ALSO THE INFAMOUS "PORRIDGE" (OR OATMEAL) FROM CHILDREN'S BOOKS AND MOVIES.
I VISITED FINLAND RECENTLY, AND THE PORRIDGE THERE WAS DELICIOUS. IT WAS ON THE SAVORY SIDE, NOT THE KIND WITH BERRY SAUCE.
SO IF YOU TAKE THIS TO BE A KIND OF HISTORICAL FANTASY MANGA, IT FALLS WOEFULLY SHORT. I HOPE YOU CAN APPRECIATE IT WITH LESS SCRUTINY THAN THAT.
ALL THE RESEARCH THAT PEOPLE DO INTO THESE TOPICS...
MANGA HAS A TENDENCY TO REWRITE THINGS TO SUIT ITS OWN NEEDS, SO IT CAN ACTUALLY BE FUN TO LOOK UP THINGS IN REAL LIFE AND SEE HOW THEY DIFFER!
...HELPS IMPROVE OUR UNDERSTANDING AS TIME GOES ON.
HOPE TO SEE YOU IN VOLUME 3!
PRRR

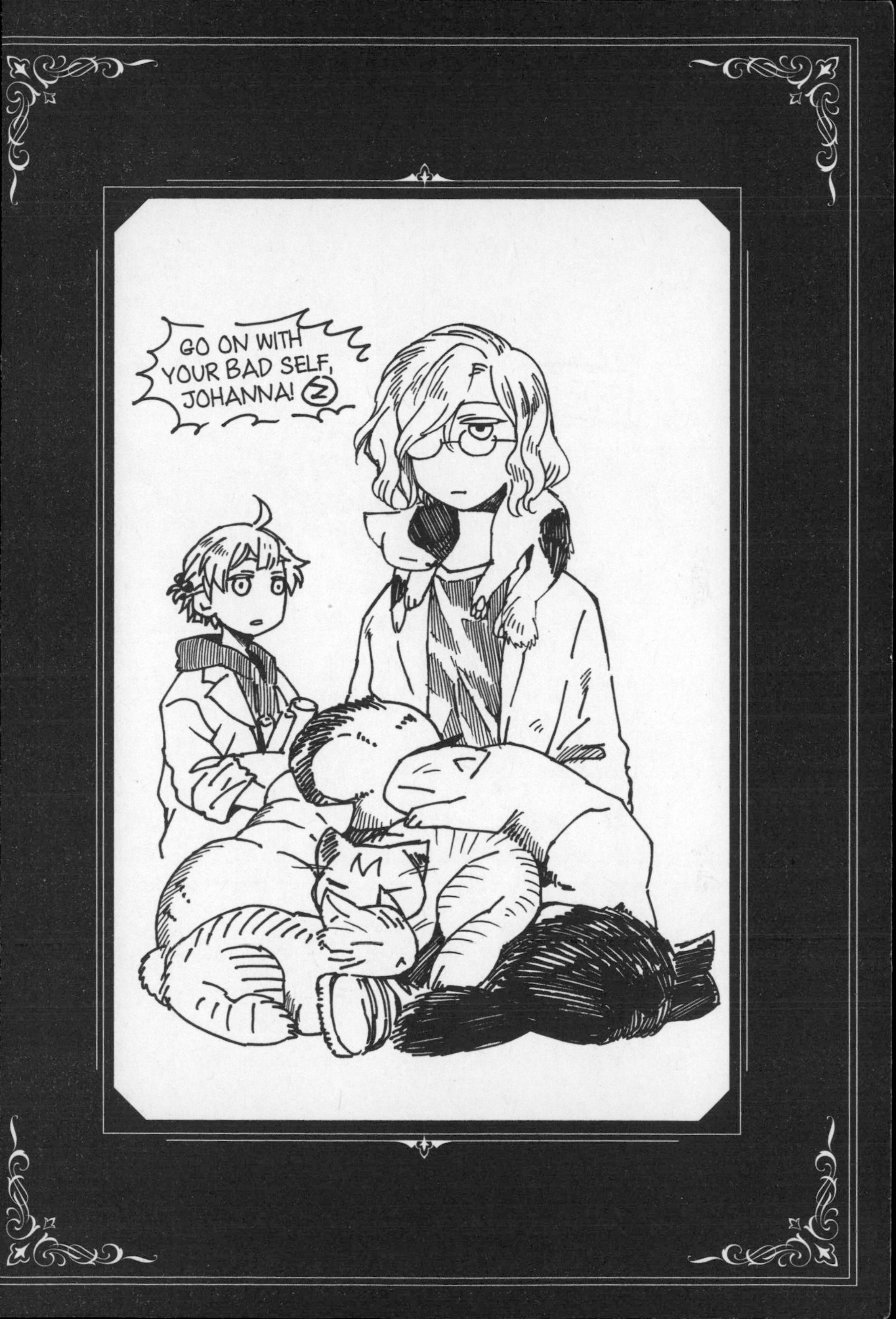
GO ON WITH YOUR BAD SELF, JOHANNA!

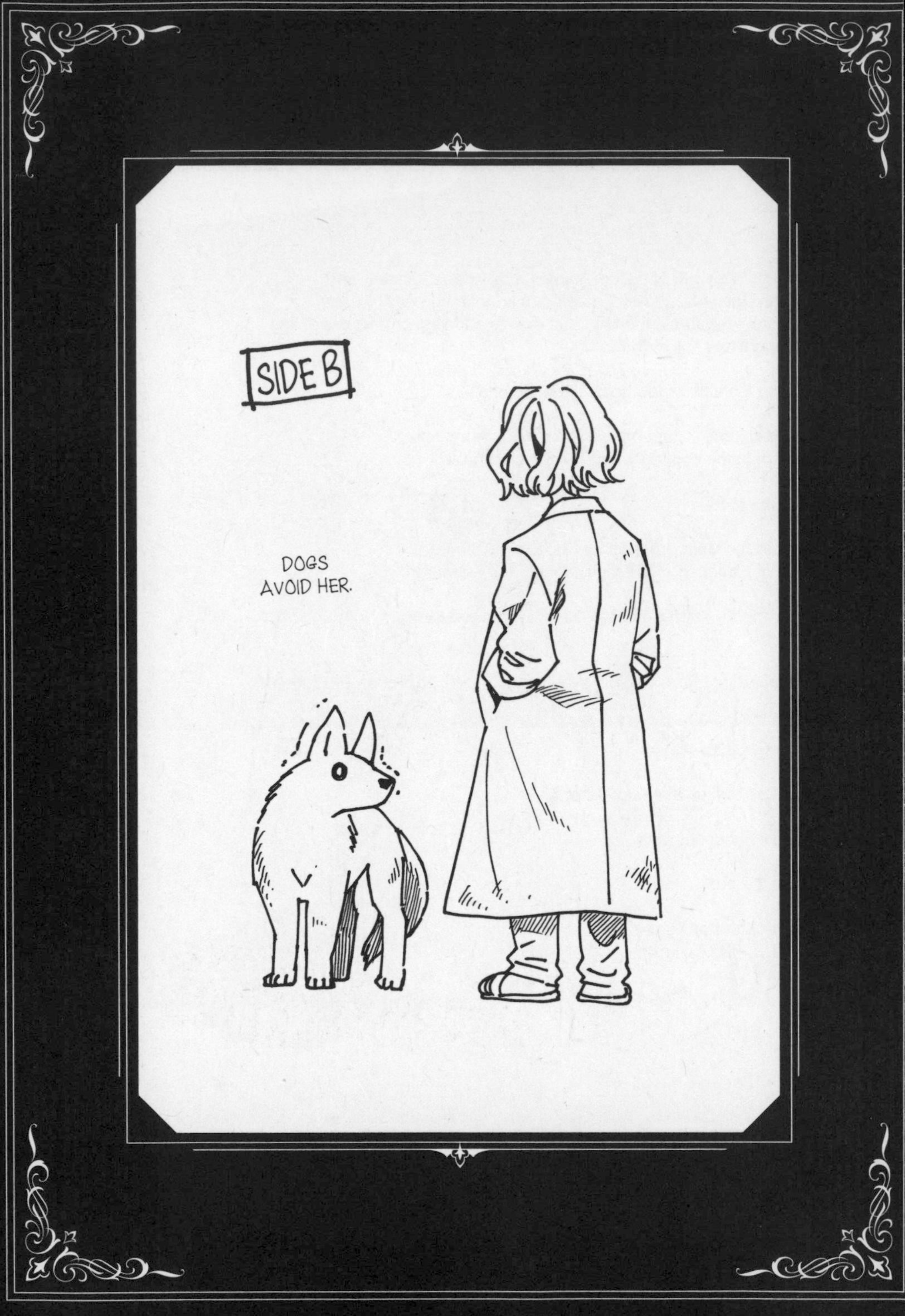
SIDE B
DOGS AVOID HER.

A Kodansha Comics Trade Paperback Original.

Frau Faust volume 2 copyright © 2015 Kore Yamazaki
English translation copyright © 2017 Kore Yamazaki

All rights reserved.

Published in the United States by Kodansha Comics, an imprint of Kodansha USA Publishing, LLC, New York.

Publication rights for this English edition arranged through Kodansha Ltd., Tokyo.

First published in Japan in 2015 by Kodansha Ltd., Tokyo, as *Frau Faust* volume 2.

ISBN 978-1-63236-481-4

Printed in the United States of America.

www.kodanshacomics.com

9 8 7 6 5 4 3 2 1

Translation: Stephen Paul
Lettering: Lys Blakeslee
Editing: Ajani Oloye
Kodansha Comics edition cover design: Phil Balsman